THE STATE AND THE ARTS

THE STATE AND THE ARTS
Articulating Power and Subversion

Edited by

Judith Kapferer

Berghahn Books
NEW YORK • OXFORD
www.berghahnbooks.com

First published in 2008 by

Berghahn Books

www.berghahnbooks.com

© 2008 Berghahn Books

Part of this volume was originally published in *Social Analysis*, volume 51, issue 1.

Library of Congress Cataloging-in-Publication Data

The state and the arts : articulating power and subversion / edited by Judith Kapferer.
    p. cm.
Includes bibliographical references and index.
ISBN 978-1-84545-578-1 (pbk. : alk. paper)
1. Art and state. 2. Arts—Political aspects. I. Kapferer, Judith.

N8725.S77 2008
700.1'03—dc22

                  2008028018

British Library Cataloguing in Publication Data

A catalogue record for this book is available from the British Library.

Printed in the United States on acid-free paper

CONTENTS

ACKNOWLEDGMENTS

Countless colleagues, friends, and relations have generously contributed to the production of this book. While individuals have tendered their own individual acknowledgements, I take this opportunity to mention some others to whom we are collectively grateful.

We were very fortunate to have Professor Sigmund Grønmo (Professor of Sociology and now the Rector of the University of Bergen) to open the workshop/seminar of which this volume is the result. His warm welcome and that of many other people in the university and the town set the tone for an extremely enjoyable and productive few days.

Professor Bruce Kapferer of the Institute for Social Anthropology and director of the Challenging the State project at Bergen gave us all tremendous support and encouragement, contributing incisive and imaginative comments to our debates. He enabled us to fashion our disparate ideas into a framework within which we all felt invigorated.

We owe an immense debt of gratitude to the Norwegian Research Council, which funded the workshop through the Challenging the State program. It is through the generosity of bodies like this that scholarship and learning are maintained, advanced, and kept alive in an increasingly narrowly focused pragmatic world.

The labors of Shawn Kendrick are at the heart of the contents of this entire volume. We have all, separately and collectively, had cause to thank her for her intelligent and patient editing and her light touch on our various idiosyncrasies. Her understanding of and empathy with us all have greatly added to our own writing experience.

Vivian Berghahn of Berghahn Books has been a kind and helpful mentor to whom I am much indebted. The Berghahn publishing house is one of the few to resist the crassly commercial pressure to churn out anodyne textbooks for an uncritical mass audience. Long may it endure!

INTRODUCTION
The Architectonics of State Power—Complicity
and Resistance

Judith Kapferer

> We are not going to protect art. The more cultural protection we enact, the more
> waste we have, the more false successes, false promotions there are. It puts us
> in the marketing realm of culture. (Baudrillard 2005)

The development of the arts as a collective modern phenomenon is intri-
cately woven into its genesis in the milieu of princely Renaissance courts
of varying size, complexity, and indeed grandeur that provided sustenance
and shelter to artists of all kinds during the fifteenth to eighteenth centuries
(see Burckhardt [1860] 1990). The protection of artists was the province of
aristocratic dynasties that could augment or rescind their patronage at unpredictable moments; nonetheless, as Elias (1993) makes clear, artists such as
Mozart struggled constantly to maintain some kind of independence from
their noble benefactors.

By the eighteenth century, such a degree of freedom had already been afforded
writers unattached to the court by the spread of literacy and the growing body
of aristocrats and the bourgeoisie that constituted their readership. This latitude

Notes for this section are located on page 11.

was granted to essayists, poets, and dramatists despite not infrequent lapses from grace as the result of circulating overly critical or even scurrilous views that offended the objects of their attacks. In places like France or Britain, with centralized imperial courts that were almost entirely separated from the provinces, the punishment for plain-spoken or libelous critiques included ostracism, horsewhipping, imprisonment, or bankruptcy. But given the centralized nature of the court society and the stimulation of the metropolis, the option of exile was not greatly utilized. Conversely, the patronage of princes in Italy and Germany allowed those not so dependent on literacy—painters, and musicians, for example—to flourish. Contravention of courtly codes still attracted severe sanctions, but for these artists, relocating to another, more congenial court was indeed a possibility.

It was in this period and in this kind of cultural environment that the public sphere was generated (Habermas 1992). Here was an arena for political debate and social criticism in which the ideals of the Enlightenment took root and provided fertile ground for the development of a range of philosophers, scientists, artists, and writers—an intelligentsia, in fact. The space of the intelligentsia was still the world of the rich and powerful, but they too were drawn into the circle of critique and argumentation. As well as offering a measure of financial and moral support, their patronage allowed for the publication and dissemination of literary, musical, and artistic works. Collectors such as the architect and antiquarian Sir John Soane and Queen Anne, the patron of Georg Friedrich Handel, were among them. Later, people like the diplomat Lord Elgin and the financier and archaeologist Lord Caernavon (partner with Howard Carter in uncovering the tomb of King Tutankhamun in 1922) would be included.

The Public Sphere and the Enlightenment Project

The demise of the public sphere and its separation of public from private lives at the end of the nineteenth century also presaged the end of the Enlightenment project. Accompanied by the burgeoning power of the merchant class in the nineteenth century and the triumph of capital in the twentieth, opportunities for patronage were rapidly expanded. In particular, the enormous wealth of the robber barons of the United States, concerned for their own profit and social aggrandizement (Veblen [1899] 1970) and the prestige of their national institutions (Freeland 2001; Karp 1992; Zukin 1995), extended the international trade in artworks and the construction of museums and art galleries to accommodate them. In this instance, the interests of the national state and of capital dovetailed tidily, the one supporting the other. As in many later polities, although never since with such impact, the age of private philanthropy was born.

The conjunction of private and public interests was, and remains, a major tool for the symbolic expression of national pride and private satisfaction, although the individual interests of pecuniary emulation have given way to the power of major philanthropic foundations, which are now so much a feature

of the aesthetic concerns of North American capital in particular. The diminu-
tion of the public sphere was concomitant with the waning influence of the
bourgeoisie and the increasing privatism of corporations and their discourse
on matters relevant to the political and economic arenas. The flowering of the
power of 'big capital' went hand in glove with the rise of the 'new class' of
technocrats, entrepreneurs, and celebrities: popular musicians, film and television actors, sports stars, lifestyle 'gurus' in fields such as cuisine, fashion,
decorating, and architecture. The 'new class' had, by the mid-twentieth century, totally surpassed the influence of the eighteenth-century bourgeoisie and
its nineteenth-century remnants, which by that time had turned its attention
to the accumulation of capital and the exploitation of natural resources abroad
and human resources (the working class) at home. The relation between the
state and the arts had been transformed from a discourse on tastes and morality to one of economic rationalism and political collusion.

Throughout what has been referred to as the 'American century' of US political
dominance of world affairs, the construction of prestigious buildings has gath-
ered pace, and, as a result, the centrality of architects as representatives of the
aesthetic sensibilities of the age has been greatly enhanced.[1] We might adduce as
examples of this phenomenon the figures of Le Corbusier, Gehry, Johnson, Pei,
Rogers, Hadad, Foster, and many others whose works are celebrated around the
world. Both government-funded and corporation-commissioned structures—the
Guggenheim Museum in Bilbao (Gehry), Berlin's new Reichstag (Foster), the
Sydney Opera House (Utzon), London's Millennium Dome (Rogers)—partake of
this iconicity of concrete and symbolic expressions of power and ambition.

The association of commercially successful architects and artists with
patrons and benefactors is well illustrated by the coterie of financiers, curators,
auctioneers, valuers, and dealers engaged in the dissemination of their works.
The role of Charles Saatchi (co-founder of the British advertising company
M&C Saatchi and owner of the Saatchi Gallery) as patron and promoter of the
products of particular exponents of so-called Britart in the 1990s is a case in
point. The art market, its popularization, and the sanctification of artists and
their works (Bourdieu 1996), along with the competitive emulation of traders,
brokers, buyers, and sellers of such works (Wu 2002), compose the foundation
of the commodity fetishism that ineluctably colors the contemporary aesthetics of capital. It is due to the 'new class' (Gouldner 1979; Szelenyi and Martin
1988) of consultants, technocrats, and managers that art markets find their
clientele in regenerated and gentrified inner cities—SoHo in Manhattan and the
East End of London, for example.[2]

Cities and Civilizations

"Judge a civilisation by its cities," advises Will Hutton (2000: vi) in his introduction to Rogers and Power's (2000) *Cities for a Small Country*. Cities, he continues, are where people "work, associate, recreate, politic, scheme and love."
The city, as metonym, can also be judged a civilization by its arts and sciences,

crafts and philosophies, politics and economics; by all of its cultural and social productions and their articulations and interconnections; by its whole way of life, in fact, as the anthropologists say.

It comes as no surprise, then, to recognize the metropolitan nature of every-day life in the twenty-first century: more than half of the world's population now lives in towns and cities. Furthermore, the metropolis is the home not only of the arts and sciences of civilization but also of the values, beliefs, intellects, and imaginings of a vortex of disputation and debate about their importance to a civilized and civil way of being. Here, under late capitalism, the essentially individualist concerns of the aesthetics and commerce of the culture industry have installed themselves in the role of ideological leaders at center stage, rele-gating the concerns of other political, social, and cultural collectivities to minor roles as spear carriers waiting in the wings and anterooms of the 'total social formation'. The city provides and nurtures the critical mass wherein dwell the teachers and learners, the acolytes of an array of cultures that define it and give it its form and substance. It is the city that offers a way out of the 'rural idiocy' that, for Marx and Engels (1976), characterized the closed, narrow, taken-for-grantedness of an unexamined existence. It is also the site of the snobbery and greed that is a feature of the new capitalist class and that is overwhelmingly ignorant of anything other than itself.

The importance of architecture in current formulations of aesthetic value within the cultures of everyday life is Hutton's (2000) theme. Once the province of numerous and nameless draftsmen, craftsmen, builders, and dreamers in the execution of homes, churches, palaces, parks, and public buildings, architecture has now achieved an expanded significance of being crucial to our understand-ing of social and cultural formulations of the arts of living. Such structures, at the same time imagined and manifested in both literal and metaphorical senses, have become the property of a range of scholars, critics, and commentators who live and work in a world that constantly envisages utopian and practical means of improving or embellishing public and private living spaces.

This is a world constituted in a welter of histories, memories, heritages, and resurgent nationalism and its putative counterweight—globalization. The central importance of Eastern Europe and the Federal Republic of Germany is that the former represents the fall of the old, autocratic, nineteenth-century empires and the would-be dictatorial empires of the twentieth century, and the latter represents the rise of the new, postmodern, decentered 'Empire' of Hardt and Negri's (2000) imagining: here is highlighted the concern of Europeans to make sense of the shifting patterns of state formations in relation to under-standing the individual and society, public and private manners, and moralities and the arts of democracy itself. But Jean Baudrillard (2005: 65), in an essay titled "La commedia dell'arte" in his *Conspiracy of Art*, maintains that "art no longer seems to have a vital function," having been appropriated by a political regime within which it enacts a partnership, a collusion with politics itself, to the extent that one is a mere metonym of the other. Such a conspiracy is, as this collection of essays argues, to be resisted for the benefit of both art and (making a virtue of necessity) the state.

A critical approach to the relation between the state and the arts has as its very center the idea of administration—the assembling, distribution, evaluation, and organization of culture as a bureaucratically regulated arm of the cultural departments of cities, "disparate elements considered together as culture, at least momentarily" (Adorno 1991: 108). The role of the cultural expert is crucial in the administration of the formulation and reformulation of values in the service of the state. This is clearly seen in relation to the role of the market in determining the monetary value attached to culture and the arts; in education, it is demonstrated in the formation of new religious sects and the revitalization of old ones—in the idea of conservative 'family values', for instance. The expertly administered world is another control mechanism of dominant social orders, as Weber (1978) was well aware. Yet it is becoming less and less a seamless ideological phenomenon, with constant economic scandals and administrative restructurings testifying to the unease of observers and participants alike (Baudrillard says we are all complicit).

The arts (across all fields of creative production) have an unusually ambivalent relation to the state and other agencies of political and economic control within urban society, and it is in the cracks in between that spaces for resistance and critique are to be found. From ancient times, the arts have been used to represent and promote the forces of power in ruling socio-political regimes. But they have also been engaged in challenging those institutions of power and in breaking through those conceptions, values, and conventions that are associated with hegemonic state authority and governing social orders. Assyrian, Pharaonic, Greek, Roman, Byzantine, Aztec, Chinese, Renaissance, Reformation, Enlightenment, industrial, and post-industrial projects have long placed the arts and humanities at the centers of power through their involvement with both ideological and repressive practices of domination.

It is our purpose to address here the relation of the arts of living to institutions of order and control in current state formations and to explore some of the ways in which cultural practice may partake of and map out a range of the shifting alignments, articulations, and configurations of contemporary states. Art, or more broadly, culture, is always implicated, for good or ill, in the operation, manipulation, and legitimation of regnant social orders.[3]

'Empire' and Transnational Networks

A key concept at the turn of the twenty-first century has been that of 'Empire'. Hardt and Negri (2000: 325) characterize 'Empire' as a "decentralising force that distributes different forms of power (political, economic, cultural) through dispersed centres, yet these forms connect in global networks that cross-cut national boundaries and thus challenge national state sovereignty." Their picture is one of political, economic, and, above all, cultural networks slicing through the orders of nation-states and deployed within intermittent affiliations, mergers, and takeovers. Thus, for example, international partnerships mounting cultural festivals, traveling exhibitions and performances, world music, 'roots' festivals, and numerous conferences and seminars abound. But it is uncertain whether there remains a hierarchy of participants and venues that reflects the global power relations of such events.

The thesis of 'Empire' is imbricated with the notion of globalization, variously connoting blocs of political or economic power embodied in alliances and treaty arrangements such as the European Union (EU), NATO, the UN Security Council, the G7 or G8, and so forth. The changing social and cultural relations among the former Soviet bloc countries of the Cold War period have resulted in potentially fruitful sets of realigned and reshaped connections and disconnections that are constantly shifting, with consequences for social relations on a global scale. Hardt and Negri follow Deleuze and Guattari (1988) in their fascination with the central image of the nomadic war machine as the metaphor that describes and defines the fluid and instantly adaptable mechanics of cross-cutting ties among people in extra-territorial social relations, helping to create a decentered 'new Empire' where, it is hoped, the arts of peace will bloom.

Alain Joxe (2002), on the other hand, sees what he calls the "empire of disorder" as opening up spaces for contestation and transformation in the interstices of societal orders within and beyond national state structures and territories. These nodes and networks form what Castells (1989) and others call the 'information society' and what some (e.g., Harvey 1990) refer to as post-industrialism, post-colonialism, or even post-capitalism. Joxe's picture of this empire is a gloomy one, stressing its fracturing and fragmentary nature, while Hardt and Negri's outlook is much more optimistic (in what is perhaps a singularly American way). Their idea of 'Empire' is essentially one that promises power to the people—that is, people steeped in a carefully defined and administrated political, economic, social, and cultural world under the reign of capitalist democracy supported by military and economic sanctions and rewards. In this regime, the old notion of empire as designating colonial or post-colonial spheres of influence or imperialist takeover gives way to a series of tightrope-walking acts constantly maneuvering for extra-territorial financial and cultural advantage. Yet the dice remain loaded in favor of those states of the West and the North that have reordered their political, economic, social, and cultural arrangements to maintain their old sovereignties and forge new ones in the new global empire—satrapies within the revitalized capitalist formation of the American empire.[4]

The distinction between culture and civilization has a long pedigree (see, e.g., Adorno 1991; Elias 2000; Marx and Engels 1976) and essentially turns on the very fact of the judgment and evaluation of any specific way of life as more or less worthy of admiration and emulation than another. The distinction between the arts and art is a cognate concern. The right/duty of artists and intellectuals to interpret, criticize, and publicize the political and economic hypocrisies and prevarications of nation-states and the post-national worlds of twenty-first-century capital is as urgent as ever. Perhaps it is all the more pressing in an age in which commercial priorities, under the aegis of 'Empire', are ascendant, and exchange value outweighs the use value of education and the arts. One clear example of this process is the comparatively recent emphasis on management techniques in the area of religious administrations (often enough, complete with financial scandals and lapses in the faith of the leaders). Another is evident in the arts, where the most egregious instances of the ascendancy of commercial 'properties'—involving phenomenal sums being paid for classic or fashionable works and litigation about copyright, theft, and fraud—are to be found. A telling example is the case of artworks that, when purchased, are never displayed in public places but are instead incarcerated in vaults. These are truly the acts of patrons who know the price of everything and the value of nothing.

Culture and Critique

What is to be stressed in this context is the much-vaunted prerogative of artists and intellectuals to uphold and advance the ideals of diverse communities in exercising and practicing constitutional rights, such as the freedom of expression, as conceptualized by artists, writers, poets, dramatists, crafts people, musicians, scientists, and, above all, educated citizens. The role of the educated citizen is crucial here, and it is increasingly under attack by those intellectuals who have an ulterior motive—financial profit, cultural domination, electoral advantage, social control, or the overt and covert manufacturing of consent, for example. Perhaps, also, the unpublicized motives of administrators and politicians—and large bodies of the general public—are often little more than taken-for-granted understandings of the relation between politics, economics, and the exchange value of art in the corporate state.

Here is Adorno (1991: 116–117) again: "Culture … involves an irrevocably critical impulse towards the status quo and all institutions thereof … The concept of culture has been utilized to a great extent through its emancipation from the actual processes of life experienced with the rise of the bourgeoisie and the Enlightenment … Today manifestations of extreme artistry can be fostered, produced and presented by official institutions; indeed art is dependent on such support if it is to be produced at all and find its way to an audience. Yet at the same time, art denounces everything institutional and official."[5] This contradiction involving the role of the arts in the maintenance of the social order, as achieved through the processes of governmentality and the ideological state apparatuses (Althusser 1971), lies at the heart of the themes of this collection. Hereby, culture, as Adorno says, is transformed into a lubricant for the systems of administration and political practice that, in effect, define the state itself—the ensemble of interests that Poulantzas (1978: 16) calls the 'total social formation'.

But the arts (and, increasingly, populist 'entertainment') are more than providers of bread and circuses or the means for the execution and operation of the works of various ministries of culture and other related government departments. Culture, as opposed to what the purveyors of mere entertainment and basic primary school education call 'cultural activities', is not just a lubricant; it is a vital element of the legitimation of government policy. As such, it reaches far beyond the realms of politics, administration, and economics, as do, of course, those cultural activities masquerading as art that Horkheimer and Adorno (1972) so scorned as the 'culture industry'—the instruments of mystification produced by the mass media. Their obfuscations and half lies are indicators of the waning of the Enlightenment project, through which it had been hoped that reason would dispel the darkness of myth, superstition, and Weber's (1978) 'enchantment of the world'. The culture industry—which has since been termed the 'cultural industries' or the 'creative industries' (Caves 2000; Florida 2004; Hartley 2004; Hesmondhalgh 2002)—and the arts themselves are in fact complicit in the practices of re-enchantment and de-rationalization of the public sphere and the entire Enlightenment project (see Kapferer 2007).

The order of the 'new Empire' is premised on a preference for individualism, a style of life that overrides the order of the community. Competitive capital accumulation is attested to everywhere—in the mass media, the press, advertising, window displays, Internet sites, etc.—as a dominant concern. US citizens in particular mourn the passing of a community spirit characterized by egalitarianism, cooperation, compassion, and mutual support that was once thought to symbolize the order of the democratic small town meeting acclaimed by de Tocqueville. The works of writers such as Robert Putnam (2000), Richard Sennett (2003), Lyn Lofland (1998), Ray Oldenburg (1999), and many others illustrate the dilemma involved in balancing the public and private aspects of everyday life, no more precariously than in the ownership of property and space.

The fetishism of culture as commodity and that segment of culture called the arts is the central concern of these chapters. That concern is embodied in the relation between the state and the arts that, for good or ill, shapes our understanding of aesthetics as the central component of the politics of space, manifested in the concrete structures and abstract realizations of a capitalist dispensation. Fractious and frequently antagonistic, the often teeth-gritting[6] relationship between the various ideological state apparatuses and their couplings (art-technology, art-craft, art-warfare, art-religion, art-economy, art-politics), along with the overarching social order of the ideology-repression dyad, holds the power structures of the state together. The ensemble of these momentary connections and disjunctions is the stuff of the political administration of the arts in our time. The phases of regulation, de-regulation, and re-regulation of national economies parallel those of the market in aesthetics, and it is the understanding of these relationships that provides for the sustaining and revival of the aesthetic impulse, either in opposition or in reinforcement.

This installs both the corporate state and the welfare state at the heart of judgments of cultural value that are conceived of as advancing 'our' civilization: liberty, equality, comradeship, compassion, democracy, education, the family, religion, the rule of law, human and civil rights, etc. The state is charged with the protection of those values, including the cultural/aesthetic values that enhance the quality of life and maintain its legitimacy. In the interstices and contradictions of the legitimations of cultural practice are to be found those spaces for rebellion against the status quo and the powerful imaginaries of new formulations of the everyday acts of mundane existence, of the humanities and the aesthetics of the arts of living.

How do cultural contexts affect contemporary power formations—and vice versa? Are other social formations (religious, ethnic, multicultural, etc.) replacing the social contract between states and citizens? Does the overriding concern for personal and national security in the contemporary world benefit artistic production, or is it more a regulatory and constricting force?

The State as Socio-cultural Production

The genesis of this book lies in a workshop of eight participants convened at the University of Bergen. Over the course of a year, and with the inclusion of two other writers, our discussions eventually resolved themselves into designating three major facets of the arts-state relation. These cover, first, cultural politics both within and beyond state administrations and state policies, as explored by Malcolm Miles on public art in the UK, Monica Sassatelli on EU arts policies, and Jeremy Valentine on the auditing of bureaucratic and administrative processes linking the government and the Scottish Arts Council within the framework of Scotland's National Cultural Strategy. Terence Chong focuses on the effects of globalization in relation to the cultural politics of the Singapore theatre field, contrasting the dominant English-language theatre companies with the 'marginalized' and less well-funded indigenous theatre.

Secondly, we examine some articulations between public art and political contexts. Henri Beunders writes on artistic expression and violent reaction to such expression in the Netherlands, Rosita Henry explores indigenous–non-indigenous political art in northern Australia, and Marina Fokidis discusses resistance to state domination along the ancient Mediterranean route known as the Egnatia Road.

Thirdly, we investigate some meanings of memory, social change, and the arts of the state through the lenses provided by Karen Kipphoff on monuments in Berlin and Bucharest, by Inger-Elin Øye on private lives and social orders in the reunified Federal Republic of Germany, and by Judith Kapferer on public space and the socio-cultural public sphere in London.

This is hardly a neatly demarcated arrangement, and many of the chapters pertain to more than one of these three areas of analysis. We are equally conscious of a number of lacunae, occasioned by our inability to persuade representatives of various arts to answer our call for contributions—film, music, and literature being the most conspicuous of these. For this we apologize. Hopefully, others will later fill in some of the gaps that we were unable to cover.

The objective of our deliberations has been to focus on civil society and on cultural and social contexts within and/or beyond state borders, addressing a range of issues involving the arts, the culture industries, cultural NGOs and interest groups, and other social movements relating to creative production. To this end, we attempted to determine the extent to which the various social formations that constitute civil society act in lieu of direct state control and government power—as, to use Foucault's (1979) term, a form of governmentality. Do these formations undercut state power, constituting nodes of resistance to it? Or do they uphold and legitimate it?

In the following chapters we touch on a number of local and global questions pertaining to these issues:

- Imperialist and transnational domination of cultural practice: taste, style, and new class hegemony—cooperation and competition among museums; galleries; dance, orchestra, and theater companies; and the entertainment industries
- Spaces of resistance, legitimation, support, co-optation, and/or accommodation to changing state forms: divisions and alliances across different public arenas and public spaces
- The corporate media as sites of artistic expression and production: to what extent do they bring the arts into new relations of uneasy association with powerful controlling interests?
- Resurgent nationalism and ethnic revitalization
- Shifting modes of cultural production: moves, already well advanced, to further privatization, professionalization, and formal training in cultural fields

Is the state itself, then, a cultural production? We claim that it is, and we see the arts and the culture industry itself as all too often the fundamental prop of the dominant military-industrial complex of current state structures. Like Baudrillard's (2005: 66) Danubian peasant, "who knows nothing but suspects something is wrong," we struggle to understand the ramifications of this conjuncture, wary of the pretentiousness and associations that feed the conspiracies of art—through administrative regulation, the commercial dealings of the 'symbolic economy' (Zukin 1995), the education and training of artists, and the influence of metropolitan critics. The autonomy of the arts is constantly threatened by the cultures of affluent consumers and investors—the patrons and courtiers of post-industrial society. Artists are squeezed by state policies, on the one hand, and the arts market, on the other, thus being denied the creative space and freedom of expression to pursue their own distinctive practices. The legitimation of arts policies is the legitimation of the corporate state itself, of a contemporary ruling class in search not of a post-Enlightenment vision but of a rapacious individual identity centered on the competitive accumulation of financial and cultural capital.

Bourdieu (1998: 7) refers to civic virtue and the public interest as being embattled vis-à-vis the return of an individualism "which tends to destroy the philosophical foundations of the welfare state and in particular the notion of collective responsibility … which has been a fundamental achievement of social (and sociological) thought." He adduces here the role of the 'new intellectuals' and the economistic belief in 'blaming the victim', engaging in a social science reduced to journalistic commentary.

Thus, the current lethargy of intellectual life—with artists, writers, philosophers, and scientists increasingly failing to confront the self-serving political-administrative functionaries of the corporate state—is also complicit in lessening the force of debate and critique in the public sphere. It is these tendencies that require constant and urgent questioning and refutation in support of civilization and democratic practices, and it is these critical issues that inform the chapters we now place before you.

Notes

1. In Ayn Rand's (1943) novel, *The Fountainhead*, the figure of architect Robert Roark, whose insistence on his personal will in the face of bureaucratic intransigence brings about his own destruction, is an egregious example. One does not have to look far, however, to find other, non-fiction examples. The vision of Adolf Hitler as translated by the architect Albert Speer is a case in point. As an influential artist, Speer clearly stamped his imprimatur on his era.
2. See Hewitt's (1996) description of the rise to respectability of the formerly disreputable artists' garrets in Montmartre in the late nineteenth century.
3. Both the so-called anthropological definition of culture as humanly constructed 'webs of meaning' (Geertz 1975) and its usage in everyday life, commonly restricted to the realm of the arts, are frequently interchangeable constructs in the chapters in this volume.
4. That the empire of the East looms as a threat to Western imperialism is recognized, but that is a story that takes us well beyond the scope of this introduction.
5. An illustrative case regarding official institutions concerns the findings in July 2006 of the Charity Commissioners in the UK, with regard to acquisitions by the governing trustees of the Tate Galleries of works of one of the artist-trustees, apparently to finance that artist's imminent wedding. Despite the ubiquity of the practice, it is frowned upon as a kind of insider trading; members of the Stock Exchange face opprobrium for similar offenses.
6. The term is Althusser's (1971).

References

Adorno, Theodor W. 1991. *The Culture Industry: Selected Essays on Mass Culture*. Ed. J. M. Bernstein. London: Routledge.

Althusser, Louis. 1971. *Lenin and Philosophy and Other Essays*. New York: Monthly Review Press.

Baudrillard, Jean. 2005. *The Conspiracy of Art*. New York: Semiotext(e).

Bourdieu, Pierre. 1996. *The Rules of Art*. Trans. Susan Emanuel. Cambridge: Polity Press.

_____. 1998. "The Left Hand and the Right Hand of the State." Pp. 1–10 in *Acts of Resistance*. Cambridge: Polity Press.

Burckhardt, Jakob. [1860] 1990. *The Civilisation of the Renaissance in Italy*. London: Penguin.

Castells, Emmanuel. 1989. *The Informational City*. Oxford: Blackwell.

Caves, Richard. 2000. *Creative Industries: Contracts between Art and Commerce*. Cambridge, MA: Harvard University Press.

Deleuze, Gilles, and Félix Guattari. 1988. *A Thousand Plateaus*. Trans. Brian Massumi. London: Continuum.

Elias, Norbert. 1993. *Mozart: Portrait of a Genius*. Ed. Michael Schröter; trans. Edmund Jephcott. Berkeley: University of California Press.

_____. 2000. *The Civilising Process*. 2 vols. Oxford: Blackwell.

Florida, Richard. 2004. *The Rise of the Creative Class*. New York: Basic Books.

Foucault, Michel. 1979. *Discipline and Punish*. New York: Vintage.

Freeland, Cynthia. 2001. *Art Theory: A Very Short Introduction*. Oxford: Oxford University Press.

Geertz, Clifford. 1975. *The Interpretation of Cultures*. New York: Hutchinson.

Gouldner, Alvin. 1979. *The Future of Intellectuals and the Rise of the New Class*. London: Macmillan.

Habermas, Jürgen. 1992. *The Structural Transformation of the Public Sphere*. Cambridge: Polity Press.

Hardt, Michael, and Antonio Negri. 2000. *Empire*. Cambridge, MA: Harvard University Press.

Hartley, John. 2004. *Creative Industries*. Oxford: Blackwell.

Harvey, David. 1990. *The Condition of Postmodernity*. Oxford: Blackwell.

Hesmondhalgh, David. 2002. *The Cultural Industries: An Introduction*. London: Sage.

Hewitt, Nicholas. 1996. "Shifting Cultural Centres in Twentieth-Century Paris." Pp. 30–45 in *Parisian Fields*, ed. Michael Sheringham. London: Reaktion.

Horkheimer, Max, and Theodor Adorno. 1972. *Dialectic of Enlightenment*. New York: Continuum.

Hutton, Will. 2000. "Introduction." Pp. vi–vii in Rogers and Power 2000.

Joxe, Alain. 2002. *Empire of Disorder*. Los Angeles: Semiotext(e).

Kapferer, Bruce. 2007. "Anthropology and the Enlightenment." *Australian Journal of Anthropology* 51, no. 2.

Karp, Ivan. 1992. *Museums and Communities: The Politics of Public Culture*. Washington, DC: Smithsonian.

Lofland, Lyn. 1998. *The Public Realm*. New York: Aldine de Gruyter.

Marx, Karl, and Frederick Engels. 1976. *The German Ideology*. Moscow: Progress Publishers.

Oldenburg, Ray. 1999. *The Great Good Place*. New York: Marlowe.

Poulantzas, Nicos. 1978. *State, Power, Socialism*. Trans. Patrick Camilleri. London: Verso.

Putnam, Robert. 2000. *Bowling Alone*. New York: Touchstone.

Rand, Ayn. 1943. *The Fountainhead*. New York: Bobbs Merrill.

Rogers, Richard, and Anne Power. 2000. *Cities for a Small Country*. London: Faber and Faber.

Sennett, Richard. 2003. *The Fall of Public Man*. London: Penguin.

Szelenyi, Ivan, and Bill Martin. 1988. "The Three Waves of New Class Theories." *Theory and Society* 17, no. 5: 645–667.

Veblen, Thorstein. [1899] 1970. *The Theory of the Leisure Class*. London: Unwin.

Weber, Max. 1978. *Economy and Society*. Vol. 2. Berkeley: University of California Press.

Wu, Chin-tao. 2002. *Privatising Culture*. London: Verso.

Zukin, Sharon. 1995. *The Cultures of Cities*. Oxford: Blackwell.

Chapter 1

THE END OF ARROGANCE, THE ADVENT OF PERSUASION
Public Art in a Multicultural Society

Henri Beunders

After a decade or so of increasingly intensifying debates on controversial modern art, a decade that saw the removal or destruction of hated public art and a life-threatening *fatwa*, the physical violence against people and property has begun. In the early twenty-first century, Europe is the center stage for outbreaks of politically motivated violence against the material symbols of 'the enemy'—against writer-politicians, writer-artists, cartoonists, producers, and publishers.

Acts of violence have included the burning of 'colonial cars' in 2005 in the French *banlieus*, the ghettos where ethnic minorities live; the assassination of a controversial political candidate, Pim Fortuyn, in the Netherlands in May 2002

Notes for this chapter are located on page 27.

by a radical animal rights activist because he was "not against wearing fur" and was seen as a "danger to society in general"; and the murder of the Dutch writer and film director Theo van Gogh (a descendant of Vincent van Gogh) in November 2004 in an act of ritual slaughter on an Amsterdam pavement in retaliation for the 'anti-Islam' movie he had made. In the backlash of the van Gogh murder, a dozen schools, mosques, and churches were torched. Less than a year later, in September 2005, the 'cartoon war' started with a series of cartoons about the prophet Muhammad in a Danish newspaper, including one that portrayed Muhammad with a bomb for his headgear. A half-year later, the Danish consulate in Beirut was burned, and the Danish and Norwegian embassies in Damascus were set on fire.

All of these acts of violence against the 'symbols of oppression', the distributors of blasphemy, and the proponents of 'hate speech' have been caused by tensions within multicultural societies, which most European countries only in recent decades have turned into. Furthermore, all of these incidents have a relation to 'the arts'. They were either 'symbolic' acts, such as burning cars that represented the hated native French, or a direct reaction to the artistic publications of a writer, a filmmaker, and several cartoonists. Subsequently, when governments attempted to calm down the public and soothe public opinion at home and abroad, 'art' suffered once again. In November 2004, the mayor of Rotterdam, amidst the violent turmoil of van Gogh's murder, ordered the immediate destruction of a piece of public art next to a mosque. The mural, which featured white doves and the words "Thou shalt not kill," came under fire when Muslim citizens protested that they were unjustly associated with the murder because the artist had added "2 November 2004" (the date of van Gogh's death) to it. In February 2006, London condemned the publication of the Muhammad cartoons as "insensitive," while Washington declared that it was "unacceptable" to incite religious hatred by publishing such pictures (*Economist*, 9 February 2006). Whereas in 1989, when the British writer Salman Rushdie published his *Satanic Verses* and the Iranian ayatollahs issued a *fatwa* to kill the author for his fictional, artistic insults of Islam and Muhammad, the reaction of London, and the rest of the West, was "We stand by our man, and his art" (Gonzalez 2005).

What is left of the adherence to 'freedom of expression'? The present disarray on the value or necessity of freedoms of speech and expression to Western democracy is fueled by ethnic and religious tensions between the old Christian majorities (or those with Christian roots) and the new Islamic minorities. The September 2001 attacks in the name of Islam on the 'heart of the West' and the subsequent 'war on terror', followed by the terrorist bombings in Madrid (2004) and London (2005), have been called the proof that Samuel P. Huntington (1993, 1996) was right in predicting 10 years earlier a 'clash of civilizations'.

In analyzing the fate of public art in multicultural societies, we will see that the present disarray the West has fallen into about the meaning of 'freedom of expression' has various origins: firstly, the crisis in modern art itself; secondly, the ongoing democratization of politics; and, finally, the mediatization of all public acts. The answer to the question 'Who decides what is tolerable?' will be that in the end it is not the law, not the artist, not the art elites, not the authorities, but rather the general public or 'public opinion' that decides the fate of publicly exhibited art. To put it another way, the cultural climate in a country is the real judge. One particular question that arises is how tolerance toward controversial art can be promoted in today's tense political climate. The answer will be that the fate of public art depends on the 'art of persuasion'. It seems that, as all forms of arrogance sooner or later are bound to be punished, the era of the 'arrogance of public art' has come to an end.

The Ideology of Abstract Art

Changes in social, political, and religious beliefs have, throughout history, always resulted in parallel changes in the production of public art, as Dale Lanzone[1] has described in "The Public Voice," a short and elegant essay on public art in the US: "The 'allowed' and 'profited' meanings that are directly or indirectly expressed through a public work of art form a complex composition of ideas incorporating dreams, ambitions, myths, and fears—the many nuances of the objective and subjective self as a public entity. Works of art are necessarily encoded with the intelligence, vision, and resonating will of the dominant influences of their time."

These words on the history of public art in the US generally apply to Europe, as for any country, although Europe has, of course, a different history and especially a more traumatic twentieth century, with World War I and II as a double watershed that has resonated in the art world. For both continents, the same general historical sketch applies. In the era of bourgeois nationalism, from the mid-nineteenth century up to World War II, governments vehemently promoted art in public places. As Lanzone (2000: 3) explained the case in the US: "Fuelled by the resonance of commonly understood figurative sculptural narratives, works of art created during this time continue to attract support and interest from the general public to this day and are often looked upon by public decision makers as the standard for greatness in American public art. Public works of art of this period idealized and affirmed the officially supported social, economic, and political doctrines of the time, thereby gaining broad-based public acceptance and support." For Europe, however, this was true to a lesser extent.

In Europe, artistic developments progressed in a more diverse manner than in the United States, as Europe is more diverse. And in the world of the arts, Europe was in a perpetual state of 'civil war', much like those wars being fought in the streets and on the battlefields. There was classical, neo-classical, and naturalist public art. There was avant-gardist public art and social realist art in the Communist Soviet Union and in Nazi Germany, both denouncing the 'decadent bourgeois art' of the liberal West—"entartete Kunst" (degenerate art), as Hitler called it (Barron 1991).

These ongoing 'cultural wars' in Europe ended in 1945 when the real wars ended, and like the real ones, the results were devastating. Germany was left a vacuum, as was Italy to a lesser degree. In despair, but at the same time purposefully and willfully, Western Europe embraced all things that promised a break from its disastrous past. While in the US, 'newness' and 'modernity' formed the holy set of cultural values that legitimized the consumption-production cycle, believed to be necessary to sustain rapid economic growth and technological development. Concurrently, for the arts it meant that "the previous traditions and imperatives for public art that communicated social purposes and values were eschewed in favor of independent, forward-thinking expressions of bold, personal visions" (Lanzone 2000: 4).

In the United States, the urge for permanent artistic renewal may have been part of the triumph of capitalism and what the American economist Joseph Schumpeter (1942) once called its essence—"creative destruction." In Western Europe, the official attitude toward art was predominantly formed by the negative: everything was allowed and promoted as long as it did not resemble social realist art, the propaganda tool of defeated Nazi Germany and that of the West's powerful new enemy, Communist Soviet Union. Figurative representation and narrative idealism were de facto banned from public life (except for war memorials). In the Netherlands in the 1970s, some citizens founded an association for figurative art in protest of the "state ideology of abstract art."

The belief in many Western countries that free and modern art should be abstract instead of figurative caused a great "uncertainty of taste," but nobody wanted to be depicted as a "conservative." Consequently, this uncertainty was never expressed clearly and artists were given more or less carte blanche. It is not hard to imagine some of the reactions of the judging state commissioners when confronted with incomprehensible works of art. Former politicians and decision makers later admitted that in some cases all they were able to utter was "how interesting" or "most peculiar," while in reality being either disgusted or totally clueless (Beunders 1998: 184). Since the late 1950s, in fact, artists could unboundedly do what they liked. They became both icons and iconoclasts and were worshipped as heroic, courageous, and visionary creators of "the world to come," in which everything would be better and freer.

During the Cold War, freedom and democracy were the key words in the West, with the emphasis on the first word in order to contrast the 'better' Western world against the category of 'people's democracy' that existed in the East. While in the US the 'Red Scare' in the early 1950s led to dramatic forms of restrictions on the arts and self-censorship, Western Europe—under its own or the American nuclear umbrella—was able to celebrate freedom even more fully. Court cases for public acts of blasphemy, for insulting royalty or a friendly nation, or for corrupting morals seldom resulted in imposing a fine or jailing the offenders.

The Ideology of Human Rights

In the West, freedom and human rights were inseparable. Looking back from the early twenty-first century, it is easy to see how unbalanced the titles of the two grand official declarations on the matter were. The first was the Universal

Declaration of Human Rights (UDHR), adopted by the United Nations in 1948, at a time when the UN was dominated by Western powers. The second was the Convention for the Protection of Human Rights and Fundamental Freedoms, also known as the European Convention on Human Rights (ECHR), which was adopted under the auspices of the Council of Europe in 1950. Established in 1949, the Council of Europe was founded by 10 states: Belgium, Denmark, France, Ireland, Italy, Luxembourg, the Netherlands, Norway, Sweden, and the United Kingdom. The Convention of 1950 was the first international legal instrument safeguarding human rights.

For the following 50 years, both Western governments and the Western public read and reiterated only the words "human rights," or only one word, "rights." "Rights" were the main issue, whereas the other key words of both documents, "duties and responsibilities," were not emphasized as much. Both documents were inspired by Christian beliefs and are partly a secular rephrasing of biblical commands. Of course, the UDHR article regarded as the most important was and still is: "Everyone has the right to freedom of opinion and expression; this right includes freedom to hold opinions without interference and to seek, receive, and impart information and ideas through any media regardless of frontiers." However, in the UDHR this statement only materializes in Article 19; thus, it is preceded by no less than 18 other rights. Take Article 1: "All human beings are born free and equal in dignity and rights. They are endowed with reason and conscience and should act towards one another in a spirit of brotherhood." This proclaimed equality of everyone in "dignity and rights" is followed by a command to act "in a spirit of brotherhood." In Article 29, the UDHR commands once again: "Everyone has duties to the community in which alone the free and full development of his personality is possible."

Freedom of the arts is not included at all in the UDHR. Only once, in Article 27, is there a reference to the word 'art': "Everyone has the right freely to participate in the cultural life of the community, to enjoy the arts and to share in scientific advancements and its benefits." While Article 27 makes note of art, it is merely focusing on the public—participating, enjoying, and sharing—not on the creating artist.

In the ECHR, the freedom of expression is even more restricted. Ironically, this restriction of the freedom of expression is formulated in the very same article (Article 10.1) that proclaims it: "Everyone has the right to freedom of expression. This right shall include freedom to hold opinions and to receive and impart information and ideas without interference by public authority and regardless of frontiers. This article shall not prevent States from requiring the licensing of broadcasting, television or cinema enterprises." The second part of Article 10.1 contains an even longer list of limitations of this freedom: "The exercise of these freedoms, since it carries with it duties and responsibilities, may be subject to such formalities, conditions, restrictions or penalties as are prescribed by law and are necessary in a democratic society, in the interests of national security, territorial integrity or public safety, for the prevention of disorder or crime, for the protection of health or morals, for the protection of the reputation or rights of others, for preventing the disclosure of information received in confidence, or for maintaining the authority and impartiality of the judiciary."

It is even worse. In some national constitutions in Europe, the subject of art is not mentioned at all (Peaslee 1968). In other constitutions, there might be a paragraph merely mentioning that "the state should promote art." In other words, there is very little concern given to the arts as a basic right of freedom in European constitutional legislature. The fact that human or constitutional rights might clash with each other and with all the prescribed duties to the community was, of course, well known to domestic authorities and judges, who in court cases had to decide which of the constitutional or international rights prevailed. However, during the Cold War, both governments and public opinion kept advocating the importance and prevalence of the human right of freedom above all other interests.

Toward the end of the millennium, however, things began to change rapidly. In the 1990s, the European Commission against Racism and Intolerance (ECRI) was set up. ECRI's remit is to combat racism, xenophobia, anti-Semitism, and intolerance. This suggests a potential conflict with the freedoms of speech and expression. The fact that many people prefer other constitutional articles to the freedom of speech was deplored by the media and the Dutch politician Pim Fortuyn early in 2002. Fortuyn declared that, "when forced to choose," he would prefer the constitutional right of free speech over the first article in the Dutch constitution, the prohibition of discrimination (*Volkskrant*, 9 February 2002; see also Eckardt 2003).

I will mention only briefly another trend in recent years, which is of growing importance to the question of freedom of speech and artistic expression—the matter of copyrights. Among scholars and judges, there is a concern for the steady proliferation of intellectual property rights. The reason is that an overstretched protection may be in conflict with the general interest and may impinge on the freedom of speech. In a world where one cannot even use the words 'refreshes best' because they are copyrighted, the public domain is declining (Hugenholtz 2000). With copyrights on enormous collections of music and photographs being sold for billions of dollars to the world's richest companies (e.g., Sony) and wealthiest people (e.g., Bill Gates), general and cheap access to this cultural heritage—a basic human right—is in danger.

Public Art and the Democratization of Politics

The pseudo-religion of modern abstract art, informed and promoted by both governmental and artistic authorities, created a gap within parts of the wider public, which sometimes did not 'understand' this art at all and often openly despised it. The question of what exactly constitutes art became more and more confusing, even for the cultural theorists. This had already been the case since the early twentieth century. Avant-garde art itself was full of iconoclasm, especially in relation to museum art. Marchel Duchamp put a signed pissoir in a museum and suggested using a Rembrandt as an ironing board. Jean Tinguely built art machines that eventually destroyed themselves.

In the 1960s, some artists wanted museums to be burned down because they were "the coffins of art." Art had to be democratized and put on public display. This theory became practice in the 1970s, when the aim of art was both embellishment and giving meaning to the living environment of the ordinary citizen. Democratized art in a way became a state ideology in some countries, celebrating the welfare state and at the same time civilizing the people. However, the manner in which this ideology was produced and presented can be regarded as paternalistic.

As a result of the democratization of art since the 1970s, the definition question became clearer and lost any aura of scholarly value. As Joseph Beuys declared, every object could be considered art and everybody could be an artist (Harrison and Wood 1992: 890). The ultimate consequence is that everybody can therefore be considered an art critic, regardless of formal educational or artistic background (Beunders 2000). Up to today, Beuys's statement is still popular among cultural theorists and artists themselves: art is whatever the artist says it is, and art is sacred, to be protected forever by the authorities. This is the arrogance of the art world that caused a backlash in society against some pieces of modern art. In the center of the debate and political strife were some specific pieces of public art and the question as to whether the state had to fund artists and pieces of art that 'insulted' the very people whose taxes had paid for its production and exhibition (Mitchell 1992).

The question of what art is might have been solved by Beuys. The public and political question of what *public art* is was not. The British "think tank for public art practice," ixia, which receives funding from the Arts Council England, answers this question online: "The practice of public art is diverse … As a result public art is difficult to define."[2] Obviously, this definition does not provide much resolution for the clarity-seeking audience. Even the free online encyclopedia project Wikipedia gives a better definition: "The term 'public art' properly refers to works of art in any media that [have] been planned and executed with the specific intention of being sited or staged in the public domain, usually outside and accessible to all."[3] The advantage of this wide definition is that it puts an end to the judicial and political distinctions between all kinds of different media, of which 'the press' was historically thought of as the most prominent and most protected in democracies.

In recent times we have witnessed the transformation of all kinds of technical media and the consequent blurring of definitions, like the one on public art. Now we acknowledge that monuments, memorials, and civic statuary are public art and that architecture and the man-made landscape also fulfill that definition. Increasingly, our whole environment, whether represented by permanent materials or by temporary graffiti and festivals, is seen as public art. Initiating, funding, and sanctioning by the authorities are no longer considered the distinctive criteria.

However, from the 1960s into the 1990s state funding was the main issue. First it was a welcome vehicle for positive change, later a scapegoat for all kinds of artistic unease and societal frustration. The ideological foundations of the 'percent of art' policies in most countries in the West, in which a certain percentage of the construction costs has to be spent on public art in or outside a public building, were all about changing the environment—and the citizens themselves—for the better.

In 2005, ixia provided a list of claims that have been made over the last few decades about the value that public art brings to public places and the people in general. Among these assertions are that public art:

- Enhances the physical environment
- Creates a sense of place and distinctiveness
- Contributes to community cohesion
- Contributes to social health and well-being
- Contributes to economic value through inward investment and tourism
- Fosters civic pride and confidence
- Raises the quality of life
- Reduces crime[4]

One may notice the strong emphasis on presupposed socio-economic effects in all these claims. Furthermore, there is a total lack of the factors that caused the explosion of public art in the century before 1940: national identity, national pride, national unity, and national destiny. Although in practice the welfare state was in essence a nationalistic enterprise, resulting in great uncertainties and social unrest when it eroded, since World War II the combination of individualistic and cosmopolitan—local and global—well-being was at the heart of the public art enterprise.

As is common with new ideologies, the benefits of public art were taken for granted. As of yet, they still are not very well researched. There are dozens of case studies on specific examples of public art, but studies that examine the relationship between public art of the welfare state and the public realm over a longer period of time are rare. Incidentally, this is in sharp contrast to the multitude of studies on the political and psychological effects of public art in Christian feudal Europe and in twentieth-century United States and Europe leading up to World War II.

What happened after the launch of the 'percent for art' policy in most Western countries was that the artistic field claimed an ever more important role for artists in the public domain. In some European countries, the permanent funding of artists themselves, no matter what art they produced, was tied to the emancipation of 'the artist'. Assured of his or her income, the artist became almost totally independent. As a consequence, the post-war attitude that art had to be critical was sometimes taken to extremes.

With 'balance' as the key word in the weighing of rights and duties, public art can be used in several ways—as an effective tool of social emancipation, as a means of establishing a dialogue in tense situations (as with mural art), but also as a weapon of propaganda to achieve a political goal. It was Lenin who ordered the installation of the public art of heroes and artists in almost every village in his revolutionary Soviet Union. In the West, the line between graffiti and 'guerrilla' art is thin.

For decades, the definition of public art has been the preserve of artists, cultural theorists, and state commissioners, a peculiar fact since most definitions assume some kind of interaction with a public audience. Until the early 1980s, this audience was seldom asked for their opinion about planned pieces of public art, not even when the installations were to be put in the immediacy of their own neighborhood or in central places of the public domain. The backlash of this paternalistic neglect would be powerful, and it is still raging today. The list of controversies over pieces of public art is almost endless.

The online list of acts of censorship presented by the National Coalition Against Censorship (NCAC), founded in the US in 1974, is growing longer and longer. The main goal, formulated according to the spirit of the 1970s, was "to protect artists' rights to participate in the democratic dialogue by defending public access to their work and supporting their ability to freely express views that might be unpopular or controversial."[5] In due time the emphasis shifted to organizing educational programs, in order to counter censorship attempts. NCAC now recognizes that 'the public' is important: "Censorship has been around for as long as there has been creative expression; no doubt, censorship attempts will be part of our future. However, the degree of public support for free speech has always made a difference—the difference between silent repression and a lively debate. We keep the debate not only alive, but healthy."[6]

The NCAC over the years seems to have discovered two things: that 'public support' is necessary and that the question of censorship is not as simple as the name of the organization suggests. One example, in 2001, from the long list of acts of censorship will suffice to illustrate the recognition of the fact that in matters of free speech and censorship, there are only gray areas. "A Seattle gallery chose to move artwork from the front to the back room ... after the provocative nature of the photographs prevented patrons from moving throughout the entire gallery to view other artists' works. This incident questions where the line is between censorship and permissible curatorial discretion."[7]

One of the simplifications of the post-war era was the idea that the matter of human rights and freedom of expression was a straightforward, black-and-white affair (Garry 1993). The other simplification of free speech was the idea that censorship was an offense that only 'the establishment'—political authorities and the 'religious right'—was guilty of. In reality, censorship, although political, can neither be regarded as typically left wing or right wing, nor can it be considered categorically progressive or conservative. Censorship can, on various occasions, be demanded by all segments of society. Consequently, every society has its own specific tolerance levels that sometimes are described in the penal code (Dubin 1992). In seven European countries, Holocaust denial (*Auschwitzlüge*) is forbidden by law. In early 2006, the controversial British historian David Irving was sentenced to three years in prison by an Austrian court for having written such claims 20 years earlier. In Japan, the exposure of pubic hair is forbidden. In many countries, including the United States, the desecration of national symbols, such as the flag, is forbidden.

It is invariably the dominant culture in a country that prescribes what is allowed and what is not, what kind of social behavior is allowed and what is not, whether it is about smoking or physical contact between school pupils and their teachers. As soon as a 'counterculture' arises, questioning the dominant culture and its codes and laws, conflicts are on the horizon.

After the 1960s, the counterculture and the artists had gained the upper hand in the field of the public arts. This era came to an end during the 1990s as a result of developments in the art world itself; as a result of the changing morals, if not moral panics, in society; as a result of the ongoing politicization of small interest groups, such as gays and lesbians, Indians and Aboriginals, who were "seeking safety in an insecure world" (Bauman 2001), and environmental groups, such as Greenpeace and animal rights movements; and, last but not least, as a result of the emergence of a multicultural society. The mass immigration to Western Europe of people from all over the world, especially from Muslim countries, has caused a novel and unsettling confrontation between liberal, secular societies and new groups that are prepared to use violence in support of their fundamentalist religious beliefs.

Moreover, the concept and acceptance of avant-garde art has been eroding further. Avant-garde art used to be characterized by three main elements: alienation, innovation, and the future. The postmodern 'anything goes' mentality and the commercialization of the art world have destroyed this concept. As Stuart Hobbs (1997) describes it, postmodernism took the future out of avant-gardism. For many people, artists lost their aura of authenticity and sincerity, some of them openly admitting that they were only in it for the money. Striving for innovation and pushing boundaries were seen as conventions, and, more importantly, art increasingly became a consumer commodity. Art forms that were relatively new in the post-war period, like that of Andy Warhol and Roy Lichtenstein, by the 1980s had lost their capacity to evoke strong reactions. Some writers published books presaging turbulent times ahead, such as *The End of the American Avant Garde* (Hobbs 1997) and *After the End of Art* (Danto 1997).

In the 1990s, the art world plummeted into a state of crisis. Some artists, like Jeff Koons and Damien Hirst, deliberately chose to find ways to create art that was still able to shock people and create a scandal. Some 1990s artists openly proclaimed that provoking a strong reaction from the public was their main aim. But they meant for this reaction to be a verbal one—a discussion or a polemic in some newspaper—not a ban or the destruction of the piece of art itself. Nevertheless, destruction is exactly what has happened more and more since the 1980s. Both the general public and specific interest groups have increased their protests against works of art that insult morality, endanger the public order, and disparage their identity or religious beliefs. And here opposing positions sometimes find common ground (*les extrêmes se touchent*). In Amsterdam in 1994, two different groups of women—left-wing feminists and fundamentalist Muslims—protested a public art photograph of a half-naked woman at a bridge (Beunders 1994: 24–25).

Physical attacks on pieces of art are not a novelty. In the early twentieth century, a British suffragette attacked *The Rokeby Venus*, by Diego Velasquez, because of its masculine, sexist nature and to protest against the suppression of women (Nead 1992). Since then, many world-famous works of art have been assaulted, such as Rembrandt's *The Nightwatch* and avant-gardist Barnett Newman's *Who's Afraid of Red, Yellow and Blue*, both in Amsterdam. More recently, a painting by Roy Lichtenstein in Vienna met with the same fate (Gamboni 1997).

The backlash against the prevailing counterculture and the holiness of art and the artist came from several directions. After the early 1950s attacks by US Senator Joseph McCarthy on all political and artistic expressions that he damned as "un-American activities," in the late 1960s and early 1970s attacks on free speech and 'wrong' public art came from the extreme left, in protest against the right-wing 'yellow journalism', sexist pornography, sexist commercials on television, and commercials in general. Statues of colonial heroes were brought down, and street names had to be changed because the 'historical figure' had fallen into disgrace due to the ever-changing perspective of the past. Colonialism, collaboration during wartime, and apartheid caused bitter struggles in local communities over symbols in the public domain that had to be erased, and subsequently replaced by statues or names of people and deeds that were more in tune with the norms and values of the current times. From the 1970s onward, special interest groups claimed ownership over their own image. And, last but not least, the 'common man' started to raise his voice against specific forms of public art she or he did not want to see as a memorial or as a symbol for the nation—or simply did not want to encounter on the way to work.

When one of the best-known public controversies, the *Tilted Arc* controversy, is taken into account, we discover that the era of protest against enforced public art has already lasted a quarter of a century. Since its installation in 1981 and subsequent removal in 1989 from New York City's Federal Plaza, noted sculptor Richard Serra's *Tilted Arc* has been a touchstone for debates over the role of public art. Immediately after it was installed, the 10-foot-high, 120-foot-long curved wall of self-rusting steel became a magnet for criticism. Art critics labeled it the city's worst public sculpture, with many denouncing it as an example of the elitism associated with art, while others saw it as an obstacle to the use and enjoyment of the plaza (Senie 2001). The debate was in fact about public funding of the arts and not, for instance, about the universal right of enjoyment of the arts. After a jury voted to remove it, the piece ended up in a government warehouse in Maryland.

A few years later, Robert Hughes (1993) published his book *The Culture of Complaint*. In it, he denounced the antipathetic reactions by special identity/interest groups to all forms of public utterances or public art that they believe have insulted their private identity. Hughes's call for more moderate, modest, and tolerant behavior by citizens did not meet with a receptive audience. The culture wars continued apace. National scandals and lawsuits ensued over exhibitions of photographs by Robert Mapplethorpe and Andres Serrano, for example (Dubin 2000). Also, in many local municipalities, smaller but just as bitter struggles were fought over symbolism in the public domain.

Most democratic countries have not yet seen the end of the outbreaks of popular protests against public art and court cases involving it. For an essay on art and censorship in the mid-1990s Netherlands, I could easily sum up a list of hundreds of cases of secretly or openly vandalized or totally destroyed pieces of public art. In the Netherlands, some controversies grew into national debates, just as happened in New York with its *Tilted Arch* incident (Beunders 1994: 12–40).

What has to be noted is the difference between several countries in the West with regard to the Christian religion. Art that could be considered anti-Christian—Serrano's *Piss Christ* (1987) and Chris Ofili's painting, *The Holy Virgin Mary* (1996), depicting a black Madonna with cut-outs from pornographic magazines and elephant dung—met with much more resistance in the US and Britain than in Western European countries, such as France, the Netherlands, and Scandinavia, where secularization had become predominant since the 1960s. A Dutch judge decided not to prohibit the Serrano exhibition in the late 1990s, and what is more illuminating, the museum that displayed the photographs drew hundreds of thousands of people to a relatively remote part of the Netherlands.

Religion and Public Art

The factor of religion brings us to the last element that in the early twenty-first century makes the fate of public art even more complex than it has already become. In the struggle since the 1950s between traditional dominant national culture and the counterculture of the post-war generation, the most recent 'party' that joined the stage, Islam, has created the same panic in society as the counterculture did around 1968 among 'silent majorities' in the US, France, and elsewhere in the West. Whereas the answer of the old elites to the counterculture in the 1960s had been quite simple—giving in—this time the panic is perhaps even greater. Now the acts and counter-acts that are triggered by feelings of degradation among ethnic and religious minorities will not be resolved with sit-ins. This time protest is mainly ventilated through violent means, like death threats and acts of (mass) murder.

The current helplessness of authorities in multicultural societies in Western Europe on the issue of the freedom of expression is, as said, proof that arrogance is bound to be punished, sooner or later. After the arrogance of white supremacy in the 1950s and of the state-subsidized 'independent' artists in the 1970s, the rather arrogant idea took hold that artistic freedom and 'anything goes' could last forever because it provided us with the best of all possible worlds. Francis Fukuyama (1989), in a dramatic denial of the force of history and of the effects that changes in social, political, and religious beliefs and in demography would have on society and on the arts, saw in it "the end of history."

The idea that the secular, modern, democratic, and free Western world would remain peaceful in the aftermath of an influx of immigrants, and that the millions of newcomers from all over the world would adjust peaceably to the beliefs and practices of their new European homelands, was a dramatic error. Whatever one thinks of Huntington's views on the clash of civilizations, the fact is that in the secularized European countries, the role of religion, which was viewed as a primitive thing of the past, had been disregarded.

The first country that realized with a shock that this secularization had left it empty-handed in the face of the rising religion of Islam was the Netherlands. Because of the lack of dialogue with Muslims, and the lack of knowledge of religion in general, the panic was great after the brutal killing of writer-filmmaker Theo van Gogh by a Muslim fundamentalist in 2004 (Buruma 2006). Van Gogh, a controversial artist, pushed the envelope of freedom of expression as far as he could. He sealed his fate when, together with Ayaan Hirsi Ali, a former Somalian refugee turned member of Parliament and a fierce critic of the anti-female violence of fundamentalist Islam, he made an 11-minute movie on the abuse of women in Islam. Not long after this movie was shown on television, van Gogh was ritually slaughtered, and the killer promised that Hirsi Ali would soon follow. As a result, the Dutch authorities guarded her 24 hours a day.[8]

In September 2005, purportedly to highlight the topic of self-censorship in the media, the Danish newspaper *Jyllands-Posten* published a series of cartoons on Islam that resulted in often violent protests and consumer boycotts by Muslims throughout the world. Afterwards, the paper, according to the *International Herald Tribune* (7 February 2006), declared to have done so as an experiment to see whether political satirists were capable of being as harsh to Islam as they are to other organized religions.

What is so striking about the reactions of the authorities and most parts of the public was the lack of willingness to defend the freedom of speech and expression and the full exercise of those freedoms by artists like Theo van Gogh and the Danish cartoonists. While some political reactions to the killing of van Gogh and the burning of embassies in the wake of the Danish cartoons were of high indignation, the predominant response in politics and the press was: "Freedom of expression has to be defended, but maybe they had gone too far." On 9 February 2006, the British weekly, *The Economist*, summarized this lukewarm response of some Western governments, accompanied by apologies to Voltaire, as follows: "I disagree with what you say, and even if you are threatened with death, I will not defend very strongly your right to say it." In the US and Britain, both at war in Afghanistan and Iraq, the cartoons were not published.

The Art of Persuasion

In a fully media-oriented world, we can no longer make a distinction between different forms of artistic expression. In this globalized world of immediate communication, every art form—whether permanent or temporary—can instantly be seen all over the world. In a politically tense situation, everything can be used to create uproar or to score points in the struggle for emancipation, for beliefs, for anything people strive for, in the positive or negative sense. Among the slogans used by all proponents of maximum freedom since the Enlightenment, the words of Benjamin Franklin still endure: "They that can give up essential liberty to obtain a little temporary safety deserve neither liberty nor safety." In fact, history and politics over the centuries has proved that liberty expands in times when there is little outside resistance and shrinks when the pressure grows.

In the early twenty-first century, there seems to be more outside pressure than in many decades before. Furthermore, the pressure is now more diverse since it is coming from all directions. The restrictions that are consequently being put on public art are successful because the maxim 'victory is not caused by the strength of the attackers but by the weakness of the defenders' is as true as it ever was. The crisis in modern art itself is one of the main reasons for the half-hearted attitude of the politicians and the public to defend artistic freedom.

After a half-century of modernist dominance, both the public and the decision makers grew weary of the promises of modern art. From the mid-1980s on, they began asking for the reintegration of public art and public purpose. As Lanzone put it: "We now live in an age of mass 'realpolitik.'"[9] He could not have been more right. Groups, organizations, and even private individuals, regardless of their interests, can dramatically affect the course and outcome of public decision making through the tenacious application of well-orchestrated criticism. Our culture resonates with unpredictability, which has resulted in surprising new forms of social and political anxiety about old and new 'folk devils' (Cohen 1972). Public officials have become fearfully nervous and apprehensive in their decision making.

I call this new situation the 'revenge of the people' on the arrogance of the arts (that is, arts commissioners) and the hubris of some artists. Is there cause to be pessimistic about the fate of public art? Not really. In fact, we have returned to the pre–World War II situation in which commissioned artists predictably had to conform to the national cultural and social standards. Now, 'national' means that artists have to adjust to the demands of many interests groups and of the recipient community in particular. That is democracy: more struggles, more debate, more compromises.

The pieces of public art that have been the most successful in recent years show how great the public interest is in the narrative, well-humored, and symbolic communication of public art. It is true that the public artists who are the most successful have had to become more like well-skilled process managers, sometimes perhaps more skilled in the 'art of persuasion' than in art itself. In other words, to be successful means to build up a career of past positive performances, both as an artist and as a public diplomat. A clear example is Christo. It took him more than two decades to convince the government of the German Federal Republic that wrapping up the Reichstag, the symbolically heavily loaded Parliament building in Berlin, with recyclable man-made materials for 14 days was a good idea. But in the end, in 1995, Christo succeeded. Millions of tourists from all over the world traveled to Berlin.

One might call this new form of globalized, mass-appealing public art the 'Disneyfication' of art. The only alternative seems to be politicians with enough power to overrule all kinds of democratic processes, such as prime ministers and presidents. However, their 'great works' of public art, such as London's Millennium Dome, are not as universally admired as they had no doubt hoped. The fine truth about the fine arts is that people in the West these days yearn for common moments of experience and artistic visions of truth or beauty, and this yearning seems to intensify. Thus, there is no reason to believe that politicians will stop promoting public art. While they might have a more reluctant attitude, in anticipation of possible future criticism, making pragmatic adjustments to new socio-political circumstances is the heart of the political profession.

Although we are going through a phase of uncertainty, with restraint in public expressions and downright censorship and self-censorship in the media, the many examples of very successful public art give reason to believe that there is a need for public art in the multicultural society as well. This public art will change, no doubt. It may even occur that, thanks to the large Muslim minorities in many European countries, geometric abstract art will return, pushing aside once again the now popular figurative art. So be it. The only requirement for public art in this century is the persistence of the democratic 'art of persuasion'.

Acknowledgment

An earlier version of this essay was delivered at a symposium in the Sociology Department of the University of Bergen, 15–18 September 2005. The author wishes to express gratitude to Zihni Ozdil for his assistance in finalizing this chapter.

Henri Beunders received his PhD from the University of Amsterdam and has been Chair of History of Society, Media and Culture at Erasmus University, Rotterdam, since 1990. In addition, he is director of Postacademische Dagblad Opleiding Journalistiek, the post-graduate institute of journalism. His principal interests are history, politics, and culture of conflict and societal dynamics; mobilization of masses/citizens through action and old and new media; strategic and crisis communication; police and justice matters. He has written several books and dozens of articles, including "The Politics of Nostalgia or the Janus-Face of Modern Society" (2007) and "The People Conquer the Media: An Edifying Dumbing Down" (2004).

Notes

1. See http://www.chihuly.com/essays/lanzoneessay.html.
2. See http://www.ixia-info.com/publicart/index.htm.
3. See http://en.wikipedia.org/wiki/Public_art.
4. See http://www.ixia-info.com/research/index.htm.
5. See http://www.ncac.org/advocacy_projects/Arts_Advocacy.cfm.
6. Ibid.
7. See http://www.ncac.org/action_issues/Race_Ethnicity_Gender.cfm.
8. After remaining in the Netherlands for two years, Hirsi Ali is presently a fellow at the American Enterprise Institute, a conservative think tank, in Washington, DC. She has again been granted security protection due to death threats she has received from Muslims in the United States.
9. See http://www.chihuly.com/essays/lanzoneessay.html.

References

Barron, Stephanie. 1991. *"Degenerate Art": The Fate of the Avant-Garde in Nazi Germany.* New York: Harry N. Abrams

Bauman, Zygmunt. 2001. *Community: Seeking Safety in an Insecure World.* Cambridge: Cambridge University Press.

Beunders, Henri. 1994. *De strijd om het beeld: Over de behoefte aan censuur* [The Battle of the Pictures: On the Need of Censorship]. Den Haag: Vuga.

_____. 1998. *De verbeelding van de wereld: De wereld van de verbeelding* [The Representation of the World: The World of Representation]. Amsterdam: Jan Mets.

_____. 2000. *Wat je ziet ben je zelf. Big Brother: Lust, leven en lijden voor de camera* [What You See Is Yourself. Big Brother: Lust, Life, and Suffering in Front of the Camera]. Amsterdam: Prometheus.

Buruma, Ian. 2006. *Murder in Amsterdam.* New York: Penguin Press.

Cohen, Stanley. 1972. *Folk Devils and Moral Panics.* Cambridge: Cambridge University Press.

Danto, Arthur C. 1997. *After the End of Art: Contemporary Art and the Pale of History.* Princeton, NJ: Princeton University Press.

Dubin, Steven C. 1992. *Arresting Images: Impolitic Art and Uncivil Actions.* London: Routledge.

_____. 2000. *Displays of Power: Controversy in the American Museum from the Enola Gay to Sensation.* New York: New York University Press.

Eckardt, Frank. 2003. *Pim Fortuyn und die Niederlande: Populismus als Reaktion auf die Globalisierung.* Marburg: Tectum.

Fukuyama, Francis. 1989. "The End of History?" *National Interest,* no. 16 (Summer).

Gamboni, Dario. 1997. *The Destruction of Art: Iconoclasm and Vandalism since the French Revolution.* London: Reaktion.

Garry, Patrick. 1993. *An American Paradox: Censorship in a Nation of Free Speech.* Westport, CT: Praeger.

Gonzalez, Madelena. 2005. *Fiction after the Fatwa: Salmon Rushdie and the Charm of Catastrophe.* Amsterdam: Rodopi.

Harrison, Charles, and Paul Wood, eds. 1992. *Art in Theory 1900–1990.* Oxford: Blackwell.

Hobbs, Stuart D. 1997. *The End of the American Avant Garde.* New York: New York University Press.

Hugenholtz, P. Bernt. 2000. "Copyright and Freedom of Expression in Europe." In *Innovation Policy in an Information Age,* ed. Rochelle Cooper Dreyfus, Harry First, and Diane Leenheer Zimmerman. Oxford: Oxford University Press.

Hughes, Robert. 1993. *The Culture of Complaint: The Fraying of America.* Oxford: Oxford University Press.

Huntington, Samuel P. 1993. "The Clash of Civilizations?" *Foreign Affairs* 72, no. 3: 22–49.

_____. 1996. *The Clash of Civilizations and the Remaking of World Order.* New York: Simon & Schuster.

Lanzone, Dale. 2000. "The Public Voice." In *Chihuly Projects.* Seattle, WA: Portland Press. Citations from http://www.chihuly.com/essays/lanzoneessay.html.

Mitchell, W. J. T., ed. 1992. *Art and the Public Sphere.* Chicago: University of Chicago Press.

Nead, Lynda. 1992. *The Female Nude: Art, Obscenity and Sexuality.* London: Routledge.

Peaslee, Amos J. 1968. *Constitutions of Nations.* The Hague: Nijhoff.

Senie, Harriet F. 2001. *The Tilted Arc Controversy: Dangerous Precedent?* Minnesota: University of Minnesota Press.

Chapter 2

CONTESTING AUTHENTICITY AND THE PROMETHEAN COMPLEX
The Cultural Politics of Globalization

Terence Chong

Singapore exists because it is a global city. As a former British colonial port, the city-state, at the southern tip of the Malay Peninsula, has long been an integral part of global trading processes, supporting the assertion that contemporary global cities are 'global' because of their historical characteristics (Abu-Lughod 2001). The need for Singapore to retain its economic globalism upon independence was heightened by its lack of a hinterland when it was expelled from Malaysia in 1965. Since then, various scholars have written at length about the deep sense of globalism inscribed on the country's economic policies and its unrelenting desire to synchronize itself with world markets for nothing less than national survival (Low 2001; Rodan 1989).

In contrast to the government's far-sighted, globally oriented economic policies, the ruling People's Action Party (PAP) did not have a coherent national

Notes for this chapter are located on page 40.

policy for the arts and culture in the early years of independence. More occupied with the challenges of unemployment and housing shortages, the PAP government did not make the arts a national priority. Hence, material and social welfare and earning a living were the primary concerns of Singapore's mostly immigrant community. Culture and the arts were never seen as a basic need (Koh 1989).

Nonetheless, even though the PAP government lacked a clear vision for the arts and culture industry, it devised a specific role for it. The multi-ethnic and multi-religious complexion of Singaporean society—composed mainly of ethnic Chinese, Malays, and Indians—was a constant source of socio-political tension and worry for the government. The ethnic riots of 1964 between the Chinese majority and the Malay minority left 23 dead, and the conflict has since become a political leitmotif of the government in its discourse on race and religion. In an effort to promote the national ideology of multiculturalism and integration among the disparate ethnic groups, the notion of culture was linked to ethnic practices and traditions, resulting in the representation of 'Chinese culture', 'Malay culture', and 'Indian culture'. With culture thus linked to ethnicity, the highly visual language of the arts and culture industry became an ideal means of increasing awareness of different traditions. These diverse cultures were symbolized by respective costumes and traditional dances performed by various ethnic groups, and the collective performances often functioned as purposeful metonyms for broader inter-ethnic harmony. These presentations of state-sanctioned culture are not unusual, given that "[s]tate-building elites and officials have self-consciously used culture as an instrument of national integration" (Schudson 1994: 22). Local schools, community centers, and the media were spaces in which the arts were used to re-enact state fantasies of multiculturalism and model citizenry. One of the earliest government statements on cultural policy came in 1959. According to the *State of Singapore Annual Report*, the Ministry of Culture had clear objectives for local arts and culture, namely, "[t]he creation of a sense of national identity, the elimination of communal divisions and attitudes. The propagation of democratic values, conducive to the ultimate creation of a just society. The creation of a wide acceptance of a National Language" (quoted in Bereson 2002).

The government's single-minded intent to use culture and the arts to serve nation-building purposes was demonstrated in the 1980s when the Ministry of Community Development assumed the portfolio of the Ministry of Culture. The turning point for Singapore's national cultural policy came in 1985. The role of the arts was re-examined when economic stagnation gripped the country that year. Experiencing one of the country's worst economic recessions, the government set up the Economic Review Committee (ERC) to explore potential growth sectors. Among its many recommendations, the ERC report singled out the economic potential of the "cultural and entertainment" sector, which included the performing arts, film production, museums, and art galleries.

The ERC report was the seed of a coherent national policy for the arts and culture in that its recommendations "represented the first explicit, albeit somewhat ad hoc, acknowledgement of the economic potential of artistic and cultural activities" (Kong 2000: 413). This nascent government policy was refined four years later in the form of the *Report of the Advisory Council on Culture and the Arts* (1989). Its recommendations included the establishment of a state cultural and funding institution and a national arts center, realized in the National Arts Council (NAC) and the Esplanade: Theatres on the Bay, respectively.

A Global Cultural Policy and Its Stratification of the Theatre Community

Singapore's cultural policy took on a decidedly global orientation in 1992. The government embarked on a 'Global City for the Arts' campaign to boost local arts and cultural industries in a bid to turn the city-state into an international cultural hub. Driven by economic need, the government exploited the arts and culture as a selling point in the global competition for human talent and capital. Hence, instead of embarking on a coherent policy for the purpose of cultural preservation or the nurturing of indigenous art forms, the Singapore government formulated cultural policies that would complement and support the city-state's progression up the New International Division of Labour. It was acknowledged that Singapore's early economic models, while successful in the past, had to be restructured in order for the country to reduce its reliance on low-skill manufacturing, given the greater competition from India and China, and that the country needed to invest in creative industries and research and development. This made the government keenly aware of the arts as a means to encourage skilled global professionals to work and live in Singapore, and also as a means to dissuade highly qualified and mobile Singaporeans from leaving the country. Given the centrality of these two elite groups in the policy-making process, the Singapore government's conception of the Global City for the Arts policy was a class-based one in which the interests of the transnational capitalist class were prioritized. In fulfilling this group's interests, the Singapore government soon found that it had to recalibrate local regulations and rules in accordance to the expectations of this class.

Consequentially, in an effort to reconcile local standards with international norms, the 1990s saw several moves by the government to relax stringent censorship regulations in the arts and culture industry (see Chong 2005). This was necessary because in order to win international legitimacy for the Global City for the Arts project, there had to be (or at least there had to be an appearance of having) a "realigning of local regulations and mindsets in line with international best practices" (Chang 2000: 818). Cities desiring to meet global expectations, for instance, needed to develop local-global "reconciliatory policies" for international familiarity and standardization (Burtenshaw, Bateman, and Ashworth 1991). As such, the gradual cultural liberalization that swept through the 1990s was less the result of an authoritarian government voluntarily doing away with strict censorship regulations and more the consequence of globalization pressures that accompanied an effort to win international legitimacy. This did not mean that the government had unburdened the local arts and culture industry from its early nation-building responsibilities. Rather, state messages and discourses were put across more subtly by a fast maturing cultural industry for a more sophisticated audience. These nation-building messages and state discourses also had to be refined and made less conspicuous, because the liberalization of the arts and culture industry through the 1990s was often used as a barometer of the Singapore government's political openness.[1]

In appealing to the transnational capitalist class, it invariably became necessary to nurture and champion local arts groups that shared the socio-cultural characteristics of this class. The Global City for the Arts campaign led to the restructuring of local state grant schemes. Previously, arts groups, regardless of their track record, could apply for state funds under the generic Project Grants program. Under this inclusive scheme, all arts groups were eligible for the same amount of public funds, regardless of audience appeal or genre. In 2000, the National Arts Council introduced two other grant programs—the Annual Grants and the 2-Year Major Grants—to create a three-tier hierarchy within the arts and cultural community. At the bottom rung were the traditional Project Grants, then the more generous Annual Grants, and, finally, the exclusive 2-Year Major Grants. The beneficiaries of the Annual and 2-Year Major Grants were identified by the state as 'flagship' groups that would be nurtured for the international stage. The Project Grant is perhaps the oldest form of state theatre grant, going back as far as the existence of the Ministry of Culture in the 1970s. An ad hoc grant given on a project basis, it is limited to not more than 30 percent of a theatre company's total production costs. The Annual Grant, which starts at S$300,000, is meant to meet part of the arts organization's annual operating expenses and to facilitate the development of professional staff and resources. The 2-Year Major Grant aims to develop local organizations into world-class entities. The amount for the 2-Year Major Grant may reach S$800,000 per annum.

The Singapore government's Global City for the Arts project has, in effect, led to the stratification of the local theatre field. In an attempt to woo foreign talent and tourists, it has been found that the selection criteria for the more exclusive grants heavily favor contemporary English-language theatre companies (Chong 2005). Social factors, such as English as a language medium, the Western training of artistic directors of these theatre companies, the greater disposable income of English-educated middle-class audiences, and the ability of expatriates to access these companies linguistically, all contribute to the fact that English-language Singaporean theatre companies are over-represented in the higher state grants. At the other end of the scale are theatre groups that do not possess the cultural capital or audience size of the well-established English-language theatre companies. These smaller groups include Chinese opera, traditional Malay theatre, and Tamil drama, as well as amateur English-language theatre groups. The three-tier grant schemes have transformed the theatre community into a field of power wherein certain established and contemporary English-language theatre companies enjoy privileged positions, while other companies are located near the margins.

These 'marginal' theatre companies, for the present purpose, are those that are eligible only for the ad hoc Project Grants. Unlike established theatre companies, they are not fully professional but amateur in status. They do not possess well-defined internal administrative organization or clear-cut roles within the theatre company. Many are run part-time by university students or practitioners with day jobs. Furthermore, while professional theatre companies base working relationships on contractual obligations, many of these marginal theatre companies rely on notions of friendship and mutual understanding.

Nonetheless, it would be a mistake to assume that the uneven relations between privileged and marginal theatre companies are static or that the asymmetrical structures of power and resources have overwhelmed marginal theatre companies. In *Pascalian Meditations*, the late French sociologist Pierre Bourdieu (2000: 187) writes that each agent in the social world "pursues not only the imposition of an advantageous position of himself or herself, with the strategies of 'presentation of the self', but also the power to impose as legitimate the principles of construction of social reality most favourable to his or her social being and to accumulation of a symbolic capital of recognition." Many marginal theatre companies also pursue the construction of social reality most favorable to themselves. In this case, certain marginal theatre practitioners recognize the structural prejudices of the field, such as the specific criteria of higher state grants, and consequently avoid competing directly with top-tier English-language companies, largely because they do not possess the cultural and economic capital to do so. Instead, local marginal theatre companies strategize their resources differently in order to win recognition or symbolic capital from the field. They generally do so in two ways: first, they contest the notion of authenticity, and, second, they take on a 'Promethean complex'. The data and interviews recorded in the sections below are gleaned from ethnographic fieldwork conducted by the author within the Singapore theatre community over a period of 12 months.[2]

Contesting Authenticity: The Cultural Politics of Globalization

The concept of authenticity is one of the key issues in the globalization literature. It is usually described as being closely tied to local culture and the particularities of time and space (Featherstone 1990a), as well as being accompanied by assumptions about boundedness and rootedness (Tomlinson 1999: 129). In contrast to this, global culture is defined as a "mélange" of disparate components, "eclectic, universal, timeless and technical" (Smith 1990), such that it is "memory-less," "syncretic," and dependent on capitalist production of "mass-mediated signs and symbols" (Perry 1998). In other words, "local or national cultures have strong emotional connotations for large numbers of people, but global culture is bereft of such 'ethnic-based' appeal" (Beynon and Dunkerley 2000: 13).

Given that global processes and flows have transformed territories into a variety of transient "scapes" (Appadurai 1990), it is no surprise that the concept, appearance, and even promise of authenticity have become highly prized in the memory-less and syncretic cityscape. The notion of authenticity is prized in Singapore, not only because it is a node enmeshed in the matrix of global capitalism and therefore inundated by the unrelenting flows of an impersonal syncretic global culture, but also because, as a predominantly immigrant population that has severed its roots twice, first from its original homelands of China and India and then from Malaysia, it is a nation-state that has no 'golden past' or *ethnie* on which to predicate nostalgia, historicity, and, ultimately, authenticity. Hence, the search for authenticity in Singapore often operates on two levels. The first is a superficial level that emphasizes the importance of form, such as championing the use of Singlish (a vernacular hybrid of English, Chinese dialect, and Malay) in the media or celebrating local cuisine. Here, icons and social phenomena are used in a shorthand manner as signifiers of Singaporean-ness. This idea of Singaporean-ness is a national distillation of societal practices, idiosyncrasies, attitudes, and visual markers over a period of more than 40 years since independence.

The second level delves more deeply into the fissures of class formation and its consequences. As a hyper-capitalist society, the city-state's participation in the international economy and its pursuit of global capital has ushered in both the positives and negatives of globalization. The negatives include the widening disparity between the skilled and the unskilled, the influx of foreign human talent at the perceived expense of local workers, and the direct linkage between local employment and capricious global market forces. These negatives are played out in various ways at the local level. Firstly, an identifiable working class with traits such as English-language deficiency and particular leisure habits has been formed. This is in contrast with the smaller number of English-proficient, middle-class cosmopolitan professionals with whom political and economic power lies. Secondly, gaps in the domestic workforce have forced the Singapore government to adopt a pro-active policy to attract skilled workers from around the world. Vernacularly known as 'foreign talent', these skilled workers have become a source of tension between the government and some sections of the local population, with the latter feeling that they have been marginalized in favor of outsiders. With dichotomies such as working class/cosmopolitans and local/foreign talent, the cultural politics of globalization is often articulated as local versus global, authentic versus alien. Authenticity is thus often defined in contrast to the global and cosmopolitan and, subsequently, is imagined to be located in the working class and its social world because this class has not been the beneficiary of globalization or global capitalism.

Discourses of authenticity and Singaporean-ness are important to local theatre companies for several reasons. The first is market segmentation. Local audiences who attend the productions of local theatre companies expect to see the staging of original and local narratives and stories. Those who prefer more global or Western theatre offerings have access to touring productions of shows such as *Les Misérables* or *The Phantom of the Opera*. Second, the conception and production of local plays and narratives allow theatre companies to jostle more favorably for state funds in view of the government's public commitment to the local arts and culture industry. Third, and most significant, theatre companies become endowed with symbolic capital—that is, they acquire recognition, prestige, and reputation for articulating the local. For Bourdieu (1986), symbolic capital is self-interest disguised as being "disinterested" in order to gain obedience, deference, recognition, and the services of others within a given field.

A typical assertion of authenticity or Singaporean-ness begins with the avowal to be resolutely 'local'. Many smaller theatre companies claim to be interested in local subcultures, the lives of ordinary Singaporeans, and 'heartlander' issues, and thus (un)consciously engage in the global-local binary. The 28-year-old artistic director of a small, amateur English-language theatre company explained it this way: "My plays are about Singaporean life. I think you have to be Singaporean and be part of the culture in order to understand my stuff. I respect what the other [established] theatre companies are doing, but I want to tell the story of the 'Ah Sohs' who have to deal with their HDB neighbors and their *mahjong* sessions. I think ordinary Singaporeans respond more instinctively to local stories that are happening around them than abstract ones."[3]

Invariably, these discourses of authenticity and Singaporean-ness are designed to contrast against the productions of certain Annual and 2-Year Major Grants theatre companies that are known to engage more with concepts of pan-Asian-ness and interculturalism. A 32-year-old director of a small, amateur bilingual theatre company states: "[We have] no pretensions of who we are and what we do. We're not some jet-set theatre company like some who talk about interculturalism. My experience as a Singaporean who has lived in Singapore his whole life does not qualify me to be, you know, pan-Asian and all that fashionable jazz. I am more interested in the local. I am more interested in the 'Ah Bengs', the billiard salons, the seedy karaoke bars, the underbelly of Singapore, so to speak."[4]

Attention to the local and the life-worlds of ordinary Singaporeans suggests that marginal theatre companies compete for symbolic capital, not by being cosmopolitan or global, as Annual and 2-Year Major Grants theatre companies are groomed to be, but by being committed to local stories. The commitment to the life-worlds of HDB residents, 'Ah Bengs', and 'heartlanders' is an assertion of local culture and identity, an appeal to the pull of national culture, in contrast to the more exclusive global or cosmopolitan culture. This avowed commitment to the local is a form of capital in the field to struggle for rewards because "they are recognised as having value and they can be traded or exchanged for desired outcomes within their own field or within others" (Webb, Schirato, and Danaher 2002: 109–110). In essence, these amateur theatre companies position themselves as an embedding force against the deterritorializing and delocalizing effects of globalization. This is a particularly powerful position because the local-global dichotomy is often played out as the dichotomy between the home and the transient (Tomlinson 1999). This home-transient binary is used to good effect by those without global cultural capital or cosmopolitan values since accentuating the deterritorializing and delocalizing effects of globalization not only stirs up the specter of loss but also highlights the material disparities between those who are global and those who have no choice but to remain local.

However, Annual and 2-Year Major Grants theatre companies, in addition to professing a global outlook or vision, also claim to be concerned with Singaporean-ness and local narratives. It is not uncommon for these established theatre companies to adopt the government discourse of globality as well as localness. Take, for example, the two-pronged mission statements of theatre companies such as TheatreWorks and Toy Factory Ensemble.

> Theatreworks asks, What is Asian in this age of globalisation, internationalisation, modernisation and urbanisation? Its work exists on the tension between modernity and tradition, local and global … [TheatreWorks] promotes and produces Singapore writing, thereby creating a theatre that is Singapore and with a Singaporean voice. The company recognises its responsibility to encourage awareness of human and social issues and is dedicated to sharing the magic of theatre with arts lovers and the Singapore community.[5]

> Guided by a bold spirit and an attitude of risk taking, Toy [Factory Ensemble] has carved out an indelible niche for itself in Singapore. Its global vision resolves Singapore's constant blend of East and West, new and old.[6]

W!LD RICE, another established theatre company, goes further, co-opting the discourse of globalization literature by describing itself as 'glocal': "W!LD RICE aims to be a dynamic platform for the Singaporean and Asian voice in theatre. By producing and touring quality 'glocal' productions that are distinctively local in flavor and yet global in vision and concerns, it will provide meaningful theatrical experiences for audiences in Singapore and the world."[7] Clearly, these established theatre companies, sensitive to the government's global cultural policies, have sought to straddle the local-global axis. By claiming to be both local and global, these theatre companies seek to win symbolic capital in terms of recognition from audiences and economic capital in the form of state grants from the government. Marginal theatre companies, on the other hand, which are unable to form international links with overseas groups or initiate joint collaborations, and which rely primarily on their localness for recognition, are contesting the claims of established theatre companies. A 28-year-old playwright for a Chinese-language amateur theatre company says: "Many of [the established companies] say that they produce Singaporean plays and, in the same breath, say they are also international in vision … in character. Can you be both? I'm not sure."

Some amateur practitioners admit that it might have been true that established theatre companies like The Necessary Stage and TheatreWorks started out staging local working-class stories when they were formed in the mid-1980s. However, they argue that these pioneer English-language companies have now gradually moved toward middle-class, professional, and white-collar issues in their more recent work, leaving stories of the working class behind them. Whether fair or not, this argument is not uncommon among smaller theatre companies. Another mode of contestation is the way in which suspicion is cast over cosmopolitan or pan-Asian identities. According to a 32-year-old director of an amateur theatre company: "Its fashionable to say you're producing cosmopolitan theatre. It all fits in very well with the government's Global City for the Arts [project]. Go global, go global … but at the end of the day, you still come back for Singaporean taxpayers' money [for state funds]."

Such assertions echo historical views of cosmopolitans as 'non-citizens' and 'deviants' who refuse to define themselves by location, ancestry, citizenship, or language (Waldron 1992). The cosmopolite in mid-nineteenth-century America, for example, was perceived as "a well-traveled character probably lacking in substance" (Hollinger 1995: 89). And as Vertovec and Cohen (2002: 6) have shown, the historical cosmopolitan's perceived 'lack of substance' was measured against "a readily identifiable provenance, an integrated and predictable pattern of behavioural practice, including loyalty to a single nation-state or cultural identity." Used by local marginal theatre practitioners, such tropes seek to undermine claims of authenticity and localness made by cosmopolitan theatre practitioners and suggest a strong perception among the former that the state, through its dispersal of funds, privileges the latter. These views also parallel broader discourses over the PAP government's pro-active foreign talent policy. Many citizens, predominantly from the working and lower-middle classes, feel that they have been marginalized from jobs due to the government's policy of favoring foreign skilled workers. The citizens argue that these foreign workers have not served national service and are transient in nature, always ready to leave for better economic conditions elsewhere, while they as nationals are rooted to the locale. The fact that the state privileges self-professed cosmopolitan theatre companies while pursuing a pro-active foreign talent policy positions the PAP government as a prime initiator of globalization processes. Small, amateur theatre companies, almost by default, occupy the opposite position—they are the storytellers of local reality and truth.

The Promethean Complex: "What Makes You So Special?"

As self-professed storytellers of local reality, marginal local theatre companies claim to stage the life stories of ordinary citizens and those on the margins of society. The depiction of local realities, regardless of their grittiness—and perhaps because of it—prompts soul searching and nostalgia, both very welcomed in globally transient and impersonal capitalist sites like Singapore. The stories of forgotten, marginal, and dispensable identities are becoming fashionable as people begin to understand the darker consequences of globalization and neo-capitalism. In articulating such identities, marginal theatre companies are credited with providing a dose of truth as they perform their self-appointed 'artist-as-hero' role. This role is not lost on the larger, more established theatre companies, many of which are aware of the discourses deployed by marginal practitioners. The 42-year-old artistic director of a 2-Year Major Grants English-language theatre company comments: "Sure, [amateur and marginal practitioners] say they talk about Singaporean stories. But sometimes you get the feeling that they are more Singaporean than Singaporeans ... I mean, it's always easier to go overboard with Singlish [on stage]. Most of us [established practitioners] progressed beyond that phase back in the late eighties, early nineties." The artistic director continues: "It's sometimes a little condescending when you say you're doing local reality and Singaporean lives. People live Singaporean lives—do they need to hear you say that you're staging it for them? What makes you so special? ... They all want to be little Prometheuses, bringing fire and light to the masses."

This form of artist-as-hero self-representation wins marginal theatre companies credibility from local audiences. Theatre-goers who appreciate these companies for their position as truth bearers tend to be in their late teens or early twenties, many of them students from middle-class backgrounds with university educations.[8] In the Bourdieusian context, although many marginal theatre companies and practitioners are aware of their marginal position in the theatre field, they continue to be in illusio. Illusio, the continued belief in the rewards and aims in a particular field, keeps theatre companies from disbanding and their practitioners from exiting the theatre field completely. Despite their marginal status, many of these practitioners still purport to "love theatre" or to be "still passionate about what I am doing" or to "come alive when I am making theatre." These comments show that certain ideals, even idealism, and intangible dividends of the field prevent total disaffection and disconnection and thus ensure continued participation—or what Dreyfus and Rabinow (1999: 90) call necessary "self-deception." As the artistic director of a small Chinese-language theatre company explains: "My mother keeps asking me why I bother [making theatre]. 'You have a university degree—please go do something useful!' She belongs to the generation that believes if you're not a doctor or a lawyer then you're a bum. She is probably right ... but this is important to me, because I believe in what I'm doing."

This Promethean complex leads to strong assertions about independence and artistic integrity. Expressing the desire to be free from external influences or obligations is common among smaller and amateur theatre companies, many of them founded by university students. The lack of an overarching mission statement or objective provides marginal theatres with artistic leeway in terms of the direction of their programs. Others see their theatre companies as vehicles for their own talents; for example, a student at the National University of Singapore (NUS) set up his own theatre company because of the lack of opportunities. He explains: "I'm a student, and it's very hard for an NUS student to be involved in theatre so directly. Most of the time NUS students will end up doing front-of-house work, selling tickets and giving out brochures, which I don't really like to do. I like to direct ... but it's also very rare for people to use my script straightaway. I don't expect people to use my script, so I need to do something about it. That's why I set up my own company."

The appeal to artistic independence and autonomy is often contrasted against the Annual and 2-Year Major Grants theatre companies, which have to fulfill certain contractual obligations such as the staging of a certain number of productions in a year. Many Project Grants and marginal theatre practitioners also hint that winning higher state grants is tantamount to state co-option or 'selling out'. Such discourses are used to draw attention and reinforce their own 'independent' status, with some theatre companies even wearing their minimal state-funding status as a badge of honor. Hence, while these theatre companies do not compete with established English-language theatre companies for top state grants, largely because they do not have the cultural capital to do so, they actively compete for symbolic capital—that is, recognition, credibility, prestige, and honor—from their peers and audiences in order to enhance their reputations.

Conclusion

The early role for Singapore's arts and culture industry was largely a state-prescribed one. The PAP government, in the absence of a cohesive and long-term arts strategy, in contrast to its economic planning, saddled the arts and culture industry with significant local and nation-building responsibilities. Even as early artistic groups struggled to hone their craft and experimented with styles and creative voices aimed at a small audience, the arts and cultural space in general was often utilized by the state for the literal performance of socio-political metonyms with the aim of achieving racial and religious harmony. Ethnic costumes and traditional dresses of various ethnic groups, together with their festivals, were displayed for visual consumption to signify a multicultural society.

The Global City for the Arts project in the early 1990s was conceived as an integral plan to define and refine the city-state as a global city. In opening up the local arts and culture industry to the processes of globalization and capitalist logic, the National Arts Council introduced a three-tier grants scheme that began to separate local theatre companies on the basis of various privileged traits. In this sense, the local theatre community began to experience the consequences of globalization, including the uneven distribution of wealth, the widening gap between the haves and the have-nots, and the resultant suspicion of the new and cosmopolitan. These consequences of globalization have profoundly influenced the cultural politics within the Singapore theatre community.

In contesting authenticity and notions of Singaporean-ness, theatre companies, both established and marginal, recognize that national culture and localness appeal both to Singaporeans who are economically rooted to territory and to those who are cosmopolitan and mobile in nature. Nonetheless, different theatre companies employ authenticity differently. It is not uncommon for established theatre companies to claim to be both global and local in character. Here, tropes of globalism and cosmopolitanism are often deployed alongside concepts of the East, of tradition, and of Singaporean-ness. This is very much in parallel with the Singapore government's Global City for the Arts vision, whereby the arts and culture are used to entice tourists and expatriates to the city-state and, at the same time, to dissuade globally mobile Singaporeans from leaving for greener pastures.

The ability of established theatre companies to claim both authenticity and globality in their artistic visions and productions has deprived small, amateur, and marginal theatre companies of much-valued symbolic capital. Faced with the broader deterritorializing effects of globalization, the appeal to the local has always been a valuable source of credibility and comfort, not to mention recognition. In professing to stage uncompromising realism about the underbelly of Singapore and the life stories of ordinary Singaporeans, marginal theatre companies are animating the home-transient binary to highlight the economic gulf between the so-called cosmopolitans and those with little choice but to remain local. As a result, some have also adopted a Promethean complex, believing themselves to be artistically independent and free from contractual obligations to the state, in a heroic effort to bring Truth to Singaporeans. Implicit in this is the desire to speak for the subaltern and the working class. This desire stems mainly from the fact that symbolic capital can be won when one champions the local, which is vital in the absence of economic capital. Thus, the logic of globalization is often met with the logic of the local, whereby specific identity and class politics discourses are triggered in the interests of those who have not benefited from the rewards of globalization.

Terence Chong is a Fellow at the Institute of Southeast Asian Studies and coordinator of its Regional Social and Cultural Studies program. He has a PhD in Sociology from Warwick University, UK. His research interests include the sociology of culture and art, the Southeast Asian middle class, civil society, and nation building in Singapore. He is the volume editor of *Globalization and Its Counter-Forces in Southeast Asia* (2008) and has published in numerous journals, including *Asian Studies Review*, *Journal of Contemporary Asia*, *Identities: Global Studies in Culture and Power*, *Social Identities*, *Critical Asian Studies*, and the *Journal of Southeast Asian Studies*.

Notes

1. In July 1999, *Time* magazine wrote that "Singapore swings." The magazine report went on to explain that "once notorious for tight government control, the city-state is getting competitive, creative, even funky." This suggests that structural changes to censorship regulations seemed to have won the 'Global City for the Arts' project some international recognition.
2. The author's fieldwork, conducted from 2002–2003, consisted of participant observation, semi-structured interviews, and library research. The author attached himself to three different theatre companies and engaged in production activities. An approximate total of 120 hours of interviews with 52 informants, including artistic directors, stage crew, actors, and government officials, are recorded on tape.
3. In local slang, the term 'Ah Sohs' describes older, poorly educated women. HDB (Housing Development Board) flats are public flats in which over 80 percent of Singaporeans reside.
4. 'Ah Bengs' is local slang for uncouth or working-class youth—the equivalent of the British 'yob'.
5. http://www.theatreworks.org.sg (accessed 20 April 2006).
6. http://www.toyfactory.org.sg (accessed 20 April 2006).
7. http://www.wildrice.com.sg/aboutrice.html (accessed 20 April 2006).
8. A typical audience response was that of a 20-year-old humanities undergraduate, who told me: "I think we need more theatre companies like this. They aren't big, but they are pretty independent in their direction. They also tend to be more raw and honest, which is what I like in theatre."

References

Abu-Lughod, Janet. 2001. *New York, Chicago, Los Angeles*. Minneapolis: University of Minnesota Press.

Appadurai, Arjun. 1990. "Disjuncture and Difference in the Global Cultural Economy." Pp. 295–310 in Featherstone 1990b.

Bereson, Ruth. 2002. "An Analysis of Singaporean Arts and Cultural Policy 1957–2001." The Second International Conference on Cultural Policy Research, Wellington, New Zealand.

Beynon, John, and David Dunkerley, eds. 2000. *Globalization: The Reader*. London: Athlone Press.

Bourdieu, Pierre. 1986. "The Forms of Capital." Pp. 241–258 in *Handbook of Theory and Research for the Sociology of Education*, ed. John G. Richardson. New York: Greenwood Press.

———. 2000. *Pascalian Meditations*. Cambridge: Polity Press.

Burtenshaw, David, Michael Bateman, and Greg J. Ashworth. 1991. *The European City: A Western Perspective*. London: David Fulton.

Chang, Tou Chuang. 2000. "Renaissance Revisited: Singapore as a 'Global City for the Arts.'" *International Journal of Urban and Regional Research* 24, no. 4: 818–831.

Chong, Terence. 2005. "From Global to Local: Singapore's Cultural Policy and Its Consequences." *Critical Asian Studies* 37, no. 4: 551–565.

Dreyfus, Hubert, and Paul Rabinow. 1999. "Can There Be a Science of Existential Structure and Social Meaning?" In *Bourdieu: A Critical Reader*, ed. Richard Shusterman. Oxford: Blackwell.

Featherstone, Mike. 1990a. "Introduction." In Featherstone 1990b.

———, ed. 1990b. *Global Culture: Nationalism, Globalization and Modernity*. London: Sage.

Hollinger, David A. 1995. *Postethnic America: Beyond Multiculturalism*. New York: Basic Books.

Koh, Tai Ann. 1989. "Culture and the Arts." Pp. 710–741 in *Management of Success: The Moulding of Modern Singapore*, ed. Kernial Sandhu and Paul Wheatley. Singapore: Institute of Southeast Asian Studies.

Kong, Lily. 2000. "Cultural Policy in Singapore: Negotiating Economic and Socio-Cultural Agendas." *Geoforum* 31: 409–424.

Low, Linda. 2001. "The Role of the Government in Singapore's Industralization." In *Southeast Asia's Industrialization: Industrial Policy, Capabilities and Sustainability*, ed. K. S. Jomo. New York: Palgrave.

Perry, Nick. 1998. *Hyper-reality and Global Culture*. London: Routledge.

Rodan, Garry. 1989. *The Political Economy of Singapore's Industrialisation: National State and International Capital*. London: Macmillan.

Schudson, Michael. 1994. "The Integration of National Societies." Pp. 21–44 in *The Sociology of Culture: Emerging Theoretical Perspectives*, ed. Diana Crane. Oxford: Blackwell.

Smith, Anthony. 1990. "Towards a Global Culture?" Pp. 171–191 in Featherstone 1990b.

Tomlinson, John. 1999. *Globalization and Culture*. Cambridge: Polity Press.

Vertovec, Steven, and Robin Cohen, eds. 2002. *Conceiving Cosmopolitanism: Theory, Context, and Practice*. Oxford: Oxford University Press.

Waldron, Jeremy. 1992. "Minority Cultures and the Cosmopolitan Alternative." *University of Michigan Journal of Law Reform* 23, no. 3: 751–793.

Webb, Jen, Tony Schirato, and Geoff Danaher. 2002. *Understanding Bourdieu*. London: Sage.

Chapter 3

HIJACKING CULTURAL POLICIES
Art as a Healthy Virus within Social Strategies
of Resistance

Marina Fokidis

My official job title is curator and art critic. But I like to introduce myself as an intermediary, a creative thinker—a member of a 'terrorealist' network, to borrow a term that I had once heard in a talk given by the South African–born artist Kendell Geers when referring to his piece, *The Work of Art in the State of Exile.*[1] My current occupation, the theme of this chapter, is centrally concerned with the experience and memory of the movement of populations in the Mediterranean-Balkan region over thousands of years. I am fortunate at present to be a close witness to and an active collaborator in a process that recovers history, 'hijacks' the present, and develops cooperative networks that can eventually allow space

Notes for this chapter are located on page 51.

for an ethical and appropriate language of dissent to be heard in an international arena. What I am describing here applies to art as a space of resistance, acting as a healthy virus within the broader political, economic, and social strategies of global realities.

The project I am engaged in (in collaboration with others) is called *Egnatia Road: A Path of Displaced Memories*. It was initiated by Stalker/Osservatorio Nomade, a creative research network based in Rome, in collaboration with Oxymoron, Athens (a non-profit cultural organization of which I am a founding member and director) and Atelier d'Architecture Autogérée (AAA) of Paris, a collective practice that conducts research into participatory urban actions. *Egnatia Road* forms an interdisciplinary work that concentrates on the forced displacement of populations and transborder cultural interactions extending throughout Southeastern Europe. We have been exploring ways in which certain forms of artistic collaboration are no longer an alternative but now the *only* strategy to address the complex social and political issues that artists confront in this part of the world.

Briefly, the project focuses on the reactions to and interactions among displaced peoples ('stateless refugees' or sometimes 'illegal immigrants') in the southeastern corner of Europe within the axes of a path that once shaped the Via Egnatia (Egnatia Road), which connected the eastern and western centers of the Roman Empire. A group of artists, architects, designers, theoreticians, and writers (local to each different place, as well as visiting) follows the path actively and symbolically through research and the creation of a large network that aims to collect stories of displacement and record accounts from those who were moved or have been forced to move along the Egnatia 'bridge' on the fragmented border between East and West. At the same time, each story is being metaphorically transferred to a paving stone that will serve as testimony to the experience recounted.[2]

Before I go into details, I will briefly introduce some of the ideas attaching to the kind of artistic activism with which the Egnatia project is centrally concerned. "Fiction," the artist Marcel Broothaers declares, "enables us to grasp not only reality but that which is veiled by reality. Thus art as an unorthodox working procedure of narration usually occupies a space into reality where identity, society, memory, politics, history, language are all under close scrutiny. The intention—through storytelling—is to transfer art, as an unsettling factor, into life, and vice versa" (cited in Stiles and Selz 1996: 869).

Artists have always had a strong interest in representing the experience of being in a specific place and responding to current political issues, but the nature of their engagement has changed in the context of globalization. The avant-garde had favored the shock tactics of provocation and exposure. Today there are more peacemaking and affirmative—and sometimes more ameliorative—strategies in use. The idea of representing a local place or reacting to political issues can no longer occur in isolation from global concerns. While many artists are often very committed to the places they work in, they are also deeply aware of their links to global debates and take part in transnational dialogues on the meaning of their practice and its relevance to others. Whether we are talking of collaborations or individual works, this kind of art is not being created in the confines of one's own studio. The urban landscape, the institution, the gallery—all form the actual production spaces. The artist is not the central figure in these transactions, and the input of the audience is important, in terms not of artificial interactivity but of active participation. The idea is more to alarm people into raising pertinent social issues and to produce a resistant gesture that might change their historical direction. Projects like these succeed in giving voices to parties and issues that could not be heard if the visual culture were the only vehicle used.

Personal Reactions to State-Sponsored Terrors

Mona Hatoum, for example, a British artist of Palestinian and Lebanese heritage who was born and raised in Beirut, felt the need to respond to the climax of the previous civil war in Lebanon in her performance piece *Variation on Discord and Divisions* (1984), in which she scrubbed newspaper headlines with a blood-red liquid.[3] Living in the Western part of the world, Hatoum appears to have felt that she had to personify the Other—the victimizer and the victim at the same time—thus bringing closer to the audience what they had been passively following on the television. Personally involved in the slaughter of this war, her existence works as a social metaphor for common struggle and suffering (Brett 1993; Watson 1993).

Likewise, in a lighter and more subtle way that is indicative of the present, the Turkish artist Fikret Atay through his video work *Rebels of the Dance* (2000) makes reference to an important political problem of the Kurdish population by presenting to the viewer two children dancing and singing a traditional Kurdish marriage song inside the booth of an automatic teller machine. Atay makes visible an almost entertaining event and the spectrum of political references behind it. It is up to the viewer to complete the interpretation of the work. The piece was shown in the Istanbul Biennale at a time when the Kurdish language was not allowed to be spoken on the street. Since then, Atay has been adopted by the international art scene and has had his works exhibited around the world.

Around the same time, the artist Aleksandra Mir conceived the video work *First Woman on the Moon* (1999). Coinciding with the thirtieth anniversary of the original moon landing, the piece is a direct commentary on the lack of advancement of gender equality in our society. Ironically, this tape, in which a Dutch beach was bulldozed to resemble a lunar landscape, was later used in a news report on the future of the British space industry as an example of how space can be democratized (Doherty 2004).

A Tale of Traveling and Becoming

According to Nikos Papastergiadis (2006: 42): "Art and the politics of opposition are not pre-set positions. Art, politics and ethics are no longer external to each other ... there is no bridge that connects art and politics ... the bridging is part of the politics of art." The work on Egnatia Road, which continues in progress, has taught us the most effective ways of collaborating and the methods that can be used to 'hijack' and reformulate cultural policies. What is most importantly learned from this operation is that the real work must 'emerge' in the collaborative process (trying, of course, to be on schedule and on budget). In this way, more lively processes allow disciplined teams to discover positive outcomes so that all the co-workers elaborate the design brief co-extensively with—rather than prior to—the delivery of the resultant work of art. The process of working together *is* the project. As the historian Ross Gibson (2005: 269) argues: "This process-work presents profound challenges to the 'blueprint method' of delivery upon which most of the old industrial engineering modes of construction, legal and financial accountability and team-governance have been based for the past two hundred years." It is through the presentation of the project *Egnatia Road: A Path of Displaced Memories* that I will try to expand on topics such as the transformation of the site of cultural production into an evolving theoretical concept and the revitalization of this genre of public art that engages matters found in the hearts of 'real people' outside the art world.

The history of the Balkans has been framed by cultural collisions between East and West, uneven processes of modernization, and antagonistic structures for national integration. Past occasions of territorial conflict and the population exchanges that they engender have been influenced by several factors, including the following:

- The realigning of politically defined territories and the re-siting of borders between countries
- The geological formation of the Balkan lands, which has permitted (even if secretly) the conservation of diverse cultural manifestations
- The unification of Balkan lands as a single political identity during the Cold War
- The very character of 'Balkan blood', encompassing ethnic identities, histories, religious convictions, understandings of patriotism, and memories of place

All of these factors have contributed to a present geo-political situation that goes beyond shifting economic and territorial claims.

The untranslatable nature of current and ongoing racism, the hostility of social relations and the conflicting meanings attached to them, and the very tight bonds that have developed historically between the inhabitants of particular territories (once formed by members of the same family) have led to a unique style of semi-local immigration within the Balkan region. Such an immigration refers not only to the quest for a 'better future' in a foreign land, but also to a 'homecoming' that is worth a more formal and personal local investigation.

History proves that answers are not to be found in a common being, but, as the French philosopher Jean-Luc Nancy (1983) has observed, 'being-in-common'. The solution to tensions does not lie in choosing sides. Rather, it is better

Egnatia Road: A Path of Displaced Memories
By Osservatorio Nomade in collaboration with Oxymoron and AAA.
Photos by Andrea Rocca © Andrea Rocca, Stalker

to be able to understand a set of contradictory desires and to view seeming oppositions as sustaining relations.

The Egnatia Road project seeks to collect stories of displacement by recording the actual accounts of those who were moved or were forced to move along the Egnatia 'bridge' between East and West. Metaphorically symbolizing these stories, stones are being placed along the road, serving as testimony to the widely varying experiences of the travelers on the path. The single storyteller or the community at large will indicate where the personalized paving stones should be placed, creating veritable milestones of memories. For example, a Kurdish refugee who had left Lavrio detention camp, outside Athens, and was passing from Italy to Germany was found by some artists from the group. He was the first to tell to us about the Lavrio camp and asked for his stone to be left there. Later, the research group discovered the camp, placed his stone at the site, and set in motion a new research area that remained active for a long time, leading to other stories. In the words of Iacopo Gallico, one of the members of our group: "We are collecting stories which become memories and testimonies of the process of 'normalization' and assimilation to the main model of culture ... We have the task of translating the untranslatable."[4]

Work on *Egnatia Road: A Path of Displaced Memories* began in 2002 and is now in its fifth year. The research and the production of the project are being developed simultaneously in a range of places—what we call 'agencies'—tracked by different groups of people. The main research and post-production sites are in Rome, Athens, Paris, and Berlin, but at the same time general meetings for workshops and research have been held along the Egnatia Road itself, in Otranto (Italy), Tirana (Albania), and Thessaloniki (Greece), among other places.

It might be difficult to understand how this project could have come to life, in terms of interaction with the public/participants and also in terms of funding. It is true that art still cannot be executed outside the contingencies of locational or institutional circumstances—but it is no longer determined by them. In this case, the artists are setting the rules and at the same time are functioning as translators between the cultural realms of art and the communities they are working with.

Oxymoron's invitation to the Stalker group to present another work (*Flying Carpet*) in Thessaloniki in 2001 was what prompted a team of Italian, Greek, and Albanian artists to conduct an experimental road trip to the Balkan region, following the path of the old Egnatia Road. This was the most effective way to help us understand that this road, which covers less than 1,500 kilometers, still constitutes a matter of life and death for some people.

The Egnatia Road was built to connect Rome and Constantinople, the western and eastern capitals of the divided Roman Empire. It passed through the south of Italy, Albania, Macedonia, and Thrace. From the decline of the Ottoman Empire in the later nineteenth century, through the twentieth century, and beyond to the current movements of refugees, this road has been the site of the dramatic displacement of millions of Albanians, Armenians, Bulgarians, Greeks, Jews, Turks, Kurds, Afghanis, and Iraqis. Of central importance has been the Greek-Turkish population exchange that was mediated in the Treaty of Lausanne in 1923. This forced 1.5 million people to move from their homelands.

The Stalker group accepted conditionally our invitation to participate in the Egnatia Road project. They were happy to show their work in Greece, but only if we would allocate a percentage of the budget to their involvement and facilitate the organization of the road trip. While the work was being transported from Albania to Greece, we were physically on the Egnatia Road. The trip—which had started in Rome, passed through different places in Albania, and ended in Greece—gave the opportunity for many people to come in contact with each other. Influenced by the changing environments to which we were exposed, it provided us with a chance to give birth to new ideas for interconnected actions and creations. The phantom of the Egnatia Road, a mythic unity that still gathers up a range of people and experiences, served as a zone of mutual interest for fertile partnerships, resulting in the creation of a mobile laboratory that is still in process.

In the beginning, the project was self-funded in the sense that each of us made use of his or her institutional relations and invitations, managing to introduce the project in the exhibition places to which we had been invited. This gave birth to the agencies. Every institution that has invited Stalker for an exhibition (due to their commodified status) has had to put up with an 'agency' of people working to construct events and laboratories that relate to the traditions of the communities we visit along the road.

In this way, the 'common space' that evolves most likely occurs from the effects produced by the different actors that contextualize time and place, making it function as a polyvalent unity of even the most conflicting proximities. The scheme of parallel events around and within this context was the ideal platform with which to engage local institutions, local authorities, and local families as allies in our explorations.

In the meantime, we were successful in getting funding from the European Union. For us, this meant, together with the economic stability of the project, the beginning of a constructive dialogue with the EU and its engagement in matters that might not otherwise be observed. Who really lives in Europe, and what are we really including in our discourse?

The commodification of art becomes in these cases a kind of service. And the way to define the success of the artwork relies not on a finished object but on the interaction between artists and society in the form of a cooperative project. It is a process within which producer and consumer pursue a common goal. Via Egnatia's sculptural object is actually a device to collect people's life testimonies. Although it exists as an aesthetic art object, it could never be marketed, since, at the conclusion of the project, the sculpture will be scattered on the road—in a way, undone. The engaging of the displaced in the very process of creating their own cultural representation could be understood not only as a cultural practice but also as a strategy of political importance. The intention is to pave the Egnatia Road with its forgotten memories.

We have been observers of and protagonists in a fascinating process that is hard to define, since it is interconnected with the different strategies that have continually opened up to us new questions—of agency and control, of the relation between the state and the individual or the community. How will we continue to manage the mediation of this kind of research and this kind of art that is usually quite intimate? How will we connect communities and personal histories, communicate personal experiences of struggle, or unearth partially remembered myths and legends? Crucially, how are we to maintain and enlarge our own understanding of selves and others within an encompassing, hegemonic, and often misrecognized state formation?

Conclusion

Our answers must lie in our responses to the power of the nation-state to form and structure our artistic practice. The Egnatia Road becomes a metaphor and a reality whereby we can confront the state and transcend its territorial boundaries—both literally and figuratively. As practitioners, participants, viewers, and producers, we need to realize the complex processes of initiation, mediation, and development of this kind of art. We need to make the distinction between different types of engagements and to understand the level of support that this sort of work requires.

More importantly, we need to finance our activities without compromising our attitude and artistic stance. The art institution becomes an agency for social research, and at the same time, the public sphere becomes an institution for the mediation of contemporary art. New models of exhibition styles and spaces become dialogic and open-ended. State funding of the twentieth-century blockbuster spectacles and theme parks might encourage smaller organizations and initiatives to create collaborative platforms and maintain internal research that stimulates artistic challenge and that sense of surprise and discovery from which socio-political transformations can ensue. From our experiences on the Egnatia Road, we maintain that the state should initiate mechanisms of production and cooperate in the funding of unfinished projects. In this way we can appropriate some of the powers of the state to the benefit of ordinary people living everyday lives of large hopes and small triumphs. We can 'hijack' the state for our own purposes.

Our aims as cultural agents should always be to open up an enacted, spoken, and lived space of individual narratives of collective importance, a mindscape that will eventually generate fresh hybrid signs and languages to meet the ever-changing world. The dialogue between art and life has reached that space in which certain gestures, endlessly repeated, are in the end transformed into totally open and even uncontrollable grounds of meaning. This is so even though, for most of us, the leap into the void is still a forbidden act.

Marina Fokidis is an independent curator and critic based in Athens, Greece. She is a founding member and director of Oxymoron, a non-profit organization dedicated to the promotion of contemporary visual art in Greece and on an international level.

Notes

1. Cited in http://pswart.wdka.hro.nl/fama/programme2/archive/2003-2004/experiencememory/. To view Geers's artwork and writings, see http://www.terrorealism.net/home.html.
2. For a graphic of the Egnatia Road map, see http://www.egnatia.info/.
3. The piece on DVD was performed live on 14 December 1984 at the Western Front, in Vancouver, British Columbia, Canada.
4. From an email communication with Gallico.

References

Brett, Guy. 1993. *Exhibition Catalogue: Mona Hatoum*. Bristol: Arnolfini.

Doherty, Claire, ed. 2004. *Contemporary Art: From Studio to Situation*. London: Black Dog Publishing.

Gibson, Ross. 2005. "Attunement and Agility." Pp. 269–277 in *Empires, Ruins and Networks*, ed. Scott McQuire and Nikos Papastergiadis. Carlton: Melbourne University Press.

Nancy, Jean-Luc. 1983. *La communauté désœuvrée*. Paris: Christian Bourgois.

Papastergiadis, Nikos. 2006. *Spatial Aesthetics: Art, Place and the Everyday*. London: Rivers Oram Press.

Stiles, Kristine, and Peter Selz, eds. 1996. *Theories and Documents of Contemporary Art: A Sourcebook of Artists' Writings*. Berkeley: University of California Press.

Watson, Gray. 1993. "Interview with Mona Hatoum." *Audio Arts Magazine* 13, no. 4. http://www.tate.org.uk/britain/exhibitions/audioarts/cd3_4.shtm.

Chapter 4

ENGAGING WITH HISTORY BY PERFORMING TRADITION
The Poetic Politics of Indigenous Australian Festivals

Rosita Henry

Festivals and other public events that feature indigenous dance performances are a burgeoning phenomenon, both in Australia and in the international arena. My aim here is to trace the field of power relations in which such festivals are embedded and within which they are constituted. Festivals make for fascinating study because they present spatially and temporally contained domains in which the performative aspects of human social relations and sensual embodied expressions of social practice can be directly observed and experienced. Yet festivals are only *apparently* contained events. Although participants are meant to experience a festival for the term of its duration as a whole self-contained world, it is only a partial world. Boundaries between a particular festival event and the social order are highly permeable. Festival performances reach out beyond the festivals into the everyday world, and they can be fully understood only with reference to wider social situations and the political, economic, and social interests and state processes and practices that, in fact, produce them. In addition, the

References for this chapter begin on page 67.

state deceptively asserts its presence *within* the festivals. Indeed, agents and agencies of the state colonize the festivals, so that the festivals become prime sites for recognition of the "effects" of the state (Trouillot 2001: 126).

This chapter focuses on two contemporary festivals in northern Australia, one from Cape York and the other from northeast Arnhem Land. I explore the nature of these festivals as public events and investigate their significance as a form of political practice in relation to the presence of the state in indigenous lives. More broadly, my research concerns the role of festivals in articulating indigenous rights discourse within Australia and how indigenous groups deal with the state through harnessing the power of performance.

Dance and song are significant forms of symbolic capital. Live performances provide people not only with an avenue for presenting culture as spectacle but also with a means of political engagement, or performative dialogue, with others. Public festivals in Australia are complex sites of national identity formation (J. Kapferer 1996). Thus, festival performances must be read not as static representations of culture but as dynamic strategies of power. Similarly, the indigenous festival phenomenon should not be dismissed as a mere expression of identity culturalism or as a traditionalist revival of a long-dead past. Festivals provide opportunities for indigenous people to retrieve 'tradition' so as to put it to work to make sense of 'history' and to negotiate the processes and practices of state power as it expresses itself in Australia today.

Colonization and Folklorization

It might be argued that contemporary, state-sponsored festival performances are just another expression of the folklorization of indigenous peoples that goes hand in hand with their continuing colonization. During former decades of European settlement in Australia (as elsewhere), colonial agents, missionaries, and others perceived indigenous ritual and ceremonial activity as both a political and a moral threat. Such practices became acceptable to these newcomers only if they were rendered innocuous through theatricalization and revalued in terms of European desires and fantasies. Yet the idea of performing for colonial audiences appears to have been readily accepted by Aboriginal people as a means of communicating with the newcomers and having some control over their relationships with them. According to Parsons (1997: 46), public performances of dance and music by Aboriginal people emerged as a "cultural product" in the nineteenth century. Parsons (ibid.) identifies four major kinds of performance of this type: (1) the 'peace corroboree', staged to mark a new state of cooperative relations between Aboriginal people and the Crown; (2) the 'command performance', for official state visitors; (3) the 'gala corroboree', to mark social occasions significant to the settler populace, such as charity sporting events and annual agricultural shows; and (4) the 'touristic corroboree'.

Indigenous involvement in these kinds of performance could be read as merely the response of a powerless people to Western demands for representations of the 'primitive other'. Yet, although they evidence asymmetry in power relations, I suggest that such performances allow indigenous people to engage with settler Australians, if not entirely on their own terms, at least with some sense of agency and control (cf. B. Kapferer 1995a, 1995b). This has been the case since the early period of European contact. For example, James Morrill, one of a group of individuals who survived the wreck of the ship *Peruvian* in 1846 on the mid-north coast of Queensland, describes a "grand corroboree" in which his party was induced to participate. It was staged "by the original group of Aborigines who had encountered the survivors for the benefit of a gathering of various regional clans" (Hayward 2001: 4). Morrill writes (cited in ibid.): "The first thing they did was lay us down and cover us over with dried grass, to prevent our being seen till an appointed time. They then collected from all quarters to the number of about fifty or sixty—men, women and children—and sat down in a circle; those who discovered us stepped into the centre, dressed up in our clothes, with a little extra paint, danced one of their dances, at the same time haranguing all present, recounting how they discovered us … from whence they had brought us, and all they knew about us …and then as a finale we were uncovered, and led forth into the centre in triumph."

Performances such as that documented by Morrill in reaction to first encounters with Europeans were the responses of reflexive, adaptive, creative people dealing performatively with powerful new forces in their lives. The agency of Aboriginal people is similarly evident in the present context. Indigenous performances should not be read top down as merely complicit responses to colonial agendas (cf. Magowan 2000: 310). For example, perhaps one of the most enduring and powerfully symbolic images of the indigenous fight for rights and recognition within Australia today is that of a Wik woman dancing her victory dance outside the Australian High Court in 1996 after the landmark case in which the court ruled that pastoral leases did not necessarily extinguish native title. As Magowan (ibid.: 312) argues, through her dance, Typingoompa substantiated her "claim to indigenous rights and her authority to dance for land." Indigenous Australians have on numerous occasions attempted to harness the power of performance by drawing politicians and government bureaucrats into the performance events as participants. For example, in 1997 on Elcho Island, Yolngu clan leaders led the prime minister of Australia, John Howard, through a secret part of a ritual, and Wik women danced on the lawns of the Parliament House with Senator Harradine, who at the time held the balance in the Senate over the Wik native title legislation. According to Magowan (ibid.: 318): "The effect of leading the prime minister through the ritual was to place him in a particular performative dialogue, one that was bound by Yolngu models of political control and authority embedded in the corporeal dispositions of the dances." More recently, on 17 December 2004, Djabugay elder, Enid Boyle, danced at the official event organized to mark state recognition of Djabugay native title over the Barron Gorge National Park. In each of these cases, the Aboriginal participants actively sought to harness the poetic power of performance as an expression of their own agency and that of their people, to mark their presence in relation to the state, and to secure recognition of continuing connection and entitlement to land in the face of a history of dispossession.

Anthropologists and other scholars have long debated conceptual oppositions between tradition and history and, in relation to Australian Aboriginal
people, "the issue of the supposed absence of historical consciousness among
traditionally oriented Aborigines" (Beckett 1994: 97; see also Kolig 1995, 2000;
Merlan 1994; D. Rose 1984; Rumsey 1994; Swain, 1994; Urry 1980). It has
been argued that 'traditionally oriented' Aborigines frame the past in terms of
mythic thought rather than history. However, as Beckett (1994: 99) writes: "We
should not scorn to look at humbler, less structured forms such as jokes, songs,
genealogies, stories" as ways in which Aboriginal people articulate memory
and engage with history. Similarly, I argue that festival performances can constitute a form of strategic communication of historical consciousness.

Disinheritance and Cultural Revival

Many Australian Aboriginal people today express a great sense of loss over
disinheritance, not only of their land, but also of the cultural practices and
performances that linked them to land and to one another. They mourn the
cultural dispossession they see as resulting from their forcible removal, dispersal, and confinement to reserves and missions after European colonial
expansion into northern Australia. As an Aboriginal woman noted about her
life on the Mona Mona mission: "When I was growing up we had ... most of
our corroborees ... but the missionaries when they heard the clapstick, you
know, they didn't like to hear that ... They sort of cut it out and it gradually
died out then until now this generation is trying to revive it" (Florence Wil-
liams, interview July 1994).

'Cultural revival' became a catchphrase during the 1970s and 1980s among
indigenous peoples in northern Australia and elsewhere. During the early 1970s,
the Aboriginal Theatre Foundation was established, with encouragement from
the Australian Council for the Arts, "to preserve, to restore and to sponsor
Aboriginal dancing and singing" (von Sturmer 1973: 2). The Foundation was
officially incorporated in 1970, with a National Executive Committee (mainly
composed of non-indigenous members) that met three times a year. The Foundation provided an avenue for indigenous peoples to address an increasing sense
of cultural disinheritance and a very real fear that they were indeed 'doomed'
to extinction—that is, cultural extinction, not racial extinction as the 'doomed
race' theorists had assumed (McGregor 1997). One of the two indigenous members of the original committee, from the Northern Territory, had this to say
about the Foundation: "I am deeply worried that our young people could forget
our culture. It is our sacred song and dance that expresses, and is the root of,
our law and our discipline ... I believe that the Aboriginal Theatre Foundation
can help us to make our culture live forever. I also believe it is just as important
that the Foundation help non-Aboriginal people to understand how deep and
important is the meaning of this culture, through dance and song" (Aboriginal
Theatre Foundation 1972: 15). Thus, indigenous people sought new means to
express and transmit memories of cultural beliefs and practices that they feared

would soon be forgotten and that they believed to have been in existence at "the threshold of European colonization" (Keen 2003).

Authenticity and the Invention of Tradition

Cultural revival in Australia, as elsewhere, has been evaluated as being less about revival than about the fabrication or invention of culture. These ideas can be linked to works focusing on the politics of identity, as well as to debates over the idea of the past as 'constructed' in the present and of tradition and/or heritage as mere invention (see Beckett 1988; Friedman 1992; Handler and Linnekin 1984; Herzfeld 1982; Hobsbawm and Ranger 1983; Linnekin 1991; Merlan 2000; Tonkinson 1997).

In accord with constructivist concepts of tradition as something that has been invented are assertions that dances staged for tourists are mere concoctions aimed at the tourist dollar. It has been argued that indigenous Australian dance festivals, the hula in Hawaii, and other such performances are not authentic expressions of traditional culture, but are in fact products of colonialism. Yet as Sahlins (1993: 8) argues with regard to the hula: "[T]he hula as a sign of Hawaiianess, of the indigenous, was not born yesterday nor merely as the construction of the Hawaiian Visitors Bureau and prurient Haole interests. The hula has been functioning as a mode of cultural co-optation for more than 150 years—a significance, moreover, that was already inscribed in the meanings of hula performances before the first White men set foot in the islands."

Sahlins's point is that although the hula, as part of the current Hawaiian renaissance, may be an 'invention', it is not a colonial invention. It is not "a Western fabrication of Hawaiianess," nor is it "an Hawaiian fabrication in response to the West" (Sahlins 1993: 11). As Sahlins (ibid.: 13) writes: "We are not dealing with people who have nothing and are nothing." According to Sahlins, innovations follow logically from the people's own principles of existence. They are not simply imposed from outside by the colonial order or by the commercial forces of a global economy. Like hula, contemporary Aboriginal dance festivals are not an invention divorced from cultural forms and historical contexts.

The Aboriginal cultural renaissance is clearly not just state-sponsored and generated for the tourist industry. It is a political response by indigenous people, an attempt to control their relationships with the state. An ethnographic study of festivals celebrating the indigenous cultural renewal reveals the role that dance performances play in a fraught political arena in which the criteria for indigeneity are continuously being contested and negotiated.

Cultural Festivals

I provide here a comparative account of two indigenous Australian cultural festivals held in the north of the country: the Garma Festival, which is staged on an annual basis by Yolngu clans from northeast Arnhem Land, and the Laura

Aboriginal Dance and Cultural Festival, which is held biennially in Cape York (cf. Henry 2000a, 2000b, 2002). Both festivals are relatively recent institutions. The Garma Festival was first held in 1999, while the roots of the Laura Festival in Cape York can be traced to 1972, when a regional festival was sponsored by the Aboriginal Theatre Foundation and hosted by Aboriginal people from Lockhart River, Cape York.

Some festivals in Australia are staged by indigenous people who are familiar with one another's practices and who have relationships in the lived-in-world beyond the event. This is the case with the Garma Festival. By contrast, the Laura Festival brings together many unrelated and culturally distinctive peoples from all over Cape York Peninsula. Although similar in substance, the festivals are different both in flavor and in terms of the "logics of their design" (Handelman 1990: 7). These differences reflect not only the cultural differences of Cape York and Arnhem Land peoples but also their different histories and experiences of European colonialism.

The Laura Festival, Cape York

The pragmatics of organization of the first Cape York Festival, at Lockhart River, necessitated some rapid adjustments in performance practices by the participants. The festival, as a newly forged intercultural space, brought together distant groups to perform in the presence of one another for the first time, and this led to some disquiet and debate concerning the ritual protocols that should be followed.

For example, von Sturmer (1973: 4) writes that some of the dance leaders were concerned about "the intermingling of sacred (though public) and secular dances" at the festival, and were disturbed by "the failure to carry out the proper ritual procedure which should follow the introduction of unfamiliar and powerful dances." According to von Sturmer (ibid.), it took many behind-the-scene consultations among various groups before correct protocols were thrashed out and the dancing went ahead.

Because these early festivals were envisioned as a means of 'cultural revival' of 'traditional' song and dance, they generated lively debate and competition among groups concerning the relative traditionality of the performances. In this politics of knowledge, as Chase (1980: 419) observed, "whoever had the greatest range of 'old fashion' dance was thought to be the most successful."

The Lockhart River Festival spawned the idea for an annual Cape York Festival, hosted by a different community each year and supported by state government funding. It was held in a number of different Cape York Aboriginal communities, which had been established during the mission and reserve era, before a permanent site was chosen. The festival is now held biennially near the tiny town of Laura. While allowing Cape York peoples to celebrate their social and cultural differences, the festival fosters connections that have contributed to an emerging regional Cape York identity (Chase 1980: 421).

The festival was initially staged solely for indigenous people of Cape York Peninsular, not for tourists. The organization of the festival was for many years under the control of the State of Queensland Department of Communities, through a committee of elected indigenous representatives. It was organized much like a sports carnival, with a competition between dance groups representing their respective ex-mission/reserve communities. However, during the 1980s the festival began to attract an increasing number of domestic and international tourists. To accommodate the demands of the tourist audience for cultural authenticity, the organizing committee decided on a number of rules to be followed by groups wishing to participate. Included among these were that all dance performances "must be properly cultural and traditional," dancing costumes "must be traditional," and "no modern instruments (such as kerosene tins) are to be used" (as related in a document titled "History of the Laura Dance and Cultural Festival," released to the media by festival organizers in 2001).

There was some discontent among the participants regarding the control and influence of the state ministry and the rules and regulations imposed by the committee. In particular, people objected to the fact that the dance festival was staged as a competition with prizes awarded to the winning dance teams. Some argued that competition was contrary to Aboriginal spirituality. There was ambivalence about, or disquiet concerning, an increasing accommodation of the performers to the demands of the tourist audiences. Initially, 'revivals' of ritually performed dances of the past were showcased, with an accompanying attitude of solemnity and a sense that the participants were being drawn into the presence of the sacred ancestors (and vice versa). Yet with time, and in articulation with the demands of state agencies and domestic and international tourist audiences, the festival became increasingly like a sports festival.

Among indigenous groups, there is an apparent hierarchy in terms of which groups can demonstrate a stronger continuity of traditional knowledge and practice, with certain groups recognized as 'more traditional' and therefore culturally stronger than others. The criteria upon which this recognition is based include the participation of 'song men' who are able to accompany the dancers in language and of elders with knowledge of 'remembered' dances that may have been performed in the past in a ritual context. If an unprecedented event occurs (e.g., as when a member of a dance team died as a result of a heart attack), the advice of elders from these more traditional groups is often sought, as they are considered to be more knowledgeable about how to handle the contingencies of life in a culturally appropriate way.

It is interesting to observe the different responses among the audience to the performance capabilities of the dancers. A person sitting next to me at the 1999 Laura Festival complained that he could not take good photos of some groups because the dancers had their backs to him (they had not adapted their performance for the tourist audience). He praised other groups for their virtuosity and obvious audience appeal. Yet for indigenous members of the audience, the less showy dances have a symbolic power that the dances of the more tourist-oriented teams lack. They are accompanied by song men singing in language, which signifies that they have closer links to traditional culture. In 1997, the dance team from Kuranda danced for the first time to songs newly composed in Djabugay. They were complimented by an elder from another group who said he was happy to see that they were getting their language back and were now able to produce their own song men. He had felt "sorry" for them at earlier festivals. Here tradition is 'rediscovered' in contemporary innovation. The words of the songs were composed with the help of a linguistic anthropologist, but their source is still believed to be the dreaming ancestors. The anthropologist is thought to be merely the conduit, the tool that enabled the revelation of what was/is always in existence.

The Laura festival ground was handed back under the *Aboriginal Land Act* of 1992 (Qld) to the Western Kuku Yalanji people in a special ceremony at the 1997 festival. That same year, rather than trophies being awarded to winning teams, all the dance groups were presented with certificates of acknowledgment for participation. The traditional owners of the area now control the running of the festival. In 2003, in an attempt to revitalize the festival, the dance competition was reintroduced. Some performers expressed discomfort over this decision, suggesting that it was culturally inappropriate for the performances to be staged in terms of a competition. Others disagreed, arguing that such competition is not alien to Aboriginal tradition and operates to enhance virtuosity.

While the festival organization is in the hands of the traditional owners, the state's presence at the festival remains strong. Various bureaucratic welfare and other state agencies, including the National Native Title Tribunal and numbers of Aboriginal representative bodies, promote themselves and their products and services at the festival. The Laura Festival is as much a competition for Aboriginal clients by the welfare state and by state agents—referred to by Collmann (1988) as "boundary riders" or "brokers" (including lawyers and anthropologists)—as it is a dance competition. Thus, the state reproduces itself through the festival, sustaining itself by feeding upon the very Aboriginal lifeworld that it claims to support.

The Garma Festival, Arnhem Land

The Garma Festival, at a place called Gulkula near Nhulunbuy, is an annual event hosted by the Yolngu, indigenous people of northeast Arnhem Land. The festival is organized through the Yothu Yindi Foundation (2003), a non-profit charitable organization that was established in 1990 by representatives of five of the Yolngu clans—Gumatj, Rirratjingu, Djapu, Galpu, and Wanguri—to "support and further the maintenance, development, teaching and enterprise potential of Yolngu cultural life." The Foundation is working collaboratively with a number of Australian universities to develop the Garma Cultural Studies Institute to facilitate sharing of Yolngu and Western knowledge. It has also established a Music Development Centre to support local songwriters and musicians and to facilitate the documentation of traditional song cycles. The Garma Festival is funded partly through various state and federal government bodies and programs as well as through sponsorship of a number of non-governmental organizations and industry bodies.

Garma is a Yolngu name/concept. It condenses, or distills, many different but related meanings. We were told at the festival that it 'implies balance' between indigenous and non-indigenous peoples (see Yunupingu 1993). It is also the abstract idea of "a place from which cultural meanings flow" (Verran

2004). In other words, it is a place of learning where Yolngu people of different clans, affiliated with that country, come together and where the first (public) stages of initiation are performed. Garma also refers to a public genre of ceremonies that include songs (*manikay*), accompanied by didjeridu (*yidaki*, the Yolngu *dhuwa* moiety name for didjeridu) and clapsticks, and associated dances, painted designs, sand sculptures, and objects (Keen 1994: 138). In other words, it is a concept of a kind of social relationship or a moral principle of how people should relate to one another (i.e., in a balanced way), a place, a type of ceremony, and a level of knowledge. It symbolically condenses the link between people, knowledge, and place.

Unlike the Laura Festival, the Garma Festival is relatively closed to tourists. Attendance is by invitation only. A limited number of invitations are issued to members of the general public by the Yothu Yindi Foundation, upon receipt of an expression of interest. The majority of people attending the 2003 festival were not tourists but invited politicians, government bureaucrats, academics (e.g., anthropologists, ethno-musicologists, lawyers, linguists, and other scholars), media personnel, and people linked in various capacities with the indigenous arts industry and indigenous education, employment, health, and welfare (e.g., community arts coordinators, community development workers, and indigenous artists). In addition, there were participants from all over the world who were specifically at the festival for the purpose of attending the *yidaki* master class (didjeridu students from Germany, Japan, Iceland, and elsewhere). Very few of the participants could be classed simply as tourists. Yolngu people outnumbered all other participants.

The Garma Festival takes an interesting form. It is predominantly a set of educational workshops and a conference organized around a particular topic and embedded within a festival of Aboriginal dance, music, and other expressive cultural practices. Each year, a different forum or academic program with a specific theme has been organized as an inherent part of (or an umbrella for) the festival. To date, these have been: "'Bush University': Natural and Cultural Resource Management" (1999), "Gathering of Indigenous Scholars" (2000), "Ngarra Legal Forum: Indigenous Australians and the Criminal Justice System" (2001), "Djakamirri Wangawu Forum: Indigenous People and the Environment" (2002), "Dhuni: Indigenous Art and Culture" (2003), "Indigenous Livelihoods and Leadership" (2004), "Indigenous Cultural Livelihoods" (2005), "Indigenous Education and Training" (2006), and "Indigenous Health: Real Solutions for a Chronic Problem" (2007).

The forums are structured very much like a regular academic conference with invited keynote speakers and plenary sessions that break up into a number of different panels and/or workshops. It is mostly Yolngu people who lead the sessions and workshops, thereby sharing their concepts and ideas on the relevant theme. Concurrent with the forum sessions are cultural workshops, such as women's basket weaving, painting, woodcarving, spear making, the *yidaki* master class, and tours for gathering bush foods and painting materials. It is thus possible, if one is not a panel member or a speaker in a session, to come and go, to move in and out of the forum proper, and to escape the talkfest, if one is so inclined.

Celebrated as a means of marrying Yolngu and *balanda* (non-indigenous) knowledge systems, the Garma Festival is very much 'entangled' with the state through its links with the tertiary education sector. In particular, the University of Melbourne and Charles Darwin University play a key role in aspects of the festival. At the 1999 Garma Festival, Yolngu leaders prepared a message stick that they sent to invite the vice-chancellors of Australian universities to travel to Gulkula (the Garma Festival site) to attend a Garma ceremony. At this meeting, the Australian Vice-Chancellors' Committee (AV-CC) formed a working party that facilitated a gathering of indigenous scholars at the 2000 festival, during which the Garma Declaration, a statement about indigenous higher education in Australia, was developed. The festival and its accompanying academic program are envisioned as being part of a 'bush university' and of an ongoing development of the Garma Cultural Studies Institute, established to "sustain and extend Yolngu intellectual traditions and knowledge systems" and to "develop partnerships and collaborative relationships with places of learning, other Indigenous peoples and the wider community" (Yothu Yindi Foundation 2003: 11).

The logic of the organization of the Garma Festival is thus much like that of a conference or convention. It is a highly orchestrated event, entangled with the tertiary education sector and with high-level state and federal political institutions and industry bodies. A Yolngu participant in one of the forum sessions referred to the Garma Festival as a "window to the nation." It could also be interpreted as a space of governmentality. Trouillot (2001: 127) argues that the state has no "institutional fixity or geographical fixity" and that its materiality resides "in the reworking of processes and relations of power so as to create new spaces for the deployment of power" (cf. Aretxaga 2003; Das and Poole 2004; Foucault 1991; N. Rose 1999). I suggest that one such space is the cultural festival, where effects of the state—in particular, the identification, legibility, and spatialization effects, as described by Trouillot (2001)—are clearly recognizable. Festivals foster the construction of, desire for, and consumption of indigeneity (the identification effect). They are sites where knowledge of, and the means for governance of, indigenous people is produced (the legibility effect) and where social and political boundaries are generated (the spatialization effect).

The Poetic Politics of Dance: A Politics of Knowledge

Dance is the main focus of the three-day Laura Festival, and different dance teams are scheduled to perform one after another, all day long. At the five-day Garma Festival, however, the dance performances are the climax of the academic/educational activities of each day. The *bunggul*, a Yolngu performance of dance and song, takes place just before sunset (*bunggul* is the Yolngu term for dancing but also the generic term for ceremony; see Tamisari 2005: 179). It restates what might have been lost during the day's talkfest, that is, that Yolngu people (of a number of related clans from northeast Arnhem Land) are in charge. It clearly re-establishes the identity of the hosts and the guests at the festival.

The two festivals, Laura and Garma, bring non-indigenous participants into an indigenous space. The remoteness of the festival grounds, out in 'the bush', means that the participants are captured for the time of the festival. Unlike a city festival, there are no hotels, motels, or lodgings available as a means of escape: visitors are expected to camp at the festival ground. The participants are granted autonomy in choosing the level and nature of their participation. At both festivals there are a number of different activities going on simultaneously, and participants can choose to connect to the festival through any one or more of these.

Although the Laura Festival dance performances are more obviously geared to a tourist audience than the Garma *bunggul*, in both cases the performances are not aimed just at visitors. Constituting instead a performative exchange among indigenous groups themselves, they evidence a dynamic continuity of social relations and a display of power politics. Although there is an emphasis on the cultural continuity of the performances, culture is not represented as something static or fixed in times past. Rather, culture is performed as a dynamic process. Elders can be observed instructing the junior dancers on the dance ground during their actual performances. The significant point here is that the dances are not necessarily presented as finished products. According to Smith (1997: 60), in her study on Wik ancestral dance, the performances by Wik peoples at festivals such as Laura are a public proclamation of their "continuing link with land, with Ancestors, and with the past." I suggest that such presentations are also a public statement of the continuity of cultural transmission. The performances are as much exhibitions of a process of teaching and learning as they are displays of song and dance routines. Festivals are an opportunity to evidence cultural vitality by publicly performing a process of transmission and acquisition of embodied knowledge. At Garma, the children dance with their elders on the *bunggul* ground. At the Laura Festival, in 1995 there were 170 child performers of a total of 478 dancers, while in 1997 there were 202 of a total of 467.

By placing an emphasis on the ritual, ancestral aspects of the performances, indigenous people claim authenticity in terms of embodied knowledge of the past and of sacred connection with the ancestors and the land. However, virtuosity in dance is valued as a powerful means of capturing not only the attention of the ancestors but also of the audience. However, if it is allowed to dominate, virtuosity leaves the dancers vulnerable. According to Franca Tamisari (2000: 283), who has written of Yolngu responses to, and understanding of, virtuosity in their dance performances: "As for virtuosity, the full extent of one's power makes one vulnerable … the capacity to act on and change others requires a disposition to be in turn acted upon and changed, or as the Yolngu would say seeing the other's feeling and inner desires is paralleled by being invaded by them." While dancing at public festivals opens up the possibility of acting upon the sentiments of the participant audience, including agents of the state, the dancers are also in danger of being invaded and transformed by the inner desires and feelings of that audience.

The dances are a means not only of continuing the links with ancestors and the past but also of creating connections in the present. Through the festival performances, the dynamics of the relationships between individuals and

groups is publicly restated. For example, as the two dance groups were introduced at the Garma Festival, the announcer (Galarrwuy Yunupingu) noted that
they had recently, in the lived-in-world beyond the festival, ritually exchanged
colors, so that the group that was dancing under the red flag had at the last
festival danced under the yellow flag. (In this way, it was also made clear to
the visitors that Yolngu 'business' is alive and well outside the festival context,
and that the performances in the festival are not just a reconstruction of a past
long gone.) Neparrnga Gumbula and De Largy Healy (2004) provide a fascinating account of the complexity of contemporary political relationships between
different Yolngu clans attending the festival (cf. Preaud 2005).

The dance performances can also be read as a commentary on the morality
of the colonial encounter and the colonial practices of the European settlers.
Examples at the Laura Festival include comic, lighthearted dances, such as one
that depicts Aboriginal first encounters with the European bee (which has a
sting, unlike the native bee). Another dance mimes the strange antics of European gold prospectors and miners. However, there are also more direct political
statements through performance. At the 1997 festival, the Aurukun dancers
marched onto the dance ground in T-shirts screen-printed with a map of Cape
York identifying Wik territory, while a spokesperson explained the Wik High
Court decision on native title (*Wik Peoples v. Queensland* [1996] 141 ALR 129)
to the audience. In the "heterotopic space" (Foucault 1986) of festivals, indigenous people reconstitute cultural symbols to address contemporary realities
and confront their social situation.

At the Garma Festival, Yolngu call attention to the inequitable nature of the
relationship between indigenous people and Europeans. For example, some
of the performances concern narratives associated with Indonesian fishermen
from Macassar (Ujung Pandang), who had trading relations with Yolngu until
just after the turn of the century. A *beche-de-mer* (trepang) industry continued
from the early seventeenth century to 1907. The spiritual significance of the
Yolngu-Macassan connection to particular Yolngu clans has been documented
in the film *Spirit of Anchor* by Barker and Glowczewski (2002). The songs and
dances at the Garma Festival acknowledge the moral application of the principle of reciprocity in exchange relations between the Macassans and Yolngu.
According to McIntosh (2000: 144): "Despite episodes of violence and blood-
shed, with the passing of time and the blurring of memories, the seafarers are
remembered with great fondness, particularly when compared with the European missionaries … miners and bureaucrats who came in their wake."

In highlighting the moral principles employed by Macassans in their relationship with Yolngu, the performances at Garma operate as a form of admoni-
tion, underscoring the amoral practices of the Europeans who, in contrast to
the Macassans, invaded and took without fair return. The songs and dances
concerning Yolngu relations with the Macassans can be interpreted much like
Deborah Rose (1984) interpreted the Aboriginal narratives about Captain Cook
in the Victoria River District of the Northern Territory. Unlike the Macassans,
the Europeans did not employ the valued moral principles of "reciprocity,
balance, symmetry and autonomy" in their relations with Yolngu people. The

Yolngu-Macassan relationship is thus held up as a model of what constitutes moral social engagement between different peoples.

At the Garma Festival, a six-meter representation of the ancestor figure Ganbulabula (the sugarbag hunter), carved by Yolngu leader Galarrwuy Yunupingu, is erected in the center of the *bunggul* ground for the period of the festival. What is Ganbulabula's role in relation to the festival? Perhaps he is, as Handelman (1990: 133) puts it (but in relation to the Madonna in the Palio Festival of Siena), a kind of "ideological underwriter," a means of legitimizing the festival according to principles, precepts, and regulations that are higher than (or beyond) those of the state. In other words, Ganbulabula embodies a higher moral law that is above and beyond state law and embraces all of the participants in the festival, Yolngu and visitors alike. The visitors are meant to leave the festival, not radically transformed in terms of their nature, but with recognition of the moral precepts of Yolngu law and an understanding of the immorality of *balanda* law (i.e., European law or 'Captain Cook's law').

At the festival, Yolngu present a way of being, a philosophy of respect, and a basis for mutual and equitable relationships between Yolngu and *balanda* (European). The festival is not independent of the lived-in everyday world, since it, in fact, springs from it and is in response to it (see Handelman 1990: 27). Nevertheless, the festival, albeit for just a short time, is experienced by Yolngu and their visitors as autonomous from everyday life, operating according to its own law—Yolngu law.

The Laura and Garma festivals are public events that re-present the lived-in-world. According to Handelman (1990: 49): "Events that re-present do the work of comparison and contrast in relation to social realities." In other words, an event that re-presents raises "possibilities, questions, perhaps doubts, about the legitimacy or validity of social forms, as these are constituted in the lived-in world" (ibid.). Such events comment upon and call into question the world as it is by inverting it (but not necessarily transforming it), by neutralizing distinctions, and by proposing alternative possibilities of being.

For example, at the Garma Festival it is Yolngu who are in charge. They are the lecturers at the Garma bush university, while the academics and bureaucrats and politicians become their students, their 'initiates'. During the festival we were told by a number of Yolngu participants that *garma* is but the first stage of a ceremonial complex involving public or 'outside' knowledge and that there are other levels of knowledge or 'inside' knowledge that Yolngu initiates are taught after they have first participated in *garma*. Nevertheless, even in the context of *garma* ceremonies, there is secrecy, or what Keen (1994: 226) refers to as "secrecy in public." It is this secrecy in public that is the key to the politics of knowledge. At the Garma Festival, it is made clear to the participants that there is much more to the story/performance/painting than is being revealed. We were repeatedly told in various ways that what was being conveyed to us at the festival was open knowledge (*garma*). Yolngu teachers stressed that *garma* is only the first level of a system of knowledge consisting of a number of restricted deeper levels.

Therefore, even though songs, dances, and designs are performed in public, they may have their secret interpretations. As Keen (1994: 226) notes, performances in public may in fact operate to emphasize "the ignorance of those without access to knowledge of this secret significance and the privilege of those with inside knowledge." *Balanda* visitors to the festival are thus placed in the position of powerless initiates under the authority of powerfully knowledgeable Yolngu elders.

Festival visitors are advised not to ask too many questions but to learn by watching and listening, and also, where appropriate, by doing. Visitors are invited to try weaving, to participate in making a didjeridu or a spear, and to taste bush food. They are also taught where it is not appropriate to observe or do these things—that is, they are taught Yolngu intellectual property law. It is through a complex dynamic interaction between processes of concealment and revelation that knowledge is transmitted among Yolngu people (see Keen 1994; Morphy 1991; Tamisari 2000). Emphasized again and again is the idea that there are levels of knowledge that are not revealed but that are generative of what *is* revealed. The visitors are allowed access only to the public realm of knowledge (*garma*). Bureaucrats, government officials, politicians, academics, and others become neophytes, and hierarchies of the lived-in-world are inverted.

Conclusion

The phenomenon of the indigenous cultural festival has burgeoned in Australia in tandem with state multicultural policies that foster the celebration of culture as a factor in the government of people. Festivals such as the Garma Festival and the Laura Aboriginal Cultural Festival are 'governmental technologies' in that they work to constitute the collective identities necessary for the task of "governing through community" (N. Rose 1999: 189–190). Yet through participation in these festivals, indigenous people are able to confront creatively the contradictory social forces that affect their lives by engaging with state agencies and bureaucratic realities according to their own terms. What De Soto (1998) has argued for the carnivals of the German peasants of the Black Forest also holds true for festivals of indigenous Australia. Through such festivals participants "express contemporary existential fears and economic insecurities arising from national and transnational political communities, markets, and bureaucratically enforced policies and regulations in which their lives are embedded" (De Soto 1998: 482).

The festivals allow Aboriginal people to bring various parties into a spatial and temporal frame that they themselves regulate and direct. These events provide a means of creating, albeit only momentarily, a micro-world in which the vagaries and uncertainties of their interactions with state agents can be controlled, or at least can be more easily controlled than in everyday life. In this way, indigenous people are better able to confront the state and the asymmetrical and oppositional relations that they have with its agencies. Governmental and non-governmental agents of the state, removed from their familiar social spaces and their bureaucratic agendas, are drawn, if only briefly, into a web of relationships and obligations that are not of their own making but of Aboriginal fabrication.

Through these public events, and in particular the use of media coverage, indigenous people are able to reach an extended audience, so as to communicate their concerns as widely as possible, both nationally and internationally. Through the festivals they attempt to show publicly not only how they view the world but also how their worldview might provide a moral discourse (or moral principles) through which their relationships with the state and with other Australians might be transformed.

By using the performances as a mode of cultural transmission and acquisition of embodied knowledge, indigenous people challenge the idea that their dances are a mere theatricalized presentation of fixed traditional forms. They question the dominance of a discourse that, by producing and celebrating a peculiar concept of 'traditional culture', might deny them the contemporary reality of their lived experiences and any agency to control this reality. At festivals people do indeed celebrate tradition, but they do so in order to put it to work to make sense of history and to negotiate their way through the myriad government technologies that have invaded their life-worlds. Festivals allow Aboriginal people to be not only custodians of the past but also agents of change. As Mary Douglas (1995: 23) has aptly reflected: "Time past is remembered, privately or publicly, when it can be used in time present to control the future."

Acknowledgments

This chapter draws on a paper that was originally presented as a public lecture in Mexico City at the invitation of the Comision Nacional para el Desarollo de los Pueblos Indigenas (CDI) and the Australian Embassy (8 July 2004) and again at James Cook University at the colloquium "Indigenous Strategies of Communication: Cultural Festivals and New Technologies" (18 July 2004). Although, of course, the responsibility for the substance rests with me, I am grateful to the colloquium participants, particularly Barbara Glowczewski-Barker and Marcia Langton for their comments. I am also indebted to Franca Tamisari for generously taking the time to read the essay and provide valuable feedback and to my colleagues at JCU, especially Michael Wood and Douglas Miles. The field research on which this chapter is based was conducted with the help of a Merit Research Grant from James Cook University. I especially acknowledge my friends, filmmakers Magdalene Wilson and Christine Togo-Smallwood, for accompanying me in the field, for helping me to record the festivals, and for sharing their insights on the festivals. Finally, I thank Judith Kapferer for her invitation to submit this essay for publication and for her encouraging suggestions on how to strengthen my analysis.

Rosita Henry is currently the Head of the Department of Anthropology, Archaeology, and Sociology at James Cook University. Her ethnographic field research in Australia focuses on the performative relationship between people and the places they call 'home'. Her research publications to date concern indigenous dance festival performances and the political economy of indigenous and non-indigenous identity politics. She is co-editor of *The Politics of Dance* (2000) and *Le Defi Indigene: Entre Spectacle et Politique* (2007).

References

Aboriginal Theatre Foundation. 1972. *Aboriginal Theatre Foundation Newsletter*, no. 1 (May).
Aretxaga, Begona. 2003. "Maddening States." *Annual Review of Anthropology* 32: 393–410.
Barker, Wayne Jowandi, and Barbara Glowczewski. 2002. *Spirit of Anchor*. Documentary video featuring Yolngu narrators from Arnhem Land: Tim Murrmurrnga Burarrwanga, Nancy Gaymala Yunupingu, Barbara Burarrwanga. French and English subtitles. Production/distribution, CNRS Images/Media.
Beckett, Jeremy, ed. 1988. *Past and Present: The Construction of Aboriginality*. Canberra: Aboriginal Studies Press.
_____. 1994. "Aboriginal Histories, Aboriginal Myths: An Introduction." *Oceania* 65, no. 2: 97–115.
Chase, Athol. 1980. "Which Way Now? Tradition, Continuity and Change in a North Queensland Aboriginal Community." PhD diss., University of Queensland.
Collmann, Jeff. 1988. *Fringe-Dwellers and Welfare: The Aboriginal Response to Bureaucracy*. St Lucia: University of Queensland Press.
Das, Veena, and Deborah Poole, eds. 2004. *Anthropology in the Margins of the State*. Santa Fe, NM: School of American Research Press.
De Soto, Hermine G. 1998. "Reading the Fool's Mirror: Reconstituting Identity against National and Transnational Political Practices." *American Ethnologist* 25, no. 3: 471–488.
Douglas, Mary. 1995. "Forgotten Knowledge." Pp. 13–29 in *Shifting Contexts: Transformations in Anthropological Knowledge*, ed. Marilyn Strathern. London: Routledge.
Foucault, Michel. 1986. "Of Other Spaces." *Diacritics* 16, no. 1: 22–27.
_____. 1991. "Governmentality." Pp. 87–104 in *The Foucault Effect: Studies in Governmentality*, ed. Graham Burchell, Colin Gordon, and Peter Miller. Chicago, IL: University of Chicago Press.
Friedman, Jonathan. 1992. "The Past in the Future: History and the Politics of Identity." *American Anthropologist* 94, no. 4: 837–859.
Gumbula, Joe Neparrnga, and Jessica De Largy Healy. 2004. "Murrayana Is Coming to Garma this Year: Acting Out Clan Engagement and Dynamic Networks on a Public Stage." Paper delivered on 18 July 2004 at the colloquium, Indigenous Strategies of Communication: Cultural Festivals and New Technologies, James Cook University, and on 1 October 2004 at the Australian Anthropological Society Conference.
Handelman, Don. 1990. *Models and Mirrors: Towards an Anthropology of Public Events*. Cambridge: Cambridge University Press.
Handler, Richard, and Jocelyn Linnekin. 1984. "Tradition, Genuine or Spurious." *Journal of American Folklore* 97: 273–290.
Hayward, Philip. 2001. *Tide Lines: Music, Tourism and Cultural Transition in the Whitsunday Islands*. Lismore, New South Wales: Music Archive for the Pacific Press.
Henry, Rosita. 2000a. "Dancing into Being: The Tjapukai Aboriginal Cultural Park and the Laura Dance Festival." *Australian Journal of Anthropology* 11, no. 3: 322–332.
_____. 2000b. "Festivals." Pp. 586–587 in Kleinert and Neale 2000.
_____. 2002. "Plesanje v Povezanost: Aboriginski Plesni in Kulturni Festival v Lauri" [The Laura Aboriginal Dance and Cultural Festival]. Trans. Darja Hoenigman. Pp. 31–48 in *Ples življenja, ples smrti* [Dance of Life, Dance of Death], ed. Borut Telban. *Poligrafi* 7, nos. 27–28.
Herzfeld, Michael. 1982. *Ours Once More: Folklore, Ideology, and the Making of Modern Greece*. Austin: University of Texas Press.
Hobsbawm, Eric, and Terence Ranger, eds. 1983. *The Invention of Tradition*. Cambridge: Cambridge University Press.
Kapferer, Bruce. 1995a. "The Performance of Categories: Plays of Identity in Africa and Australia." Pp. 55–79 in *The Urban Context: Ethnicity, Social Networks, and Situational Analysis*, ed. Alisdair Rogers and Steven Vertovec. Oxford: Berg.

_____. 1995b. "Bureaucratic Erasure: Identity, Resistance and Violence—Aborigines and a Discourse of Autonomy in a North Queensland Town." Pp. 69–108 in *Worlds Apart: Modernity through the Prism of the Local*, ed. Daniel Miller. London: Routledge.

Kapferer, Judith. 1996. *Being All Equal: Identity, Difference and Australian Cultural Practice.* Oxford: Berg.

Keen, Ian. 1994. *Knowledge and Secrecy in an Aboriginal Religion.* Oxford: Oxford University Press.

_____. 2003. *Aboriginal Economy and Society: Australia at the Threshold of Colonisation.* South Melbourne: Oxford University Press.

Kleinert, Sylvia, and Margo Neale, eds. 2000. *Oxford Companion to Aboriginal Art and Culture.* Melbourne: Oxford University Press.

Kolig, Eric. 1995. "A Sense of History and the Reconstitution of Cosmology in Australian Aboriginal Society: The Case of Myth versus History." *Anthropos* 90, nos. 1–3: 49–67.

_____. 2000. "Social Causality, Human Agency and Mythology: Some Thoughts on History-Consciousness and Mythical Sense among Australian Aborigines. *Anthropological Forum* 10, no. 1: 9–30.

Linnekin, Jocelyn. 1991. "Cultural Invention and the Dilemma of Authenticity." *American Anthropologist* 93: 446–448.

Magowan, Fiona. 2000. "Dancing with a Difference: Reconfiguring the Poetic Politics of Aboriginal Ritual as National Spectacle." *Australian Journal of Anthropology* 11, no. 3: 308–321.

McGregor, Russell. 1997. *Imagined Destinies: Aboriginal Australians and the Doomed Race Theory, 1880–1939.* Carlton, Victoria: Melbourne University Press.

McIntosh, Ian. 2000. "Sacred Memory and Living Tradition: Aboriginal Art of the Macassan Period in North-Eastern Arnhem Land." Pp. 144–145 in Kleinert and Neale 2000.

Merlan, Francesca. 1994. "Narratives of Survival in the Post-Colonial North. *Oceania* 65, no. 2: 151–174.

_____. 2000. "Representing the Rainbow: Aboriginal Culture in an Interconnected World." *Australian Aboriginal Studies*, nos. 1 and 2: 20–26.

Morphy, Howard. 1991. *Ancestral Connections: Art and an Aboriginal System of Knowledge.* Chicago, IL: University of Chicago Press.

Parsons, Michael. 1997. "The Touristic Corroboree in South Australia." *Aboriginal History* 21: 46–69.

Preaud, Martin. 2005. "Cultural and Multicultural Red Flag: Same Culture, Different Performance." Paper presented in the School of Anthropology, Archaeology and Sociology Seminar. Townsville, James Cook University.

Rose, Deborah Bird. 1984. "The Saga of Captain Cook: Morality in Aboriginal and European Law." *Australian Aboriginal Studies* 2: 24–39.

Rose, Nikolas. 1999. *Powers of Freedom: Reframing Political Thought.* Cambridge: Cambridge University Press.

Rumsey, Alan. 1994. "The Dreaming, Human Agency and Inscriptive Practice." *Oceania* 65, no. 2: 116–130.

Sahlins, Marshall. 1993. "Goodbye to Tristes Tropes: Ethnography in the Context of Modern World History." *Journal of Modern History* 65: 1–25.

Smith, Naomi. 1997. "Body, Land and Performance of Identity in Wik Dance." Honours diss., Macquarie University.

Swain, Tony. 1994. *A Place for Strangers: Towards a History of Australian Aboriginal Being.* Cambridge: Cambridge University Press.

Tamisari, Franca. 2000. "The Meaning of the Steps Is in Between: Dancing and the Curse of Compliments." *Australian Journal of Anthropology* 11, no. 3: 274–286.

_____. 2005. "Writing Close to Dance: Reflexions on an Experiment." Pp. 174–203 in *Aesthetics and Experience in Music Performance*, ed. E. Mackinlay, D. Collins, and S. Owens. Cambridge: Cambridge Scholars.

Tonkinson, Robert. 1997. "Anthropology and Aboriginal Tradition: The Hindmarsh Island Bridge Affair and the Politics of Interpretation." *Oceania* 68, no. 1: 1–26.

Trouillot, Michel-Rolph. 2001. "The Anthropology of the State in the Age of Globalization: Close Encounters of the Deceptive Kind." *Current Anthropology* 42, no. 1: 125–137.

Urry, James. 1980. "Aborigines, History and Semantics." *Journal of Australian Studies* 6: 68–72.

Verran, Helen. 2004. "Garma Festival Workshop." http://www.garma.telstra.com/gbackground.htm (accessed 14 January).

von Sturmer, John. 1973. "Lockhart Dance Festival." *PCC Forum* 1, no. 3: 2–5.

Yothu Yindi Foundation. 2003. *Garma Festival 2003: Yothu Yindi Foundation Garma Festival of Traditional Culture, Gulkula, Gove Peninsula, Arnhem Land, Australia. August 8–12, 2003.* Festival program and background notes.

Yunupingu, Mandawuy. 1993. "Yothu Yindi—Finding Balance." Pp. 1–11 in *Voices from the Land.* Sydney: ABC Books.

Chapter 5

URBAN DESIGN AND STATE POWER
City Spaces and the Public Sphere

Judith Kapferer

State power and democratic process have always been inscribed in the material structures of urban contexts, particularly in the capital cities of powerful contemporary social formations such as the United Kingdom. Well before the advent of democratic regimes, state power—republican (e.g., Bologna), monarchical (e.g., Paris), or imperial (e.g., Vienna)—was furnished with the buildings, statuary, and 'townscapes' (Jacobs 1996; see also Carmona et al. 2003: 147) believed to inspire awe, respect, or fear, if not love and loyalty, in the breasts of those citizens who peopled the streets and squares of the city and/or the state. This is still true today of such global postmodern world cities as London, Tokyo, and New York (Beaverstock et al. 2001; Marcuse and van Kempen 2000; Sassen 1991), dominant financial centers of great ideological, economic, and political significance for the lives of ordinary citizens in the

Notes for this chapter begin on page 85.

new imperial order posited by Hardt and Negri (2000) or the disorder proposed by Joxe (2002).

I explore here the city as a constructed formation, as a work of art. Jakob Burckhardt ([1860] 1990), in his classic *Civilization of the Renaissance in Italy*, made this observation long ago. He saw in the built form of Italian city-states an expression of the logic of the society and the politics of the age. The architecture of the city revealed its creative spirit as much as, if not more than, its paintings, sculpture, music, and literature. Burckhardt, I hasten to add, was no Hegelian (overtly he eschewed such a theory of history), yet he saw in Renaissance cities—which he regarded as works of art—the dynamic innovative forces engaged in Italian social realities of the time. The built form of the cities enshrined a new individualism that Burckhardt recognized as the defining characteristic of the Renaissance spirit.

Burckhardt did not treat the city as merely reflective of the spirit of the age. He certainly viewed the city and the built forms that crowded it as expressing the nature of political power, and he understood how they came to be constructed. Cities are rarely, if ever, singular systems of power. As historical phenomena, they are sedimentations (in their memorials, public spaces, living areas, etc.) of often very different alignments of power and its effects. The city as a built formation materializes, houses, and gives substance to its social and ideological structures.

This is a study of the changing cultural and historical significance of central public city space in generating the socio-political structure of social formations, with specific reference to London. I aim to examine the life of public spaces as crucibles of the expression, resistance, and constant formation and re-formation of the social order of the city and the state. Concentration on these public centers permits a focus on their critical importance as places of social mix (cultural, ethnic, political, economic, and other forms of social diversity), where the complexity of the city and its wider environment achieves intense expression. As Lefebvre (1996: 142–143; emphasis added), whose work informs much of my analysis here, points out: "Before our eyes, under our gaze, we have the spectre of the city, that of urban society and perhaps simply of society ... Before us as a spectacle ... are disassociated and inert elements of social life ... The city and the urban cannot be recomposed from the signs of the city ... *The city is a [social] practice.*" The effort to maintain the cohesion and integration of productive *spaces* is paralleled by the ability to maintain a segregation of productive *practices*—in the marketplace, the church, law courts, schools, government offices, and so on.

This study views the public spaces of the city as crucially important in understanding the social, political, and cultural forces engaged in the creation and change of the orders governing contemporary social life. The work of Camillo Sitte ([1889] 1965), for example, illuminates many of the ideological uses to which social space is put in the creation of politically and/or culturally significant buildings, monuments, and streetscapes.[1]

I focus on the functions of public spaces in the control and direction of traffic flows and physical movement, but I also emphasize and highlight particular 'readings' of those spaces that support hegemonic ideologies and practices circulating around ideas of power, prestige, social orders, and their legitimation in everyday life. That is to say, the flows and movements I am concerned with are also metaphorical in their signposting of consensually received understandings of customary practice in diverse situations. Conversely, I have also sought out some evidences of resistant or oppositional social and cultural practices and their environing contexts and appointments, whether these sites be officially designated places of temporary misrule or spontaneous gathering grounds for the expression of popular feeling.

Public buildings and monuments do more than represent or symbolize the power of dominant groups or the class nature of social subordination and egalitarian struggle. I will argue here that the material structures with which I engage actually constitute a way of looking at and seeking to understand the workings of the national state in its liberal democratic manifestation under late capitalism. To this end, I hope to develop a picture of the meanings of certain social productions of political and cultural reality as these are manifested in the material constructions of the city. These meanings and ideas may allow us to think of the state as articulating both consent to and dissent from the orders governing social and cultural practice—sometimes simultaneously. As well, I hope to probe the notion of the social and cultural power of various state apparatuses to control the image and the substance of state legitimacy in a globalizing world. In this I seek to refocus currently popular discussion away from questions of moral 'governance' and globalization—the dominant focus of international political economy and ethical development programs—toward a more sociological emphasis on urban culture and ideology.

I propose, therefore, to analyze and deconstruct a number of public sites (squares, streets, parks, and built environments) and their furnishings (principally monuments, but also plaques, fountains, and play spaces) in an attempt to situate living people in the center of the urban spaces that they inhabit as they go about their daily round of 'getting and spending', as Wordsworth has it. In short, I want to put some substance into the notion of a public culture that is not confined to the works and interpretations of public persons, celebrities, or the mass media, focusing instead on the mundane places and spaces in which people throughout the city interact, work, play, argue, converse, and extract meaning from quotidian existence.

The public spaces that I focus on are, in the first instance, Bank Junction and 'the Square Mile' or 'the City' (the business district) and, in the second, Trafalgar Square and Speakers' Corner in Hyde Park. My intention is to map what might be called spaces of the people and spaces of power onto the buildings and monuments of these central loci of inner urban social interaction (see Debord [1955] 1996; de Certeau 1988). I do so in order to make some sense of the treasury of information—memories, myths, emotions—reposing in spaces and monuments, and to begin to conceptualize and actualize connections between people and state as the lived experience of civil society and its power relations. The journey from Lloyd's of London to Trafalgar Square bypasses and takes detours around numerous important sites, any of which could form a basis for exploration in the manner advocated by Debord ([1955] 1996). But those are excursions reserved for another time and place.

The Square Mile: Confrontations with Capital

Along the route from Lloyd's to Trafalgar Square, one can detect a change of atmosphere, a shift in the auratic (Benjamin 1999) tone of the streets and squares as they merge—albeit untidily, demonstrating what Dirlik (1997) calls the porosity of borderlands—between one central activity and the next. The same unevenness and porosity apply to the narrative history of London: the absence of a clear linear progression from one era to the next mirrors the irregular psycho-geography of the city. The material structures of the city range over time and space, building up the sedimentation and traces of people and events that have left their mark on the city itself. Accordingly, our journey takes us from the merchant City of Mammon through ecclesiastical and judicial landmarks to Trafalgar Square and Hyde Park.

The focus of this initial part of our journey is the Bank underground station and the complex of seven streets leading off it. Here, almost within sight of each other, are the Bank of England,[2] the neo-classical columns of the Royal Exchange, and Hawksmoor's English Baroque Church of St Mary Woolnoth; the nearby Lloyd's of London offices in Lime Street and, hard by, at St Mary Axe, the Swiss Re(insurance) Company's building (familiarly known as 'the Gherkin' or 'Towering Innuendo'); and, finally, the Mansion House to the southwest, wherein dwells the Lord Mayor of London. This personage gathers up and focuses the multi-vocal meanings and intimations of historical and legendary memories of the financial power of the City itself. The Lord Mayor and the Corporation of the City of London sit in uneasy juxtaposition with the Greater London Authority and its democratically elected mayor. The election—more properly, the selection—of the Lord Mayor reflects the deeply inegalitarian manner whereby the elevation to office is grounded in a property qualification, a reminder of the rising confidence and power of the merchant class at the time of Magna Carta in 1215. The annual pageantry of the Lord Mayor's Show (featuring the gilded mayoral coach and the ubiquitous heraldic motifs and images of a griffin and wyvern, with the motto *Domine Dirige Nos*) throughout the Square Mile does more than provide a spectacle for tourists and sightseers.

The office of Lord Mayor and those of the aldermen and members of the Corporation all forcefully display and concretize the significance of traditional influence and the continuous authority of the merchant class for over 800 years. Most of these personages are engaged in the business of the City: finance, trade, insurance, and banking. Many have been honored for their contributions to the furtherance of City concerns (and the rendering of good works beyond the immediate purview of narrow business interests) with knighthoods and other ennoblements. These awards not only enhance the prestige of City activities, while expressing and emblematizing them, but also signify and legitimate the overriding dominance of commerce and finance in today's power arrangements with the national state.

The complex of all these buildings is dedicated to the continuation of the trading and financial puissance of Great Britain established in the sixteenth century. It is in one of the oldest parts of London, as its street names attest: Threadneedle Street (the Bank of England is known as 'the old lady of Threadneedle Street'), Cornhill, Lombard Street, Eastcheap, Leadenhall Street, Milk Street, and Poultry. Here, the commerce of England was carried out and financial transactions were conducted, as they are to this day, albeit with trade in different commodities. Not far away is the Guildhall, whose offices, a very grand banqueting hall, a small but important art gallery, and an adjacent guild church of the Corporation of the City of London, St Lawrence Jewry, are all grouped around a courtyard. Here is the hub of the City's operations and the guardian of its global financial reputation.

Two of its most significant buildings, evocative of ruling class mores and values and demonstrating Gottdiener's (1994) or Harvey's (1990) concern with real estate as the central expression of physical property as commodity, are those of the Lloyd's of London offices and the Swiss Re building. Here, the vast majority of 'monuments' are the actual buildings that compose the City itself. The Lloyd's of London building at One Lime Street, built in 1986 by Richard Rogers (now Lord Rogers of Riverside)—all postmodern stainless steel, reinforced concrete, gleaming glass, and exterior riveting—provides a telling demonstration of capitalist power. The impression of consequence and potency is heightened by the vision of a red-coated and top-hatted doorman welcoming important clients and, at the top of the steps, two stolidly uniformed guards to repel those with no identity card.[3]

The symbolic economy expressed by the architectural style and the style of dress—ceremonial and practical uniforms versus business apparel—reflects and indeed expresses the social relations of capital itself (see Harvey 1990). Design and demeanor combine to form a 'monument' to the purpose of the building, a metonym of high finance. Lloyd's of London's position at the center of the commercial world of global finance and insurance underwriting is itself both a symbol and a realization of the world of the City, its power and its influence. Established in a Thames-side coffee house in 1688, Lloyd's is now housed, according to its Web site, in premises "slightly more befitting the multi-million dollar industry it serves."[4]

The demise of City coffee houses parallels the decline of the bourgeois public sphere identified by Habermas ([1962] 1989). What were once centers for the convivial company of gentlemen for whom the news of the day was full of mercantile and political developments, as well as gossip and literary and scientific discovery, metamorphosed into mercantile companies with their own buildings. Known as 'penny universities', the coffee houses played an important role in circulating the news of the day to all who could read and afforded opportunities for engaging in mostly congenial debate with like-minded burghers. Today, the fast-food and down-market cafés, such as Starbucks in Paternoster Square and Leadenhall Street, are unequivocally stark demonstrations of the extinction of small businesses and family-owned enterprises by transnational business interests in the heart of the City.

The Lloyd's building, reminiscent of the Centre Pompidou (which is, along with the work of Renzo Piano, another of Rogers's designs), exudes the power of capital—hard-edged and uncompromising. Apart from its core commercial activities, Lloyd's prides itself on its community programs and a number of trusts and foundations that fund fellowships and business scholarships, financial assistance to ex-servicemen and -women and their dependents, and several charities. The firm's Web site maintains that Lloyd's "believes that employers should demonstrate a commitment to social responsibility. It makes a substantial contribution to the community by supporting a variety of separate initiatives."[5] This is the ideal of 'corporate citizenship', of 'giving something back', popularized since the 1980s as a mutually beneficial partnership comprising financial might, a compassionate social conscience, and ideological imagery. "Focusing on education, training and enterprise, Lloyd's aims to make a real difference to the quality of life in East London and its success has been reflected in the presentation of three Dragon Awards by the Lord Mayor of London."[6]

Of particular interest is the Lloyd's Community Programme (LCP). It is worth summarizing the firm's view of its corporate mission to those who actually live in the City and around its eastern edge, and who are at the very center of the ideological public culture of the community: "The LCP was first established in 1989 to promote community involvement, both within the Corporation of Lloyd's and across the companies that form the Lloyd's community."[7] Volunteers from Lloyd's and other City companies engage with local schools in reading programs and literacy improvement; mentoring of skills such as job interviewing, cricket coaching, and storytelling; and practical projects such as clearing wasteland. In addition, LCP's 'mission' is to encourage enterprise, predominantly in the Borough of Tower Hamlets and neighboring boroughs working with Tower Hamlets Education Business Partnership and East London Business Alliance, where LCP funding is much utilized in providing and administering loans to local small businesses.

In the process of fulfilling this program, Lloyd's and their partners have garnered a number of awards for corporate good works. As its chairman reported in the LCP Annual Report for 2004, Lloyd's employees have been recognized for their services to businesses and charities and for their police mentoring program. This relationship between business and community, between the firm and the people living around it, is structured around the notions of corporate citizenship, of returning something of value to the local inhabitants, and of fostering the public culture of the area. Focusing on education, sports, and business is at the center of ideologies of good citizenship, for both individuals and groups.

The Lloyd's image of itself as a good citizen is polished by its awards for good works and its reputation for not only extending help to the needy but also supporting young people who might otherwise be led into a life of unemployment, poverty, and crime. Tower Hamlets, one of the poorest boroughs in the United Kingdom, is still composed of high-rise tower blocks provided by the local council, making Tower Hamlets an address that is a far cry from the corporate prestige of One Lime Street.[8]

Swiss Re at 30 St Mary Axe is another remarkable (some would say 'iconic') building that has slipped into the catalogue of important London structures. Headquartered in Zurich, the firm's London building, designed by Foster and Partners, was opened in 2004. Its ground floor windows actually advertise 'Tall Buildings', 'Landmark Architecture', and a 'World of Real Estate'—a self-promotion of the structure and its site—as well as signs announcing that 'Retail Space is Available'. Swiss Re constitutes a metonymic statement: the building is its meaning. The senior partner of the architectural firm, Norman Foster, is now (since 2000) Lord Foster of Thames Bank. Significantly, some 30 years before, the site of the old Baltic Exchange (on which the building now rests) was bombed by the IRA. Declared irreparable, the building was demolished. The East End of the city has often been the site of insurgent or rebellious uprisings, not altogether unexpected for a place wherein the conjunction of financial and state power is so clearly displayed.[9] The Baltic Exchange itself, a maritime ship-broking company, began its business in 1744 at the Virginia and Maryland (later the Virginia and Baltick) coffee house, a meeting place for merchants and sea captains engaged in matching cargoes to ocean transport providers.

Swiss Re highlights its corporate citizenship by focusing on three areas: life and health insurance, property and casualty insurance, and financial services. Research and training in areas of risk—which can be seen as of direct financial benefit to the company itself and, indirectly, to its clients—are emphasized. Thus, its remit in the fields of life and health insurance is to support research on environmental sustainability, including spheres such as climate change and conservation of water resources.

In the immediate vicinity of Swiss Re and Lloyd's there are several definitive memorials grouped around the older buildings such as the Bank of England and the old Royal Exchange at Bank Underground station. The streetscape itself is so constructed as to facilitate the impression of momentous financial activity. Around Lombard Street there are hanging signs—often gilded and decorated with an ornament, such as a cricket or a sailing ship—announcing the offices of venerable insurance companies and banks. In front of the original Royal Exchange (now a mini-shopping arcade), a statue of the Duke of Wellington—one of London's favorite subjects, invoking imperial, even jingoistic sentiment—turns its back to the red poppy–bedecked war memorial "to the immortal honour of the officers, non-commissioned officers and men of London who served their king and empire in the Great War 1914–1918."[10] On the same plinth is a kind of postscript to mark the memory of those who fell in World War II. Across the road is a statue of the engineer Greathead, inventor of the tunneling equipment that made the underground possible. But art that might be construed as public art is in general not prominent in the City proper. Public art here is embodied in the very buildings of the city itself. It is the expression of the postmodern creative spirit highlighted by intimations of historical consciousness, by sedimentations of former places and spaces, such as the remnants of the London Wall that are incorporated within the Museum of London.

In common with the rest of the precinct, the postmodern buildings are thought by apologists to blend with and give point to the older structures of the Square Mile, enhancing the townscape.[11] The aggressively thrusting new buildings of finance companies are hailed by architects, engineers, and designers as expressing the dominance of the City's status as a World City and winner of the struggle with Frankfurt to be the pre-eminent finance center of Europe. The City buildings are also monuments in themselves, symbolizing and materializing the mercantilist and financial power of capital. Others view the same cityscape as a desecration of history and tradition, an obscuring of historic vistas, and an excrescence on the London skyline. A current local problem highlights this antagonism. A long-running battle between an eminent architect and a private individual, the owner of a rusty Thames-side barge, has been waged, the issue of contention being the placement of the barge (which houses its owner's artworks and an art educational facility for London children) and a sympathetic neighboring barge-owner. The architect's complaint cites the spoiling of the view from a riverside building (designed by his own firm) situated on the bank opposite to where the hulks are anchored. The barge-owner is supported by the mayor of the Greater London Authority, the energetic self-and-city promoter Ken Livingstone, and others concerned with the preservation of the history and heritage of the London Docklands.

Trafalgar Square and the Fourth Plinth: Empire and People

While Jane Jacobs (1996), referring to Niels M. Lund's painting *The Heart of the Empire*, places Bank Junction at the center of the British Empire, Rodney Mace (1976) claims that it is Trafalgar Square that best fills this role.[12] The aura of Trafalgar Square—half-tourism, half-ideology—is of course entirely different from that of the sober and business-like Square Mile. Surrounded on all sides but one by dense traffic, the Square with Nelson on top of his column, the guardian lions at the base of the column, the confident fountains and the three imperiously mounted bronze soldiers (Havelock and Napier, both of the Indian Army, and George IV)—all unequivocally bespeak the power of an imperial past. This is a past founded on military and naval supremacy and the efforts of merchants and traders like the East India Company to subdue the populace and extract the wealth of colonies around the world. These statues are complemented by the busts of other military heroes such as Jellico, Beatty, and Cunningham, reminders of the crucial importance of sea power in protecting and furthering Britain's historic overlordship of worldwide trade and commerce into the twentieth century.

But Trafalgar Square is different from the City in a number of crucial respects. First and foremost, it has long been the great gathering ground of the British people in times of triumph, jubilation, tribulation, and rage. Traditionally, it has been the people's preferred venue for celebration (on VE Day, for instance) and protest; from 1848 on, a vast number of contentious issues have been fought over here, with 'riotous assembly' ensuing. During the 2003 anti–Iraq war rallies, there was some dispute between Parliament and people over protests being staged in Hyde Park rather than Trafalgar Square. The authorities wanted the demonstration to be removed from the central square, citing traffic considerations, while the protestors deemed Hyde Park to be too far removed from the action of the day. Perhaps such opposition can be seen as another example of the fracturing of democratic forces in the contemporary world of the global Empire.[13] One notes here the proximity to Trafalgar Square of the offices (diplomatic, trade) of former colonies—South Africa House, Canada House, Australia House, and so forth—again recalling imperial grandeur and the tight rein held by the state on the people at home and abroad.

The question of control, both physical and ideological, is well illustrated by the so-called pedestrianization of Trafalgar Square. Tourism and traffic dominate the atmosphere of the Square, and the imprint of the Greater London Authority's populist mayor of London, 'Red' Ken Livingstone, is ubiquitous. Charged with the responsibility of running metropolitan traffic, the Greater London Authority (GLA) has, under Livingstone's baton, focused on the Square as its flagship townscape. The pedestrianization of the Square, a project instigated by Lord Foster's World Squares plan, lasting from 2000 to 2003, was designed to ease congestion through the redirection of traffic and at the same time to make the center of the Square more easily accessible to the throngs of tourists who visit it annually. One of the triumphs of its design has been the opening up of the spaces within the Square itself, as well as the vista afforded by the merging of the Square and the National Gallery, now unbroken by the surging traffic of an earlier era (*Topos* 1993). The impression of a contemplative island in a sea of metropolitan industry is only partly successful, however, given the still insistent traffic on three sides, the frequent swarming of young people climbing the flanking lions of Nelson's Column, and the jostling camera-obsessed multitude.

The pigeons of Trafalgar Square appear to have a special place in its iconography. Fat and swaggering, they roost insolently on Nelson's head and menace those who would feed them. At the end of 2003, six pieces of contemporary art were short-listed (with great controversy) by the Committee of the Vacant Plinth, chaired by Sir John Mortimer, for installation on the fourth plinth of Trafalgar Square. One of the winners of the planned rotating installations was Sarah Lucas's *This One's for the Pigeons*—a small car painted with resin and acrylic to simulate being covered in pigeon droppings. Its creator hopes that the local pigeons will help the sculpture to "grow organically," and says of the work that it "would be a nod to the hopelessness of [efforts to keep cleaning up the Square] and a recognition of the abandoned car culture of less salubrious areas in London."[14]

The case of the fourth plinth is an object lesson in pitting the arts establishment conservatives against the new guard espousing populist representation. In 1950, there had already been plans to replace all the Victorian generals with "figures of socialist democracy—railwaymen, merchant seamen and miners,"[15] but Mayor Ken Livingstone himself famously declared in October 2000 that "I think the people on the plinths in the main square in our capital should be identifiable to the generality of the population. I have not a clue of who the generals [in the Square] are, or what they did."[16]

While most of the six place-getters for the fourth plinth would not be recognizable to the generality of Londoners, one statue, *No-o-war-r No-o-war-r*, by Nigerian artist Sokari Douglas Camp, perhaps the most traditional of the six, celebrates Trafalgar Square's history of famous protest speeches and demonstrations, acknowledging "the contribution made by our forebears to our democratic rights and our duty to continue to recognise those same rights." Inspired by Rodin's *The Burghers of Calais*, Camp says, "My aim is to depict ordinary people as heroes."[17]

Hyde Park and the Voices of the People

While Trafalgar Square is the site of major demonstrations of public anger and frustration with ruling groups, Hyde Park Corner, traditionally a venue for the expression of popular debate and the airing of contemporary contention, has lately (despite the anti-war disagreement noted above) focused mainly on smaller-scale, more personal and individual airings of opinion. These opinions are still voiced by a range of speakers, but the scope of debate has narrowed, and the number of participants, hecklers, and ordinary onlookers has declined since the 1980s, coinciding with the rise of neo-liberal, individualist, and privatized understandings of particularly political engagement in local and world affairs.

On a sunny Sunday afternoon in 2004, with infants in strollers and tourists sitting on the grass or on deck chairs rented by the Park authorities, the prosecution of debate appears passionless and desultory in the extreme. The speakers include a pair of US evangelists, one in a white Stetson and both in 'Western' cowboy boots and Levi's shirts and jeans. They take turns speaking about their convictions as Bible-based Christians and the importance of the Lord in their daily lives. There is little opposition raised. A dialogue is indeed carried on between one of the two and an elderly lady from Hackney, a regular visitor to Speakers' Corner over many years, but the topic of conversation is confined to the lovely weather—a gift from the Lord—and in answer to my question, commenting on the dwindling numbers of the crowd. A speaker for the Christian atheists is holding forth on another soapbox across the path, but the two groups do not appear to communicate with one another, and both are only small gatherings. A speaker nearby, a black London resident preaching evangelical salvation, also seems not to have any connection with the two orators from the US. Nor do a Chinese born-again Baptist speaker and another Christian expounding an anti-Muslim theme.

Those speakers with more overtly political interests include a white anti-feminist, an opponent of the building of the Israel-Palestine wall, a young man from the Socialist Workers' Party (quoting Marx to a minuscule audience), and a black anti-Bush speaker. The last speaker's argument is corroborated by a crowd member with a US accent, speaking of "we" (the US) and inveighing against the Iraq war and the installation of an Iraqi puppet government.

Audience members are largely tourists—Australians, New Zealanders, some French and Italians, and a large contingent of North Americans. None seems inclined to join in argument with the speakers, venturing only the opinion that a Speakers' Corner like this one is "good for democracy." None of those who address the small audiences evince any sign of heartfelt engagement. This may be an expression of the generally tolerant attitude of both speakers and listeners toward a multi-faith, multicultural society, or it may be a demonstration of their aversion to the risk of being receptive to or of rejecting the individual assumptions of others—the critique of pure tolerance put forward by Robert Wolff, Barrington Moore Jr., and Herbert Marcuse (1965). The idea that tolerance is tantamount to indifference is demonstrated by the members of this gathering and indicative of a public sphere that is withering under the onslaught of incessant calls to tighten security and control oppositional thinking.

The largest single audience group is a party of 13 students and their leader from the Church of the Nazarene in California. The students have been charged with the task of listening to and analyzing the speakers' arguments; the professor in charge says that they take a completely open-minded attitude to the views being put around them. Discussion will take place at the end of the day when they return to their hotel. There is no suggestion here that the students or their teacher might offer counter-arguments to those put forward by the speakers, no insistence on debate, no hint of haranguing. While such ideas might be broached in the privacy of the hotel and vehemently disputed, the phenomenon of Speakers' Corner seems to have deteriorated to the extent of its being only a day out in a round of tourist sightseeing—an outmoded practice of little relevance to the daily concerns of a citizenry, informed or otherwise.

Deeper into the park we find another reminder of the stated purposes of public debate in London—a mosaic of white and black pebbles depicting a spreading branched tree, designed to commemorate 'Reformers' Tree'. Its dedicatory inscription relates that "'Reformers' Tree' was a venerable tree which was burnt down during the Reform League Riots in 1866. The remaining stump became a notice board for political demonstrations and a gathering point for Reform League meetings. A new oak tree was planted by the then Prime Minister James Callaghan on 7 November 1977 on the spot where 'Reformers' Tree' was thought to have stood."

From observations made on a number of visits to Speakers' Corner, it is clear that contemporary topics of popular concern have been shifting in terms of both their content and their expression over the last 25 years. The major material for the speakers in Hyde Park has become fundamentalist religious belief and experience, on the one hand, and non-party political opinion, on the other. Very occasionally passions are aroused, but the experience of media intervention and influence has taught protestors and proselytizers alike that to be heard requires a media presence and the participation of large bodies of supporters organized around a broadly common cause. Trafalgar Square, highly regulated as it is, remains the site of choice for the voicing of strong public opinion. Increasingly, visitors to Speakers' Corner have become marginalized, now primarily tourists and disinterested onlookers rather than participants in a democratic debate about important local and global issues among the ordinary citizens of the metropolis. The ambit of the public sphere has here been diminished to the point of extinction.

The hallmark of this kind of speaking out is the individualism of identity politics in conditions of postmodernity. It is the kind of individualism that fractionalizes people, pitting single-issue politics against collective action in neo-liberal-dominated economic and political arenas. Over the past few years, elections in the US, for example, have been remarkable for the ways in which formerly private issues (abortion, in vitro fertilization, family planning, religious practice and belief) have been transposed into issues of *public policy* while cleaving to a resolutely hands-off *fiscal policy* at all levels of government. Nonetheless, Hyde Park is increasingly used, by the GLA in particular, as a venue for spectacular 'feel-good' popular gatherings, secular and all-embracing, such as the "Live 8" band performances in 2005 in aid of starving Africa or the ostensibly complementary (to the Notting Hill Carnival) Summer Festival, subsequently renamed the Caribbean Showcase.[18]

The reappropriation of Hyde Park as a venue for mass entertainment is transparently a pretext for controlling and directing popular sentiment, a reconfiguring of the public sphere in the hands of spin doctors and purveyors of the kind of public culture that caters to a privatized and individuated clientele (cf. Putnam 2000). The Summer Festival was publicized as "fun for all the family," with a thinly veiled suggestion that children and the law-abiding citizenry would be securely protected from the traditional 'lawlessness' (drunkenness, drug dealing and usage, confrontations with police, disputes among participants, etc.) of the Notting Hill Carnival. Here there is also a vague insinuation of a kind of divide-and-rule ploy among official GLA managers of public space in their bailiwick: the Notting Hill event is billed as a celebration of Caribbean identity within London, even though outsiders from other ethnic groups are welcome and even encouraged to swell the numbers in a spirit of multicultural empathy. The Hyde Park event is a manufactured festival (as opposed to the organic expression of ethnic identity) for all and can be seen as designed to control and direct traffic and the movement of people in the interests of security and public safety.

The 'Caribbean community', as it is often designated, while clearly composed of different factions, both traditional and contemporary, nonetheless partakes of the notion of a collective fellow feeling that other groups, especially those centered on class and status relations, have not been able to sustain. The destruction of the trade unions and the ever-encroaching privatization of public goods and services in such areas as housing, health, and education are both cause and consequence of this atomizing of social relations. The transformation of the public sphere, as Habermas ([1962] 1989) claims, has meant both the polarization of sociality and intimacy and a collapsing of the public-private distinction. It has resulted in the replacement of a culture-debating sphere with a culture-consuming society. Features of the social order, such as organs of mass communication, principally television and video, have the capacity to homogenize and render innocuous the production of public opinion. The public culture is thereby diminished; the wild streets and theatrical displays of Carnival are hived off and marginalized, while what is publicized as the main stream of cultural and social practice is tamed and controlled.

Challenging the State in the Spaces of the City: Public and Private Partnerships?

Thus, the ideological discourse of the state sustains the generation of belief in a hegemonic social-cultural order. I have been suggesting that such a discourse continually produces and is produced by the very monuments and edifices of the physical and symbolic structures of state forms, such as the Square Mile streetscapes, Trafalgar Square, and Hyde Park. It is a discursive practice deeply implicated in the ideological ordering of relations between politics and the economy, the dominance of economic considerations in political thinking, and the co-optation of artistic and creative endeavor into a market economy. It is a discourse that segues into the taken-for-granted sanctioning (and perhaps sanctifying) power of the church and the law in manufacturing and administrating the financial-political partnership of the City, the Greater London Authority, and the state. *Plus ça change ...*

But some things do change. The egregious celebration of what might be called 'celebrity structures'—their openings by distinguished personages, their prize-winning architectural feats—is iconic with the dominant economic values of a post-industrial era in a World City. Buildings such as Lloyd's and Swiss Re proclaim their postmodern operations through the very style of their construction. Whereas the Bank of England breathes Victorian solidity, these new masters of the City announce their financial power, not only through elegant advertising promotions with operatic arias and minimalist logos, but also through their arrogant height, dazzling façades, and neo-industrial-cum-astronautical design. High-rise office spaces and expensively rebuilt and gentrified residential apartments (Hamnett 2003; Smith 1996; Zukin 1995) further contribute to the aura of daring financial manipulation and to the high excitement of stock market trading that characterizes the City and its workers. Not solidity and probity, but risk and profit are their watchwords.

The sweeping-aside of the works of the past—of its monuments, institutions, and accompanying ideologies—is characteristic of an age that values the immediate present and the ability to eschew the remembrance of time past and, as current idiom has it, to 'move on' without regret. In an era of constant and increasingly out of control consumption, which is indeed the hallmark of that capitalist expansion without which capitalism itself would be starved of the wherewithal to grow, the continual renewal of concrete spaces and symbolic structures of power signals the might of the market and the state itself. The old spaces (the Baltic Exchange at 30 St Mary Axe being a prime example) make way for the new Swiss Re building; No 1 Poultry is already becoming neglected and denigrated as a failed structure (see Jacobs 1996). And yet the remains of each period are sedimented in the very stones of the City, in the carefully preserved churches, the gilded re-creations of old street signs, and the street names themselves—all these traces of earlier financial triumphs and disasters can never be totally erased. The denizens of the East End are never completely forgotten through more than 2,000 years of change and adaptation.[19] The new Paternoster Square at St Paul's, with its statue of the Good Shepherd, only adds another layer to the ecclesiastical postmodernity of the Square Mile.

The spaces of the people are contested throughout the City with regard to the use and ownership of beloved landmarks, squares, and memorial structures in and around churches like St Paul's and St Martin's-in-the-Fields, at Nelson's Column, and in Hyde Park. In Paternoster Square, the workers of the Stock Exchange share their lunches with Starbucks patrons, tourists, and workers from other parts of the city. Yet unlike St Paul's or Trafalgar Square, the Stock Exchange and Lloyd's are still unequivocally private places, belonging to an elite in-group of business people, investors, and traders with security guards and identity cards (continually advocated for all citizens by parliaments and police) to permit entry to and egress from these temples of financial power. They are not public spaces, and they are not to be understood as the expression of a public culture, except in the sense of the ideologized representations and manifestations I have been discussing here.

Today, in Speakers' Corner and Trafalgar Square, movement is largely unquestioningly under surveillance and controlled by CCTV monitors (see Alÿs 2005) and police (occasionally on horseback, unconsciously mimicking the military heroes of the Square), ensuring that visitors or participants do not overreach the limits of decorum established by parliamentary fiat. Preceding the GLA's control of the streets by almost a century, the Asquith government (1908–1916) established "regulations which curtailed the availability of the Square to progressive movements ... but enabled the State ... to decide who should and who should not be allowed to use the Square to advocate their cause" (Mace 1976: 214).

Trafalgar Square and Lloyd's, Hyde Park and Swiss Re are all, to varying degrees, contexts of work and play, business and entertainment. Their street furniture can be construed as relatively permanent site-specific 'installations', as can their streetscapes, in themselves distinct art objects, installations that can be read as "contexts within contexts" (art historian and critic Miwon Kwon, cited in Valentine 2004), neighborhoods and urban villages embedded in the fabric of the city as a whole. The accretion of these haphazard and often accidental urban effects is what makes the city what it is, while expressing the power of the state and the spirit of the age.

The power of the elected representatives of the people is, as ever, heavily filtered through the myriad devices of the administrative formulations and apparatuses of the national state, on the one hand, and the operations of private and public organizations and individuals advancing widely varying interests (political, economic, social, and cultural), on the other. The conjunction of art and administration allows for controlled expressions of the public culture (as in urban regeneration projects, for example) to be uttered and negotiated through formalized bureaucratic channels. The culture industry—particularly film and television—is of course highly complicit in this, as critiques over many years attest (see, e.g., Adorno 2001; Lippman [1922] 1965; Marcuse [1964] 2002; Mattelart 1979). But none of this is to say that resistant forms of creative endeavor are not to be found, even at the heart of establishment citadels of great art galleries and national repositories of particular heritages (however, see Hurley 2006). The role of the arts in opposing state-authorized cultural production is still an important facet of the challenges thrown out by people acting on the fringes of the law, as frequent recourse to censorship and libel lawsuits brought by the state, corporations, and others testify.

I return here to the spirit of the age and its architecture, both concrete and symbolic. The ownership and control of urban space—buildings, monuments, open spaces, streets, and squares—and the corresponding structure of the social, cultural, and ideological relations of the city, all manifest the kinds of freedom and independence (of movement, of action, of association) that have been cumulatively expropriated by governments and financial markets. At the same time, governments and markets have ignored or even denied those same rights and liberties to others beyond an inner circle of the rich and powerful. This is a circle that might, in another age, have been thought of as the laity, one that has recently been called 'civilian' by members of the 'market militant'—the culture-consuming society of the media and entertainment industries, the upper echelons of the 'new class,' hangers-on and courtiers to the financial and political sovereigns of our world. The authority of wealth, legitimated by government decree, produces the no-longer democratic temper of a public sphere displaced by an urge to control and manipulate the fears of disruption, dissent, and even terror that sustain the society of surveillance adumbrated by Foucault (1979) and the society of control that Deleuze (1995) further delineated.

Contrary to Hardt and Negri's (2000) dream of a triumphant and freeranging multitude of networked activity in the arts and elsewhere, everything points to the continuation of the numerous "cruel little wars" described by Joxe (2002) and attested to by the failure or the unwillingness of Empire, the borderless imperial state, to maintain order and control within its satrapies. The challenges to state power—posed not only by the ordinary voters and citizens of the nation but even more so by the dominant economic, legal, and ideological institutions of the state and the globalizing Empire—remain. The globalizing empire and its constituent state formations both foster and are fostered by precisely that kind of ideological support that the arts, no more, no less than any other cultural or social organizations and movements, encourage. The possibility of the arts standing in opposition to the power of the state and the political-economic objectives that the latter embodies and symbolizes remains severely restricted, signaling a death blow to the traditional Enlightenment project (see Horkheimer and Adorno [1944] 1972), while witnessing a newly resurgent reverence for the pragmatism of the market. The project of the national state, an economic, social, and political practice, has now been consciously developed as a cultural production, which to some extent it always and already was.

Judith Kapferer teaches and conducts research at the University of Bergen where she has been Professor in Sociology since 2000. Her interests are in urban sociology and the sociology of the arts. She has published on education, nationalism, egalitarianism, and social theory in Australia, Norway, Sweden, the United Kingdom, and Zambia. She is the author of *Being All Equal* (1996).

Notes

1. For a different perspective on social space, see Edmund Hall (1969).
2. Founded in 1694, the Bank of England was described by one of its founders, Sir William Petty, as "a Bank which shall furnish Stock enough to Drive the Trade of the Whole Commercial World."
3. The pomp-and-ceremony effect, juxtaposed with the somber, uniformed presence of security guards, is heightened by the wariness that periodically grips London during particular events construed as threatening a way of life or at moments of political tension—which are often, thanks to the concerns of the media, the same thing. The increased numbers of uniformed police at such times bear witness to the close relationship between the repressive apparatuses of state control, on the one hand, and the centrality of the commercial ideologies and practices of a 'nation of shopkeepers', on the other.
4. http://www.lloyds.com/About_Us/
5. http://www.lloyds.com/About_Us/Lloyds_in_the_community/
6. Ibid.
7. Ibid.
8. Parts of the borough are increasingly subject to gentrification, indicated by the influx of working artists and the opening of private galleries, although many 'black spots' remain in the East End.
9. Note particularly the riots on the occasion of the South Sea Bubble traders in 1720, the Stop the City protests in 1983 and 1984, and the Carnival against Capital in 1999. Over centuries, the London 'mob' has had recourse to arson, window smashing, and the looting of important buildings such as the Mansion House. Insurance against property damage is one of Swiss Re's central areas of operation.
10. In passing, it might be noted that it is difficult to find memorials to the Unknown Soldier in Central London, in contrast to those in the French capital and the omnipresent *poilu* figures of the French countryside.
11. But there has been bitter controversy here. See Jane Jacobs (1996) on the Prince of Wales's and the charity English Heritage's condemnation of the building known as No 1 Poultry and the obscuring of the vista to St Paul's.
12. Others might adduce the Albert Memorial as the master symbol of confidence and optimism in the nation's destiny, celebrating, as Rudyard Kipling had it, "dominion over palm and pine."
13. An apposite parallel is the enactment in 2005 of an anti-terrorism regulation forbidding demonstrations and placards in and around Parliament Square in Westminster and within half a kilometer of the Houses of Parliament. The ban—precipitated by the refusal of a long-time peace protestor, Brian Haw, to move from the Square (later depicted in an installation by Mark Wallinger at Tate Britain in 2007)—is symbolic of the curtailment of freedom of speech and the relocation of expressions of protest to Hyde Park.
14. http://www.fourthplinth.co.uk/sarah-lucas.htm
15. http://guardian.co.uk/arts/story.htm
16. http://www.guardian.co.uk/uk_news/story.html

17. http://www.fourthplinth.co.uk/sokari_camp.htm
18. Early in 2005 there were suggestions that the famous Notting Hill Carnival might be shifted at the request of the GLA from the suburban streets of Notting Hill to Hyde Park. The reason given for this change of venue (the Carnival had been a movable feast for the first few years of its existence in the 1960s) was the enormous crowds, which hindered public safety, the securing of property, and crowd control. Members of the Caribbean community, incensed by this attack on their traditional celebration, persuaded the GLA to abandon the idea, but meanwhile the GLA organized a Summer Festival that could be (and often was) construed as a rival carnival to that of Notting Hill—and one that could be funded by the GLA, not the Carnival Board, which was perennially in debt.
19. See Jeremy Gavron's (2005) absorbing history-cum-fictional re-creation of Brick Lane.

References

Adorno, Theodor W. 2001. *The Culture Industry: Selected Essays on Mass Culture*. Ed. J. M. Bernstein. London: Routledge.
Alÿs, Francis. 2005. *Seven Walks, London 2004–5*. London: Artangel.
Beaverstock, Jonathan, Michael Hoyler, Kathryn Pain, and Peter J. Taylor. 2001. *Comparing London and Frankfurt as World Cities*. London: Anglo-German Foundation for the Study of Industrial Society.
Benjamin, Walter. 1999. *Illuminations*. London: Pimlico.
Burckhardt, Jakob. [1860] 1990. *The Civilisation of the Renaissance in Italy*. London: Penguin.
Carmona, Matthew, Tim Heath, Taner Oc, and Steven Tiesdell. 2003. *Public Places—Urban Spaces*. Oxford: Architectural Press.
Debord, Guy. [1955] 1996. "Introduction to a Critique of Urban Geography." Pp. 18–21 in *Theory of the Dérive and Other Situationist Writings on the City*, ed. Libero Andreotti and Xavier Costa. Barcelona: Museu d'Art Contemporani de Barcelona.
de Certeau, Michel. 1988. *The Practice of Everyday Life*. Trans. Steven Rendall. Berkeley: University of California Press.
Deleuze, Gilles. 1995. *Negotiations*. New York: Columbia University Press.
Dirlik, Arif. 1997. *The Postcolonial Aura: Third World Criticism in the Age of Global Capitalism*. New York: Westview.
Foucault, Michel. 1979. *Discipline and Punish*. New York: Vintage.
Gavron, Jeremy. 2005. *An Acre of Barren Ground*. London: Simon & Schuster.
Gottdiener, Mark. 1994. *The Social Production of Urban Space*. 2nd ed. Austin: University of Texas Press.
Habermas, Jürgen. [1962] 1992. *The Structural Transformation of the Public Sphere*. Cambridge: Polity Press.
Hall, Edmund. 1969. *The Hidden Dimension*. Garden City: Anchor.
Hamnett, Chris. 2003. *Unequal City*. London: Routledge.
Hardt, Michael, and Antonio Negri. 2000. *Empire*. Cambridge, MA: Harvard University Press.
Harvey, David. 1990. *The Condition of Postmodernity*. Oxford: Blackwell.
Horkheimer, Max, and Theodor Adorno. [1944] 1972. *Dialectic of Enlightenment*. New York: Continuum.
Hurley, Clare. 2006. "A Barometer of the American Cultural Zeitgeist: The Whitney Biennial 2006." http://www.wsws.org/articles/may 2006/whit-m11/prm.shtml.
Jacobs, Jane. 1996. *Edge of Empire*. London: Routledge.
Joxe, Alain. 2002. *Empire of Disorder*. Los Angeles: Semiotext(e).
Lefebvre, Henri. 1996. *Writings on Cities*. Trans. Elenore Kofman and Elizabeth Lebas. Oxford: Blackwell.
Lippman, Walter. [1922] 1965. *Public Opinion*. New York: Free Press.

Mace, Rodney. 1976. *Trafalgar Square: Emblem of Empire*. London: Lawrence and Wishart.

Marcuse, Herbert. [1964] 2002. *One-Dimensional Man*. London: Routledge.

Marcuse, Peter, and Ronald Van Kempen, eds. 2000. *Globalising Cities: A New Spatial Order*. Oxford: Blackwell.

Mattelart, Armand. 1979. *Multinational Corporations and the Control of Culture*. Brighton: Harvester.

Putnam, Robert. 2000. *Bowling Alone*. New York: Touchstone.

Sassen, Saskia. 1991. *The Global City*. Princeton: Princeton University Press.

Sitte, Camillo. [1889] 1965. *City Planning According to Artistic Principles*. Trans. G. R. Collins and C. C. Collins. London: Phaidon.

Smith, Neil. 1996. *The New Urban Frontier*. London: Routledge.

Topos. 1993. *Urban Squares*. Munich: Callwey.

Valentine, Jeremy. 2004. "Art and Empire: Aesthetic Autonomy, Organisational Mediation and Contextualising Practices." Pp. 187–214 in *Art, Money, Parties*, ed. Jonathan Harris. Liverpool: Liverpool University Press.

Wolff, Robert, Barrington Moore Jr., and Herbert Marcuse. 1965. *A Critique of Pure Tolerance*. Boston: Beacon Press.

Zukin, Sharon. 1995. *The Cultures of Cities*. Oxford: Blackwell.

Chapter 6

SELF AND THE CITY
The Politics of Monuments

Karen Kipphoff

> The past is never dead. It's not even past.
>
> — William Faulkner, *Requiem for a Nun*

The public spaces of historical importance of the twentieth century in Europe feature monuments representing the factual and figural expressions of the cultural politics of the time. As the political, social, and cultural developments of the twentieth century unfolded, these spaces and their monuments were in some cases destroyed, in others neglected, forgotten, altered, or redefined. New concepts of power and ways of displaying it emerged. In consequence, different models of how these societies should present themselves were inserted into the public sphere. In fact, architecture and urban planning today still offer considerable potential in meeting the pressing need for erasing, rewriting, and overwriting history with new material that is deemed more suitable for the present.

References for this chapter are located on page 97.

As the demand for places of consumption, living, and working evolves further and coincides with the representational agenda of political and economic powers, cities are subject to considerable efforts in stylizing the urban atmosphere. The individual's sensation of urban space, lived experience, and wishes are not taken into consideration in an environment where culture is produced simply by inserting new shopping areas—as monuments—into the cities, which are otherwise governed by economic interests.

The cultural anthropologist Thomas Csordas (1994), in *Embodiment and Experience*, discusses the idea that culture is grounded in the human body. In this anthology, embodiment, this "being-in-the-world," is established not simply as a prerequisite for an otherwise text-based culture. According to this position, embodiment cannot be reduced to a mere representation of the body, or to the body as a representation of power or as the center of individual consciousness.

While Michel de Certeau (1984), in *The Practice of Everyday Life*, qualifies the city as a text, he also presents the traditional view of the layers of space of a city as inconsistent with a description focusing exclusively on architecture or other material elements. His own idea of a city, developed using the example of New York, also includes different layers of time, people, sounds, movements, emotions, behavior. He uses the image of a pedestrian to describe a metaphorical, wandering city, perforating and penetrating into the clear, planned, and easily readable text of a city.

Just as cities and countries struggle to come to terms with the present while the past casts its shadow, how can the preoccupations of individuals with their own personal history—moving between future, present, and past—be described? Where do people find themselves positioned in the daily drama of the staging of cultural hegemony that they witness in their surroundings, at once familiar and bewildering? Is a person strolling through the Brandenburg Gate in Berlin the same person who stood there on either side of the wall in 1989? Will the monument of the Soviet worker and the Kolchos farm girl carry the same meaning when placed on top of a shopping mall in Moscow as it did when symbolizing the achievements of the USSR at the 1937 World Exposition in Paris? In Bucharest, the locating of the Parliament and the opening in 2004 of the Museum for Contemporary Art in what was known as Ceausescu's Palace were attempts first to neutralize past associations and then to assign new meaning to the building. It remains to be seen whether the redefining of this symbol of totalitarianism is acceptable to the Romanian public. In Moscow, the appealing features of Stalinist architecture have been rediscovered, and wherever possible this style is fused with postmodern elements in the construction of huge neo-Stalinist apartment and office buildings, both in the center and at the periphery of the megalopolis. The Orthodox Church succeeded in rebuilding the Cathedral of Christ the Savior in record time in 1996. In combination with all of the massive and nationalistic monuments that were installed in Moscow throughout the 1990s, the overall picture today is that of a city undecided and fluctuating between the virtues and pitfalls of the nineteenth century, the Stalinist era, and today's capitalism.

Berlin, in turn, decided to undergo a costly but thorough face-lift. Following the sell-off of prime properties to companies such as Mercedes and Sony in the early 1990s, the entire area along the site of the Berlin Wall, including the center of the city that had been destroyed during World War II, was completely built over with government buildings, embassies, and entertainment industry complexes. Spaces for monuments, especially the Memorial to the Murdered Jews of Europe and the required public art commissions, were hotly debated, assigned, and constructed. In consequence, not a single reminder of the Berlin Wall and the barren stretches of land resulting from the devastation of wartime and the Cold War division of the city remains. While tantalizing speechlessness and misunderstandings between the post-Communist East and the post–Cold War West at times seem to dominate the daily politics in Germany, hardly a blemish tarnishes the outward calm of the surface of the city. One of the last unresolved issues concerns a derelict former palace (the Palace of the Republic) that the communist German Democratic Republic had built on the site of the Stadtschloss, the city palace of the Prussian kings, which had been damaged during World War II and later torn down. The derelict building is in the process of demolition and is expected to make way for a reconstruction of the Stadtschloss, which is supposed to contain, among other things, parts of the library of the Humboldt University and the city of Berlin as well as some museum collections.

FIGURE 1: Memorial to the Murdered Jews of Europe, Berlin 2005

Bucharest's historical center was destroyed and built over by Romania's former dictator, Nicolae Ceausescu, and his aides from the 1970s onward. Caught between the former Soviet empire, the now dominant West, and the quagmire of the Balkans, the city is being forced to develop another style of renovation in accordance with the local political and financial framework. The monolith of Ceausescu's former palace, one of the largest buildings in the world, stands tall. With its sheer material dominance, it overshadows any attempt to touch up the adjacent boulevards and the rows of building blocks through the addition of large numbers of banks, investment companies, convenience shops, and travel agencies. Meanwhile, the Orthodox Church of Romania is planning, similar to the Russian model, the construction of a central cathedral, the necessity and function of which is debated in Romania. The present plan (in 2007) is to construct the cathedral in the immediate proximity of the Parliament and museum, located at the former Ceausecu palace. This country is burdened with the power plays of the immensely wealthy and successful few, who have managed to come out on top of the remains of the former state and profit from it, while the general public struggles for a minimum of health, income, and education benefits.

Photo by Karen Kipphoff

It can be noted that even if some of these spaces in Berlin, Moscow, and Bucharest are of strongly symbolic and highly political significance, they are empty scars inflicted upon the urban landscape by history and neglect. Architect Rem Koolhaas comments on the visionary quality of the empty spaces of Berlin: "[W]here nothing is, everything is possible" (Koolhaas 1985). This virtual 'nothingness' or 'no-where-ness' of urban voids suggests a structural linkage between abandoned zones beyond their historical or cultural specificity. Within a global perspective, the erased traces of past architecture—public sites or residential areas, once vivid centers of urban life—are now turned into blank spots of post-urban wasteland (ruins of construction sites), hypermodern service structures (shopping malls, freeways), or temporary architectural structures (parking lots, festival sites, or container villages). They seem to denote the unifying features of a post-industrial era, where bleak economic interests erase the historical emergence once inscribed in a place. The void, seen as a space disconnected from its social meaning and cultural context, could be looked upon as potentially redefining the presence of past stages, now invisible, and containing the possibility of highlighting the relocation of the context of these abandoned areas. Disconnected from their historical context, these "voided voids" (as architect Daniel Libeskind describes them) are peripheral zones within the centers of hypermodern cities. In spite of their unspecific character, they are part of daily operations and acquire new functions or become sites of social activities and interaction

Figure 2: Location of the Former Monastery of Vacaresti, Bucharest 2004

that may or may not reflect their former collective function. Here, the individual feels that his or her personal experience especially connects to the city, as these spaces invite projections of memory.

On a personal level, these sites represent the fundamental void of death, which both attracts and polarizes our emotions, along with the at once random and persistent memories of the past that play games with our consciousness. Between the far ends of early childhood and the moment of death, our personal life span unfurls in its seemingly very private and individual course. Of course, we know that our life is subject to social, political, and historical conditions. In his studies, Philippe Ariès (1962, 1974) wrote on the history of the concepts of childhood and death. He described private life in modernity as pertaining to the "collective non-conscious," which is modified over a long period of time and which has settled deep in our collective memory, formed by traditions and history. Ariès was also interested in the politics of memory and the way it becomes evident in the history of the commemorative traditions of our societies. In his works, he described the modern ideas of childhood and death as inconsistent with, and their concept as even non-existent in, the ideas of earlier generations and eras.

All of this may pertain to traditions no longer existent in our own times. Certainly, however, in the Russia, Romania, and Germany of today, the collective tragedies of the millions of people who were either victims or perpetrators of war and persecution, set against the backdrop of each individual family's losses

Photo by Karen Kipphoff

and guilt, have taken on a mythological quality. This mythological aspect is used and commented upon in literally all manifestations of public art today.

History and politics have many effects on the collective consciousness, as well as on the individual's memories. Pierre Nora (1998) is the editor of *Realms of Memory*, a project about the French national memory, which has broken the ground internationally with regard to the concept of the history of the politics of memory. Here, memory is not investigated as the grand unifying national narrative within which certain topics can be placed; rather, memory and history are looked at in their distinguishing and separate features. They are described as opposing each other, divided and localized in specific and diverse sites of micro-narratives, which refer to the elements that lie at the basis of the understanding of what composes the French collective history. In his introduction, Pierre Nora (ibid.) explains, among other things, the difference between memory and history:

> With the appearance of the "trace," of distance and mediation, however, we leave the realm of true memory and enter that of history ... Memory and history, far from being synonymous, are thus in many respects opposed. Memory is life, always embodied in living societies and as such in permanent evolution, subject to the dialectic of remembering and forgetting, unconscious of the distortions of which it is subject, vulnerable in various ways to appropriation and manipulation ... History, on the other hand, is the reconstruction, always problematic and

FIGURE 3: Potsdamer Platz, Berlin 2005

incomplete, of what is no longer. Memory is always a phenomenon of the present, a bond tying us to the eternal present; history is a representation of the past.

Nora (ibid.) goes on to describe the self-alienation from what we perceive to be our own lives and our own observations through the influence and omnipresence of media: "We used to know whose children we were; now we are the children of no one and everyone. Since the past can now be constructed out of virtually anything, and no one knows what tomorrow's past will hold, our anxious uncertainty turns everything into a 'trace', a potential piece of evidence ... Our memory is intensely retinal, powerfully televisual ... We seek not our origins but a way of figuring out what we are from what we are no longer."

In his study of medieval political theology, Ernst H. Kantorowicz (1957) develops the subject of medieval jurisdiction, which attributed two bodies to a king: the natural, private, personal, and thus mortal body, as well as the supernatural, royal, and immortal body. Kantorowicz describes this originally juridical construction and its implications and effects from the early medieval times onwards. Theological and political concepts here merge into one and the same figure, the king as the divine representation of God and state on earth and, at the same time, as a human, even private, figure and political leader. Transferred into the understanding of our own lives and how we figure in it, we can recognize some of the same dilemmas. One is the necessity to position ourselves

Photo by Karen Kipphoff

in terms of public and private duties and rights; another is our ambiguous relationship to the politics of the country we live in and to the public leaders embodying these politics in the media. It is also our public versus our private standing, that is, the outside and inside perception of our position and what we stand for, that is at the basis of how we would perceive of this problem today.

Returning to the initial subject of this text—the monument in the urban space designed after dominant ideologies of the day—we feel flattered when we compare our own body, our lively way of thinking and feeling, to the stiff and cold form of the heavily idealized figure represented by the monument. It is easy to read the meaning of the mounting and dismantling of these figures as acts of consolidation and reaffirmation of public memory. It is also easy to read the meaning of the newly actualized and reconfigured monument in today's settings. Time has definitely expired for this form of visual representation in public spaces. It is, in fact, easy to read any of the performative aspects of the genre of public art and architecture. We do not feel scared or intimidated or embarrassed on that kind of public ground. What we do feel, however, is the long shadow that culture and history have cast upon us and on our understanding of how and where we stand as private bodies—as male or female, as young or old, as bodies of citizens, visitors, or strangers. Public spaces, however, are being redefined and overtaken by media and other manipulative spaces. These are making obsolete the staging of the individual human body as a figure in public display against the backdrop of the city. In consequence, the idea we entertain of having both a private and a public body might become redefined into a notion of having only one body on continuous display. Our private-public body, and here I am not thinking of the physical properties alone, might never be quite our own in the future, as it becomes not only publicly viewable but also accessible at all times.

FIGURE 4: Former House of the People, or Ceausescu Palace, Bucharest 2004

Karen Kipphoff, a visual and performing artist who exhibits, performs, and publishes, is Professor of Fine Arts at the National College of Arts in Bergen, Norway. For years she has been interested in public spaces of importance in twentieth-century Moscow, Berlin, Bucharest, and Montreal. Using panoramic photography, video, and other techniques to record and explore, her work touches on dichotomies such as public/private, absence/presence, and high-tech/low-tech.

*This essay is revised from its initial publication in 2006 as "Self and the City—the Politics of Monuments" (Bergen: KHiB).

References

Ariès, Philippe. 1962. *Centuries of Childhood: A Social History of Family Life*. Trans. Robert Baldick. New York: Alfred A. Knopf.
_____. 1974. *Western Attitudes toward Death: From the Middle Ages to the Present*. Trans. Patricia M. Ranum. Baltimore: Johns Hopkins University Press.
Csordas, Thomas J., ed. 1994. *Embodiment and Experience: The Existential Ground of Culture and Self*. Cambridge: Cambridge University Press.
de Certeau, Michel. 1988. *The Practice of Everyday Life*. Trans. Steven Rendall. Berkeley: University of California Press.
Kantorowicz, Ernst H. 1957. *The King's Two Bodies*. Princeton, NJ: Princeton University Press.
Koolhaas, Rem. 1985. "To Imagine Nothingness." *L'architecture d'aujourd'hui*, no. 238: 67.
Nora, Pierre, ed. 1998. *Realms of Memory*. Vol. 3: *The Construction of the French Past*. Trans. Arthur Goldhammer; ed. Lawrence D. Kritzman. New York: Columbia University Press.

Photo by Karen Kipphoff

Chapter 7

THE CULTURE INDUSTRIES
Symbolic Economies and Critical Practices

Malcolm Miles

Art is now ubiquitous in urban development. It is seen in the insertion of new cultural institutions in post-industrial areas, the designation of cultural quarters, and commissions for art in new public spaces. Artists who reject the art object to make ephemeral or process-based work, too, are co-opted to the agenda of urban regeneration as agents for the solution of a range of socio-economic problems. This has produced a rise in state support for the arts at the price of an expediency by which artists are required to deliver outcomes well outside their expertise. Meanwhile, an increasing number of artists now refuse the prescription and opt instead for practices of dissent. This chapter identifies contradictions in cultural policy and examines the work of the British artists'

Notes for this chapter are located on page 110.

group Hewitt + Jordan as a case of dissent. It asks whether art that criticizes the system contributes to a democratic public sphere.

Context: Contesting Narratives

Since the 1980s, the arts and cultural industries (including design and media production) have been used by UK governments in the redevelopment of de-industrialized cities. In the face of a decline in manufacturing, due to the shift of labor markets to the less regulated conditions of the non-affluent world under the regime of globalization; the rise in the immaterial sectors of information and communications technologies, financial services, tourism, and the cultural industries; and the eclipsing of material by symbolic economies in competition for inward investment, the arts are seen by politicians, city marketers, and business elites as offering key leverage. The result has been a proliferation of cultural quarters, museums of modern and contemporary art, conversions of redundant industrial buildings for arts uses, and commissions for public art or the design of new piazza-like spaces.

The notion of a creative city has been influential in cultural and urban policy in the UK and elsewhere. But if cities such as Glasgow and Barcelona demonstrate the success of cultural redevelopment, questions arise as to whose culture is being used for whose benefit; whether cultural strategies can be replicated, or if they depend instead on the non-replicable specifics of place, history, and infrastructure; and whether the arts can solve non-art problems. Perhaps the gloss of the cultural turn in urban policy hides intractable difficulties. Inherent contradictions, now combined with a lack of evidence that culturally led redevelopment delivers the benefits claimed by its advocates, have produced a shift in UK cultural policy. The arts remain instruments of social and economic improvement but are also to be valued for their intrinsic qualities.

A Turn in the Cultural Turn?

The rationale of UK cultural policy from the 1950s to the 1970s was that public subsidy through bodies such as the Arts Council could raise standards of production in, and widen access to, the arts. This may be resurfacing today, but in the 1980s, emphasis was put on the arts as meeting socio-economic needs (Arts Council 1986, 1990, 1991, 1993). Foremost among these needs was the regeneration of de-industrialized cities in a world of increased mobility of capital and fluidity of labor markets. Advocacy from arts professionals and recognition by the government of the extent of the cultural economy have fueled an expansion of arts projects and the establishment of new cultural institutions in run-down areas to the extent that culturally led redevelopment is now the norm.

Following the growth of community-based arts in the 1970s—notably in London, through the support of the Greater London Council—many artists in the 1980s saw working on non-gallery projects as a way to contribute to social justice. The management of such projects entailed an expansion of art's bureaucracy and, in turn, of arts management courses in further and higher education, while the arts funding system began to require arts organizations, including public art agencies, to run as viable businesses. Art produced for the public good was thus quickly linked to an entrepreneurial outlook in arts organizations. In the 1980s, the agencies (initially established as fully funded departments of regional Arts Councils) began to compete against each other nationally, becoming more concerned with gaining a competitive edge on rivals than with sharing information or identifying best practices. The 1980s and early 1990s saw a proliferation of arts agencies and consultancies, further extended by the opportunities offered by the national lottery. Persuasive advocacy from arts professionals, based on a desire to expand the arts economy, coincided with a willingness to listen on the part of the government. This produced a consensus in which the arts could play a leading role in urban regeneration. One expression of this was the concept of a creative city (Arts Council 1993; Landry and Bianchini 1995). As Esther Leslie (2005) puts it: "Cultural policy, scrabbling for justification and cash in gloomy days, when social policy amounts to surveillance, punishment and privatisation, moulds art policy into a plus, the only plus, an ameliorative measure recruited to lighten blighted lives and neutralise zones of anti-social behaviour in the city."

A strategy that began with the insertion of new cultural institutions into de-industrialized urban landscapes, using public subsidy to lever further private-sector development, became, under New Labour after 1997, an action plan for culturally led urban renewal. This strategy embraced social as well as economic agendas, as reflected in the incidence of arts projects in 31 of 66 Single Regeneration Budgets in 1998–1999 (Selwood 2001: 60–65). A general rise in arts funding (ibid.: 183) has produced buildings such as the New Art Gallery in Walsall and the Lowry in Salford. However, not all of them have been successful: a center for contemporary music in Sheffield was closed when visitor numbers fell below expectation, as was the Earth Centre, which had been built on a disused mining site near Doncaster.

New Labour's rebranding of the UK as 'Cool Britannia' has faded into history after the failure of its most spectacular and costly project, the Millennium Dome. Added to these disappointments, as government departments trade on evidence-based policy making, is a lack of evidence for the efficacy of the arts in urban regeneration. This may explain a shift in UK cultural policy that is detectable, if not obvious, in remarks made by Secretary of State for Culture, Media and Sport Tessa Jowell to the Institute of Public Policy Research at the Royal Opera House in London on 7 March 2005.

Jowell began by supporting the license fee that funds the BBC. Calling it a regressive but popular tax that ensured the quality of broadcasting, and comparing it to an absence of good public service broadcasting in the United States, Jowell (2005: 5) asserted that "some markets deserve to be distorted … the same principle applies to the arts." Arts funding ensured the production "of dazzling new work, of far-reaching innovation, of new insights" (ibid.: 6). This almost magical notion harks back to the consensus of the post-war years, when the arts were seen as part of a process of recivilizing Europe after the Holocaust, and to the idealism in which context Jenny Lee was appointed as the first arts minister, in the Wilson administration (Willett 1967: 202–203). The post-war consensus supported artistic autonomy in the formation of an Arts Council (ibid.: 197–205; Pearson 1982: 48–66) at arm's length from government. The aim of raising quality was interpreted by John Willett (1967: 204) as a determination of standards by "the taste prevailing among dealers and critics and virtually the whole of the official art world outside a few bodies labelled Royal." In the 1980s, this became the mantra of innovation and excellence, to which widening access was an adjunct necessary to gain resources. That aside, it may have been significant that Jowell (or her speechwriter) did not rehearse the refrain that the arts produce local distinctiveness while reducing unemployment and crime or solving social exclusion; instead, she called for a public debate on how the arts can be at the center of government thinking and thus gain maximum public investment.

Jowell's remarks at the Royal Opera House are contradictory. On one hand, she sees an increase in arts support under New Labour enabled by "stressing the contribution the arts could make to other agendas" while "we had to take a technocratic approach … where every aspect of government was able to be measured" (Jowell 2005: 6). She adds that working in social settings enables arts professionals to speak in non-art circles, such as health and urban renewal, and that the arts are now "integral to our personal and national life" (ibid.: 7). On the other hand, she asserts that qualities cannot be measured and that arts policy should focus "on what the arts can do in themselves" (ibid.: 6). Looking to the arts as slaying the giant of "poverty of aspiration, or if you like, and as Nye Bevan put it, poverty of imagination" (ibid.: 7), Jowell treads on other people's dreams. Jowell is no doubt aware of a lack of evidence for the benefits of arts projects in urban social settings, and that what is achieved is often gentrification rather than community regeneration. But her use of a metaphorical imagination deficit as the focus of public arts policy seems an aestheticization of policy.

If relief of a poverty of imagination is too nebulous an idea to be measured statistically, it may in a quite different way reassert what Herbert Marcuse (1968: 88–133) called the affirmative character of culture—art's role in maintaining the socio-political equilibrium of bourgeois society by displacing hope to a realm of beauty or fantasy. It is overinterpretive to attribute this position to Jowell, yet when she rehearsed an evaluation of arts subsidy in terms of lower crime rates and truancy, she added, "I worry that we talked about these objectives so much that we actually rather missed the point" (Jowell 2005: 6). What was it? Jowell said that "enlightened parents have recognised the positive effects [of the arts] for some time. They've done the options appraisal for us" (ibid.: 7). But if the point is that children should grow up loving music, drama, art, and books—in an echo of the post-war consensus that privileged the kind of family life associated with the comfortable, middle-class homes in which New Labour now sees its core support—it may be lost on those whose lives do not fit the prescribed mold.

There are key issues to address. Firstly, whose culture (the culture of which class or social or ethnic group) is to be replicated for whom? Secondly, what impact will the arts have on the ways of life of those affected by culturally led redevelopment. Thirdly, does the aesthetic turn in cultural policy mask an instrumentalism aimed at remodeling society along the lines of the Victorian era—the assimilation of the working class to middle-class modes of behavior that do not include, in the Victorian context, revolution.

Public Improvement

Jowell (2005: 8) spoke of "the value the public places in institutions, organisations and concepts, above and beyond but not excluding their economic or individual use value." As Brandon Taylor (1993: 27) writes on the Tate Gallery at Millbank, which was built on the site of a penitentiary as a catalyst to the redevelopment of the area: "Pride in 'the nation' was the important trope—but a nation that was now increasingly free of poverty, artistic illiteracy, and above all crime." He adds that another role for the Tate was to show the compatibility of private philanthropy and state patronage in service of the public good. Tate's site, that of a redundant prison, is appropriate to "the real cultural work that could then be done" (ibid.) of civilizing the lower classes. Tate Modern, no longer at Millbank (which continues to house the national collection of British art), is the most spectacular success story of New Labour's arts policy. It has shifted the cultural center of London from the West End to a site south of the Thames, close to the financial district. The parallels with the establishment of the first Tate are striking (leaving aside its funding by Henry Tate, an industrialist and inventor of the sugar cube). The underpinning motive in both cases appears to be social equilibrium and the production of a middle class based on the values of the governing class. What has changed, of course, is the relation of that governing class to capital, no longer its regulator now so much as its servant. This, too, is reflected in the emphasis on commercial services in institutions such as Tate, as it competes with the more overtly commercialist Guggenheim in the branding of art as spectacle.

Cultural Instrumentalism

Cases such as Glasgow as European Capital of Culture in 1990, Barcelona in the 1990s, and the present Tate gallery network paint a picture of successful, culturally led redevelopment in which the arts shade into the cultural industries as drivers of regeneration. But there are complexities. Firstly, definitions of the cultural industries differ. John Myerscough (1988) restricts his to the visual and performing arts and museums. Charles Landry and Franco Bianchini (1995) include design, film, music, and media production, while Allen Scott (2000) includes fashion, jewelry, perfume, leather, and furniture among other mainly traditional sectors. These definitions can be counterposed to Adorno's (1991) term "the culture industry," by which he means specifically the movies, broadcasting, and mass media. For Adorno (ibid.: 80), the culture industry "does not so much fabricate the dream of the customers as introduce the dreams of the suppliers among the people." Scott (2000: 212) rejects "the alarmist views of the Frankfurt School" but concedes that "many of the outputs of the cultural economy are carriers of socially and psychologically enervating effects." He notes the cultural industries' ability to absorb social currents and its value-free—"agnostic"—ethos in which any cultural commodity that is seen to be profitable is marketed (ibid.: 213). I recently noticed, for instance, a museum in Amsterdam that specializes in the history of torture. Scott draws attention to the fact that art exists through its market, which fluctuates much like the antiques market or the housing market, although this is seldom recognized in cultural policy.

Secondly, strategies differ as much as definitions. Those strategies include the use of new flagship institutions such as Tate Modern and an emphasis on design and visual display (Teedon 2002); the designation of cultural quarters, as in Liverpool (Gilmore 2004), Nottingham (Shorthose 2004), Birmingham's central business district (with its concert hall, convention center, and redevelopment around the Ikon Gallery), and Barcelona's El Raval near the Museum of Contemporary Art (MACBA); and a residual community arts practice in which peripatetic artists target specific publics for involvement, living from project to project, grant to grant. These are public-sector strategies, but there are also market-led insertions of small-scale cultural businesses into postindustrial areas. For example, cultural entrepreneurs in popular music were key to Manchester's revival in the 1990s (O'Connor and Wynne 1996). In the Hoxton area of London, like New York's SoHo in the 1970s, an influx of artists seeking low-rent studios has given way to the establishment of spaces for contemporary art and high-rent apartments for postmodern bohemians, referred to as 'bohos' (Wilson 2003: 233–234), near sites of social deprivation. The model has been replicated in Mumbai, where the Colabas district is dubbed CoHo (Harris 2005: 39).

A strategy more common in the US but spreading in the UK is the use of historic sites as cultural consumption sites—a model evolved by the Rouse Company from mall development—including Baltimore's Harborplace, New York's South Street Seaport, and Boston's Faneuil Hall Market (Gratz 1989: 285–286, 316–326). Similarly, the Pittsburgh and Lake Erie rail station has been redeveloped as a heritage, tourism, and leisure zone (ibid.: 286–288). The US model has been used to support advocacy for culturally led redevelopment in the UK: "In a number of American [sic] cities, leading strategists of 'downtown rejuvenation' have argued that arts-led investment is the most efficient way of beginning the process of raising morale" (Bianchini et al. 1988: 14). Alongside culture malls, high-profile schemes such as Battery Park City in New York have been sites of art commissions and installations (Deutsche 1991; Phillips 1988). Sharon Zukin (1995: 22) writes: "Every well-designed downtown has a mixed-use shopping center and a nearby artists' quarter," while waterfronts become "sites of visual delectation" with themed shopping spaces, restaurants, and art galleries. The image is familiar. While the developers Olympia & York did not employ an arts strategy at Canary Wharf, Stuart Lipton included a sculpture park at London's Broadgate in the 1980s. Culture has been central, too, in marketing inner-city districts in conjunction with niche consumption, as in the marketing of downtown neighborhoods in New York in the late 1980s as an urban frontier for yuppies—the new pioneers (Rosler 1991; Smith 1996). These strategies and the varied definitions that inform them set a context for a growing instrumentalism in cultural policy on both sides of the Atlantic. It was adequate in the post-war years to speak of quality and access, as it was in the early 1980s to speak of excellence and innovation. But by the 1990s, this was succeeded by a rhetoric of efficacy and the idea that the arts, as instruments of policy objectives, can most effectively (or cheaply) deliver results.

George Yúdice (2004: 11) cites the following extract from a 1997 report by Gary Larson for the US National Endowment for the Arts: "No longer restricted to the sanctioned arena of culture, the arts would be literally suffused throughout the civic structure, finding a home in a variety of community service and economic development activities ... far afield from the traditional aesthetic functions of the arts. This extended role for culture can also be seen in the many new partners that arts organizations have taken on ... a host of social welfare agencies all serving to highlight the utilitarian aspects of the arts in contemporary society." Similar sentiments characterize New Labour's cultural policy. Does it work?

Sara Selwood (1995) is negative in her findings in *The Benefits of Public Art,* the first major evaluation of this field. There is a lack of evidence that broad public benefits and anything other than low-paid, low-skill, insecure employment were produced in Birmingham's culturally led redevelopment in the 1980s (Loftman and Nevin 1998). Jowell's department published a report in 2004, *Culture at the Heart of Regeneration,* in which the cases of Barcelona and Bilbao are differentiated. While Tate Modern is praised for increasing employment and attracting visitors, problems such as gentrification and the alienation of local publics are noted. The Guggenheim in Bilbao is cited as producing only short-term interest among local publics and benefiting mostly a middle-class minority, in contrast to which Barcelona is seen as emphasizing its own culture rather than bowing to the globalization of contemporary art. This reflects the city's move to a Catalan cultural infrastructure in the post-Franco period. But a claim that Barcelona's cultural redevelopment has led to lower crime rates might be read with skepticism. For Pam Meecham (2005: 10), "Evidence of the long-term impact of a landmark gallery ... in a post-industrial community is difficult to collect and interpret. Yet the document gives little indication of the problems of gathering data around cultural programmes."

For Zukin (1995: 49–78), the cultural recoding of public space follows the model of Disney theme parks, where non-contiguous times and places are juxtaposed, visitors mingle with fantasy characters, and complex realities are displaced by simulacra that are at root authoritarian. For city managers, this is attractive (ibid.: 54): "Take a common thread of belief, a passion that people share ... and develop it into a visual image. Market this image as the city's symbol. Pick an area of the city that reflects the image: a shimmering waterfront commercial complex to symbolize the new, a stately Beaux Arts train station to symbolize renewal, a street of small-scale, red-brick shops to symbolize historical memory. Then put the area under private management." Zukin (ibid.: 55) links cultural strategies to the control of public space, arguing that while theme parks denote a desire to escape, they are tightly structured narratives of an identity reinforced by spatial controls. Christine Boyer (2001: 51), too, observes the fictive aspect of place reconstruction in New York's Times Square, "incorporated into a larger sense of assembled space, where all its simultaneity and immediacy can evaporate into astonishing imagescapes." Boyer (ibid.) compares this to re-creations of space in the diorama and panorama in response to which spectators could "thrill at the re-creation of the real," while the real being depicted "may never have existed." Landry and Bianchini (1995: 23) state that immigrants "have different ways of looking at problems and different priorities ... [which] can give a creative impulse to a city," citing *bhangra* music as a case of cultural cross-over or interculturalism. Yet Graeme Evans and Jo Foord (1999) are critical of the relevance of cultural regeneration projects to diverse publics in East London. Yúdice (2004: 25) writes that "representations of and claims to cultural difference are expedient insofar as they multiply commodities," and Tania Carson (2005: 15) remarks that "the creation of cultural quarters is merely a kind of cultural branding."

What can I make of these positions? Culturally led redevelopment retains its impetus, I suggest, from a few frequently cited cases. It is difficult to ignore Barcelona's status as a cultural destination and world city, with a World Trade Center designed by I. M. Pei. No longer an impoverished Mediterranean port, it has achieved success through a policy that seeks cultural tourism in place of package tourism (Dodd 1999). There are, as it happens, lessons in the primacy of public-sector investment in Barcelona and its provision of more than 100 new public spaces in preparation for the 1992 Olympics. However, Barcelona's cultural history as the home of Picasso and Miró, its wealth of modernist and contemporary architecture, and its imperative to establish a cultural identity after the economic and cultural repressions of the fascist era are unique and cannot be replicated elsewhere. Signs of the city's republican past have since been reinscribed, as in the reconstruction of Josep Sert's 1937 Spanish Republic pavilion from the Paris International Exposition. Although questions remain about the aestheticization of its public spaces (Degen 2002, 2004), flagship cultural institutions like MACBA increasingly figure in redevelopment. Dejan Sudjic (1993: 5) writes: "In the post-industrial world a national museum has come to take on the national significance of a car factory or airport ... the bargaining chips that a new generation of entrepreneurs desperately fight over." Zukin (1995: 109–152) notes links between real estate speculation and the management of such institutions, as well as a shift from public-sector to private-sector redevelopment in New York's Business Improvement Districts. But this has little to do with regeneration, as a community-based aim, rather than the increased value of private property.

A further difficulty is that, despite claiming to deal with social issues, arts advocacy and cultural strategies are more inclined to ignore social actualities.

Evans (2004: 91) writes that the model of cultural quarters neglects specific histories. John Rennie Short and Yeong-Hyun Kim (1998: 74) remark: "Images of social justice are rarely presented; the just city never appears as one of the subthemes in the city as a good place to live. The poor are rarely discussed and never presented. The dominant images represent conflict-free cities, where pluralism leads to a variety of ethnic restaurants rather than competition for scarce resources, where the good life is neither marred nor affected by the presence of the poor and marginalised." Rosalyn Deutsche (1992: 158) writes of public art, in the context of policies to aestheticize public space, that such approaches "neither account for current conditions ... nor suggest terms for an alternative, possibly transformative practice," and that accounts of public art relegate "social conditions to the status of a backdrop." Meecham (2005: 12) urges the regeneration industry to listen to its own rhetoric: "Local communities have their own aspirations and values. If galleries are to develop new methods of seeing, in line with the transformatory projects of a global culture policy, it will be necessary to accept that high culture is not for everyone, that its transformatory powers are limited ... It may also be necessary for some forms of cultural activity to stay outside the legitimating remit of DCMS [the Department for Culture, Media and Sport]." This suggests, then, that if Jowell were to recognize the deficits of her department's policies over two decades, the appropriate response would be less a regression to art for art's sake—the 1890s consensus, as it were—and more a handing over of resources to communities and artists' groups. This has echoes of the Greater London Council community arts policies of the 1970s, seen as highly dangerous—as political—in many quarters of arts management.

A Return to Modernism?

Thinking back to Jowell's remarks, I wonder if her notion of art is based in the values of international modernism. There are similarities between some of her phrases and the work of Clement Greenberg. Jowell links aesthetics to social transformation, but transformation of an aesthetic rather than social type. Her view is that "what the arts do that only the arts do is most important. Out of that come other benefits but the art comes first" (Jowell 2005: 6). Greenberg began as a leftist critic in the late 1930s, haunted by the Hitler-Stalin pact and antagonistic to socialist realism. Jowell cannot have in mind the same specter, yet her prescription for an art of its own ends is close to Greenberg's ([1944] 1986: 203) comment: "Let painting confine itself to the disposition pure and simple of color and line, and not intrigue us by associations with things we can experience more authentically elsewhere." Greenberg rejected artistic illusion; Jowell seems uneasy with cultural instrumentalism. Their points of departure differ, but I wonder if art's authenticity is for Jowell a counter to the pitfalls of instrumentalism. That authenticity seems dubious. From critical appreciation of artists such as Mark Rothko, Jackson Pollock, and Clifford Still, whose work was internationally toured by US government agencies in the Cold War period, the aesthetic of international modernism added a dimension of privileged insight into the depths of the psyche (Kuspit 1993) to a Kantian aesthetic of natural beauty and sublimity.

Greenberg ([1939] 1986: 17) wrote: "In a stable society ... the cultural dichotomy becomes somewhat blurred. The axioms of the few are shared by the many; the latter believe superstitiously what the former believe soberly." Could this describe New Labour's cultural stance? Jowell's discovery of the unmeasurable in art is tied to the rhetoric of the creative city. Landry and Bianchini (1995: 11) assert that "genuine creativity involves thinking a problem afresh ... experimentation; originality; the capacity to rewrite rules; to be unconventional." The question, again, is whose creativity is at work, whose culture is utilized for whom. Andy Hewitt and Mel Jordan (2005: 107), of the collaborative practice Hewitt + Jordan, whose project I review below, state: "Art practitioners who for ideological reasons choose to work outside of the gallery market and seek to make art that is critical of capital and commodity find that the public funding of art is equally problematic, having its own set of patrons and agendas. The public realm is becoming less public as capital interests have taken over more of what we once understood to be public ... Parallel to this a functionalist agenda within the public funding of art practice channels it towards the support of economic goals." Meecham (2005: 12) comments: "Questioning the use of culture as a tool of government is to ask questions about the biased systems within which we operate and which sometimes work against our best interests." It may be worth recalling Audre Lorde's ([1979] 2000: 54) argument: "The master's tools will never dismantle the master's house."

Futurology and Dissident Art

If the tools were made in the forge of international modernism, or the cultural instrumentalism which followed it, they will not dismantle the master's house. Other tools are required. Among the tasks, as a beginning for something other than the creative city, is that of exposing lies and contradictions. This extends the role of European avant-gardes from Realism in the 1850s to Dadaism in the 1920s; in another way, though, it departs not only from the post-war avant-garde's revolutions of style as a placebo for revolutions of society but also from a supposition that art can portend a better society. For Adorno ([1969] 1997), art in bleak times is inflected with bleakness yet refracts it in depictions of absurdity, as in the writings of Samuel Beckett. I would argue for a purpose of exposure and of addressing less the supposedly uncultured mass public taken as the object of instrumentalism and more the articulate and informed publics, both professional and non-professional, whose expertise molds urban design and occupation, respectively. Among the concerns of such interventionist art might be the use of art itself. For example, Hewitt and Jordan (2004: 53) describe the role of public art in a billboard work displayed at the corner of Alma Street and Corporation Street in Sheffield in 2004: "The economic function of public art is to increase the value of private property." The work was commissioned, without intended irony, by Public Art Forum, a UK network of public art agencies, consultants, and public art officers in local government. Far from widening access or provoking debate on public issues directly, the billboard speaks to the constituency of artists, intermediaries, authorities, and commissioners of public art.

The project began when the artists, asked to do something for Public Art Forum's annual conference in 2003, decided to offer themselves in a raffle. The winner would be able to commission them to make a work anywhere. As it happened, the winner gave them a high level of autonomy in deciding what to do, and the work has an almost Dadaist aspect, in sharp contrast to the reformist values of public art. The project has since extended to three texts displayed in Leeds in 2005, adding to the above: "The social function of public art is to subject us to civic behaviour" and "The aesthetic function of public art is to codify social distinctions as natural."[1] The last was also presented as a banner at the Venice Biennale ("La funzione estetica dell'arte pubblica é quella di rendere naturali distinzioni sociali"). Hewitt and Jordan write of the project in Leeds, titled *Vitrine*: "The aim of the work is to examine the tensions and contradictions that exist within public art practice; to explore how public art is integral to our culture and therefore how it functions in support of the dominant ideology."[2] And, writing on a series of projects up to 2004, they refute the notion of universal cultural benefit: "We try to emphasise that art and cultural systems are not benign; they are a significant part of society and we are deeply affected by political and ideological agendas" (Hewitt and Jordan 2004: 21). Voicing faith in art's capacity to contribute to democracy, and seeing this as more important in the face of advanced capitalism, they continue: "The projects have been our attempt to examine how functionality is given to art practice, in this case art practice that is publicly funded. Through our work we hope to articulate some of the contradictions and conflicts of interest that occur between public and private agendas within regeneration objectives. Our recent preoccupations have been art and gentrification, the functions given to art within the branding of cities, and the conflicts of interest between public and private that take place within cultural regeneration projects" (ibid.). They work collaboratively, with long periods of research in preparation for a project as well as a high level of selectivity in accepting work from clients. Confirming their refusal of user-friendliness, they comment: "We do not see our role as offering cultural cohesion for a largely self interested, middle class cultural sector" (ibid.: 22). This is enabled in part through employment in art school teaching.

While the instrumentalism of UK cultural policy has produced programs such as Creative Partnerships—in which artists are assigned to schools to provide artistic interludes or, in the worst cases, to be non-qualified teachers paid from an arts budget—Hewitt and Jordan see a possibility to engage critically with the scheme. They negotiated a research project, "Futurology: The Black Country 2024," in association with Creative Partnerships, the New Art Gallery, and the Black Country Consortium. Artists Barby Asante, Dave

Beech, Nick Crowe and Ian Rawlinson, Simon Poulter, and Becky Shaw were recruited to work with school students to examine the social, economic, and political conditions of the Black Country (formerly, a heavily industrialized region in the English West Midlands), and imagine how it might be 20 years later in 2024. For example, Asante was taken by young people to places they considered theirs, filming the journeys and playing back the footage to the group. To me, the point is that Asante "asked to be led" rather than arriving on the scene as an expert (New Art Gallery 2004). The gallery outcome was a wooden shed—"a place to hang out ... There are rules of entry and use; they might not even let us in and if they do, it is on their terms and our access could be limited" (ibid.)—which signifies a social space of arbitration in a way generally not seen in public art commissions or the design of public squares, the latter retaining largely the functionalism of post-war social architecture. The exhibition catalogue states that "they have come to realise the importance of their own voice, aware ... [of] a number of ways to articulate their needs" (ibid.)

Conclusion: Beyond the Creative City

Culturally led urban redevelopment puts power in the hands of developers, entrepreneurs, and intermediaries. The emphasis is on the production of image and the spaces that signify that image, rather than the maintenance of extant cultures as the ways of life of the inhabitants. The latter would mean handing over power to dwellers and would signify the realization that empowerment is self-empowerment (Freire 1972). Yúdice cites the case of Villa El Salvador in Peru, researched by Elcior Santana (1999), which, beginning as an informal settlement, has "some of the best social indicators in the country" (Yúdice 2004: 14). Yúdice argues that this can be explained by a way of life that, with communal labor and solidarity, involves active participation. Although he discusses Villa El Salvador in the context of cultural funding by transnational organizations seeking a return on their investment in social stability, the measures of lower infant mortality and higher literacy cited are real. However, they are not produced by art, which simply cannot achieve such outcomes. But art might have a more specific role—to open critical thinking, to widen the cracks in systems of power, including the cultural economy, and to expose contradictions while indicating that there are alternatives. This is a world away from the creative city. But then, as Jane Jacobs contends (1961: 373), *"a city cannot be a work of art."* Perhaps those who make cultural policy might benefit from rereading Jacobs instead of seeming to rehash Greenberg.

Acknowledgment

An earlier version of this chapter was delivered in a symposium in the Sociology Department of the University of Bergen, 15–18 September 2005.

Malcolm Miles is Reader in Cultural Theory at the University of Plymouth, UK, where he convenes the Critical Spaces Research Group and coordinates the research methods program for doctoral students in the Faculty of Arts. He is the author of *Cities and Cultures* (2007), *Urban Avant-Gardes* (2004), and *Art Space and the City* (1997); co-author of *Consuming Cities* (2004, with Steven Miles); and co-editor of the *City Cultures Reader* (2003, 2nd edition, with Tim Hall and Iain Borden). His next authored book will be *Urban Utopias* (2008). His current research is in a field triangulated by contemporary art, critical theory, and aspects of the social sciences dealing with social transformation.

Notes

1. See http://www.hewittandjordan.com/work/vitrine.html.
2. Ibid.

References

Adorno, Theodor W. [1969] 1997. *Aesthetic Theory*. London: Athlone.
_____. 1991. *The Culture Industry: Selected Essays on Mass Culture*. London: Routledge.
Arts Council. 1986. *An Urban Renaissance*. London: Arts Council of Great Britain.
_____. 1990. *Percent for Art: Report of a Steering Group*. London: Arts Council of Great Britain. [Unpublished report.]
_____. 1991. *Percent for Art: A Review*. London: Arts Council of Great Britain and AN Publications.
_____. 1993. *A Creative Future: National Arts and Media Strategy*. London: HMSO.
Bell, David, and Mark Jayne, eds. 2004. *City of Quarters: Urban Villages in the Contemporary City*. Aldershot: Ashgate.
Bianchini, Franco, Mark Fisher, John Montgomery, and Ken Worpole. 1988. *City Centre, City Cultures*. Manchester: Centre for Local Economic Development.
Boyer, Christine. 2001. "Twice-Told Stories: The Double Erasure of Times Square." Pp. 30–53 in *The Unknown City: Contesting Architecture and Social Space*, ed. I. Borden, J. Kerr, J. Rendell, and A. Pivaro. Cambridge, MA: MIT Press.
Carson, T. 2005. "Cultural Ambiguity in an Urban Development Masterplan: Deception or Miscalculation?" Pp. 13–28 in Miles and Hall 2005.
Degen, Monica. 2002. "Regenerating Public Life? A Sensory Analysis of Regenerated Public Places in el Raval, Barcelona." Pp. 19–36 in Rugg and Hinchcliffe 2002.
_____. 2004. "Barcelona's Games: The Olympics, Urban Design, and Global Tourism." Pp. 131–142 in *Tourism Mobilities: Places to Play, Places in Play*, ed. M. Sheller and J. Urry. London: Routledge.

Deutsche, Rosalyn. 1991. "Alternative Space." Pp. 45–66 in Wallis 1991.

_____. 1992. "Public Art and Its Uses." Pp. 158–169 in *Critical Issues in Public Art: Content, Context and Controversy*, ed. H. F. Senie and S. Webster. Washington, DC: Smithsonian. [Excerpt from "Uneven Development: Public Art in New York City." Pp. 157–219 in Wallis 1991; previously published in *October* 47 (Winter) 1988: 3–52.]

Dodd, Dianne. 1999. "Barcelona, the Making of a Cultural City." Pp. 53–64 in *Planning Cultural Tourism in Europe: A Presentation of Theories and Cases*, ed. D. Dodd and A. van Hemel. Amsterdam: Boekman Stichtung.

Evans, Graeme L. 2004. "Cultural Industry Quarters: From Pre-industrial to Post-industrial Production." Pp. 71–92 in Bell and Jayne 2004.

Evans, Graeme L., and Jo Foord. 1999. "Cultural Policy and Urban Regeneration in East London: World City, Whose City?" Proceedings of the International Conference on Cultural Policy Research, University of Bergen.

Freire, Paulo. 1972. *Pedagogy of the Oppressed*. Harmondsworth: Penguin.

Gilmore, Anne. 2004. "Popular Music, Urban Regeneration and Cultural Quarters: The Case of the Rope Walks Quarter, Liverpool." Pp. 109–130 in Bell and Jayne 2004.

Gratz, R. B. 1989. *The Living City*. New York: Simon & Schuster.

Greenberg, Clement. [1939] 1986. "Avant-Garde and Kitsch." *The Collected Essays and Criticism*. Ed. J. O'Brian. Chicago: University of Chicago Press.

_____. [1944] 1986. "Abstract Art." *The Collected Essays and Criticism*. Ed. J. O'Brian. Chicago: University of Chicago Press.

Hall, Tim, and Phil Hubbard, eds. 1998. *The Entrepreneurial City: Geographies of Politics, Regime and Representation*. Chichester: Wiley.

Harris, Andrew. 2005. "Opening Up the Symbolic Economy of Contemporary Mumbai." Pp. 29–40 in Miles and Hall 2005.

Hewitt, Andy, and Mel Jordan. 2004. *I Fail to Agree*. Sheffield: Site Gallery.

_____. 2005. "I Fail to Agree." Pp. 107–120 in Miles and Hall 2005.

Jacobs, Jane. 1961. *The Death and Life of Great American Cities*. New York: Random House.

Jowell, Tessa. 2005. "Why Should Government Support the Arts?" *Engage* 17: 5–8. [Address delivered in London, 7 March 2005.]

Kuspit, Donald. 1993. *The Cult of the Avant-Garde Artist*. Cambridge: Cambridge University Press.

Landry, Charles, and Franco Bianchini. 1995. *The Creative City*. London: Demos.

Leslie, Esther. 2005. "Fanning the Spark of Hope: On *Futurology.*" Unpublished paper.

Loftman, Patrick, and Brendan Nevin. 1998. "Pro-growth Local Economic Development Strategies: Civic Promotion and Local Needs in Britain's Second City, 1981–1996." Pp. 129–148 in Hall and Hubbard 1998.

Lorde, Audre. [1979] 2000. "The Master's Tools Will Never Dismantle the Master's House." Pp. 53–55 in *Gender Space Architecture: An Interdisciplinary Introduction*, ed. J. Rendell, B. Penner, and I. Borden. London: Routledge.

Marcuse, Herbert. 1968. *Negations*. Harmondsworth: Penguin.

Meecham, Pam. 2005. "Rethinking the Regeneration Industry." *Engage* 17: 9–13.

Miles, Malcolm, and Tim Hall, eds. 2005. *Interventions: Art and Urban Futures*. Bristol: Intellect Books.

Myerscough, John. 1988. *The Economic Importance of the Arts in Britain*. London: Policy Studies Institute.

New Art Gallery. 2004. *Futurology: The Black Country 2024*. Walsall: New Art Gallery. [Unpaginated show brochure.]

O'Connor, Justin, and Deryck Wynne, eds. 1996. *From the Margins to the Centre: Cultural Production and Consumption in the Post-Industrial City*. Aldershot: Ashgate.

Pearson, Nicholas. 1982. *The State and the Visual Arts*. Milton Keynes: Open University Press.

Phillips, Patricia. 1988. "Out of Order: The Public Art Machine." *Artforum* (December): 92–96.

Rosler, Martha. 1991. "Fragments of a Metropolitan Viewpoint." Pp. 15–44 in Wallis 1991.

Rugg, Judith, and Daniel Hinchcliffe, eds. 2002. *Recoveries and Reclamations*. Bristol: Intellect Books.

Santana, E. 1999. Remarks presented at the conference "Transnationalization of Support for Culture in a Globalizing World" held at Bellagio, 6–10 December.

Scott, Allan. 2000. *The Cultural Economy of Cities*. London: Sage.

Selwood, Sara. 1995. *The Benefits of Public Art*. London: Policy Studies Institute.

———, ed. 2001. *The UK Cultural Sector: Profile and Policy Issues*. London: Policy Studies Institute.

Short, John Rennie, and Yeong-Hyun Kim. 1998. "Urban Crises/Urban Representations: Selling the City in Difficult Times." Pp. 55–76 in Hall and Hubbard 1998.

Shorthose, John. 2004. "Nottingham's *de facto* Cultural Quarter: The Lace Market, Independents and a Convivial Ecology." Pp. 149–162 in Bell and Jayne 2004.

Smith, Neil. 1996. *The New Urban Frontier*. London: Routledge.

Sudjic, Dejan. 1993. *The 100 Mile City*. London: Flamingo.

Taylor, Brandon. 1993. "From Penitentiary to 'Temple of Art': Early Metaphors of Improvement at the Millbank Tate." Pp. 9–32 in *Art Apart: Art Institutions and Ideology Across England and North America*, ed. M. Pointon. Manchester: Manchester University Press.

Teedon, Paul. 2002. "New Urban Space: Regenerating a Design Ethos." Pp. 49–58 in Rugg and Hinchcliffe 2002.

Wallis, Brian, ed. 1991. *If You Lived Here: The City in Art, Theory, and Social Activism*. Seattle, WA: Bay Press.

Willett, John. 1967. *Art in a City*. London: Methuen.

Wilson, Elizabeth. 2003. *Bohemians: The Glamorous Outcasts*. London: I.B. Taurus.

Yúdice, George. 2004. *The Expediency of Culture: Issues of Culture in the Global Era*. Durham, NC: Duke University Press.

Zukin, Sharon. 1995. *The Cultures of Cities* Oxford: Blackwell.

Chapter 8

THE ARTS, THE STATE, AND THE EU
Cultural Policy in the Making of Europe

Monica Sassatelli

As the title of this volume recalls, normally when thinking of the public fund-ing of artistic or more generally cultural enterprises, we think of the state. For instance, Howard Becker's (1982) seminal book of the sociology of art, *Art Worlds*, has a chapter titled "Art and the State," in which the author addresses issues such as property laws (concerning the role of the state in the managing of art as of any other sector of the economic and social life) and the policing of cultural forms as a possible source of public nuisance. However, Becker reminds us that as far as states not only regulate but also actively intervene in the art worlds, they do so on behalf of their own interests. These "have to do with the preservation of public order—the arts being seen as capable both of strengthening and of subverting order—and with the development of a national

Notes for this chapter begin on page 124.

culture, seen as a good in itself and as something which promotes national unity ('our heritage') and the nation's reputation among other nations" (ibid.: 180). Naturally, we say 'interest' by way of metaphor, since, literally, institutions do not have interests. However, their acting like a subject gives them a particular style according to which reality is framed. Indeed, for the modern Western world, the nation-state has been the prime agent to frame/create reality, and to shape individuals as well, constructing an exclusive and perfect correspondence between individual and nation, a correspondence that still informs to a great extent our views of what it means to be a citizen, and an individual, in general (Calhoun 1994). Cultural policy is particularly relevant for these considerations as one of its aims is the fostering of specific identities and thus the formatting of fully socialized, compliant citizens, sharing common tastes and conduct (McGuigan 2004; Miller and Yúdice 2002). For among the interests of the state, there is of course the mobilization of citizens for appropriate purposes in appropriate ways—and the prevention of inappropriate ones (Lewis and Miller 2003).

Therefore, the arts and the state have long been a, if not *the*, relevant couple. However, today the state is no longer the sole or prime actor in cultural policy: new actors and scripts are at play, which means that the old ones are seeing their role change. In the last 20–30 years, in the same Western world where that couple was created, decentralization on the one hand and Europeanization on the other have undermined the state monopoly of cultural policies. This calls for a reconsideration of their rationale, objectives, and reach. My aim in this chapter is to contribute toward such a reconsideration, concentrating on the Europeanization dimension. If the usual solution of dilemmas regarding the policing of culture has been the reference to national identity, with Europeanization there are not only more levels to mobilize, territorial or otherwise, but also more problems to solve. In particular, there seems to be a synergy developing between the local (urban, regional) and the European that takes a specific configuration and needs analysis.

Before setting off, one more general observation can help in defining the agenda. During the process of modernization, the shift from private patronage to public (i.e., state) patronage has entailed what can be interpreted as a shift toward abstraction, both of objectives and methods, in line with one of the main characterizing features of modernization processes in general. What the cultural objects being supported are expected to display is no longer the celebration of a specific patron or dynasty (such as the Italian aristocracy or the papacy during the Renaissance), achieved through more or less obvious references in the content of the artwork itself. Rather, artworks have to contribute to a national culture and are often given a relatively high level of freedom with regard to content.[1] Sometimes state support is even concealed in order to make the propaganda more effective (see Mackey 1997). Today, we should consider whether the new actors of cultural policy imply another similar shift. To do so, we should reconsider the instruments with which we study cultural policies. Moreover, if policies in general, and cultural policies in particular, define and create their subjects, the analysis of cultural policy offers an insight into how common current concepts in the literature, such as local development and identity or urban regeneration and culture, are connected to the complex constellations of imagined communities being constructed, reshaped, and challenged. We need to examine the rationale and impact of this emerging Europeanized dimension of cultural policy.

In what follows, I will rapidly recall the history of European Union (EU) cultural policy, showing its specific style, objectives, and strategies. I will then present some results of a research on how local actors interpret this Europeanization, to see if we can derive from it some answers and, more importantly, some avenues for further research regarding this new stage of cultural policies and the general implications mentioned above.

Making the Europeans: Cultural Policy and European Identity

In the 1980s, a myth started to circulate in Europe. Jean Monnet, one of the 'founding fathers' of European integration via the European Economic Community, was rumored to have said: "If we were to do it all over again, we would start with culture." Soon exposed,[2] the myth has nevertheless persisted, continuing to be reported in the literature and to function as legitimizing rhetoric for the emerging European cultural policy.

In reality, cultural intervention in the European Communities (EC) started in the late 1970s, when the never fully overthrown federalist soul of the EC managed to put culture on the agenda. Not being backed by any treaty disposition, for a long while it has been a very marginal and disguised sector, having to 'pass' under some of the statutory fields of competence it exceeded. From the late 1970s to the early 1990s, cultural action was developed according to what has been identified as a specific policy style, characterizing those sectors in which the competence is only complementary to the national one and that are perceived as dealing with sensitive domains for national identities and sovereignty, such as culture. In these cases, it has been noted, the strategy is that the Commission of the European Communities (CEC), the organ with the mandate to initiate policies, prepares 'communications'—public documents that stimulate reflection in the relevant sectors—in order to inform and shape the debate (Mazey and Richardson 1995). Combined with programs of direct grants to the sectors themselves, this aims at creating a climate of consensus and coalition, eventually legitimating the EC proposals (CEC 1977; see also CEC 1996). Many policies not covered by the original treaties have followed a similar path; for instance, mechanisms of this type are traceable in the social and environmental policies. These policies that carry strong elements of national identity, like the cultural one, have been incrementally introduced, first with general directives that still give way to some focused initiatives, and then with financial support forging links between subnational and societal actors, thus creating a demand 'from below' for EC intervention (Majone 1996).

Having thus obtained a quite diffuse support in the sector, community cultural action could emerge from the shadow of intergovernmentalism and attain a legal status after a specific, supra-national competence on culture was introduced in 1992 with the Treaty on European Union (TEU), signed in Maastricht. The TEU contains a title on culture that, together with dispositions for a European citizenship, is often cited as among its major novelties. However, and as with citizenship, dispositions on culture are in fact rather limited and reveal an approach wherein the national state is still by far the main actor. The very formulation of the relevant article is revealing of the difficult debate from which it emerged. In essence, it only ratifies what was being done already, rather than introducing new domains: "The Community shall contribute to the flowering of the cultures of the Member States, while respecting their national and regional diversity and at the same time bringing the common cultural heritage to the fore" (TEU, Art. 151, 1).

Being classified within those domains where the EC has only complementary competence (not exclusive or concurrent) entails coordination, integration, and support initiatives, while being burdened by the requirement of unanimity in the decision-making process. The iron rule of unanimity at the same time testifies to the reticence of member states to delegate even small portions of sovereignty and has the effect of slowing down every initiative. These factors, together with the very small budget devoted to culture,[3] make up the main argument of those pointing out that a European cultural action is still rather limited. It is with ad hoc activities and projects, more than with planning and structural intervention, that such action can take place.

If we turn to the actual policy implementation that gave substance to the new legal framework, we see that in the second half of the 1990s, new cultural programs were launched: Kaleidoscope for cultural cooperation, Raphael for cultural heritage, and Ariane for publishing and reading. Since 2000, a new framework program has integrated and reorganized them, including also other previous initiatives—such as its flagship European City (or Capital) of Culture (ECOC) program—and thus unifying all EU cultural initiatives under a single heading, with the official purpose to strengthen impact and comprehensiveness. The new program was initially launched as Culture 2000 for the period 2000–2004. Extended until 2006, it was then superseded by a renovated but substantially unchanged Culture Program, due to last from 2007 to 2013 (Decision/1903/2006/EC). These programs are informed by a commitment to the protection of the "common cultural heritage," together with the promotion of a better knowledge and awareness of the cultures of the European peoples (strictly in the plural), whose variety, as it is always recalled, is the richness of Europe. On paper, therefore, the objectives are very broad and quite explicitly address the question of European cultural identity, claiming that cultural policy is there to protect and the same time foster it, providing legitimacy for the European integration project. As we can read in the document establishing Culture 2000: "Culture has an important intrinsic value to all people in Europe, is an essential element of European integration and contributes to the affirmation and vitality of the European model of society and to the Community's influence on the international scene. Culture is both an economic factor and a factor in social integration and citizenship; for that reason, it has an important role to play in meeting the new challenges facing the Community, such as globalization, the information society, social cohesion and the creation of employment" (Decision 508/2000/CE). The strategy designed to pursue these objectives still follows the thread of previous actions, that is, financial support for independent (the official rhetoric would call them 'grass-roots') projects of cultural cooperation and exchange across Europe. The criteria for evaluating projects are three: 'cultural added value', 'socio-economic impact', and—subsuming the first two and giving the program its specificity—'European added value'. The last refers to a project's 'European dimension', typically measured in terms of actual cooperation (organizational, institutional, financial) and exchange with partners of different member states. A system of direct grants to various cultural actors, operating mainly at the local level, is thus still the heart of the EU cultural policy.[4]

It is not difficult to see how, against the precedent of national cultural policy and identity, all this can be seen as limited and marginal (Forrest 1994; Shore 2000). However, interpretive difficulties and disagreement may stem from the failure to consider the particular policy style in question: we cannot interpret EU cultural policy because it does not satisfy the template we have in mind, which is, explicitly or not, the national one. But European institutions simply cannot follow step by step the path of cultural homogenization and consensus that the nation-state so successfully imagined for itself.[5] They cannot because their existence is based on that of the states and thus on a delicate equilibrium between the drive for unity and the concern for diversity, which affects objectives as well as strategies. The resulting dominant rhetoric of 'unity in diversity', which characterizes the majority of both academic and official accounts of European identity (see a review in Delanty and Rumford 2005: 52–66), is a formal solution that differs from more assertive, essentialist narratives of national identity. Furthermore, another reason why the EU cannot follow the national path is precisely that those essentialist, monolithic identities are increasingly criticized and exposed as simplistic and inadequate for the contemporary world, in Europe and elsewhere (Ifversen 2002). To consider necessary the definition of a common (homogeneous and consensual) culture, and thus a common identity, descends normatively from a comparison with the way that the nation was imagined as a community (Anderson 1983), which is flawed both historically and methodologically. Indeed, by using—even if partially, clumsily, and almost apologetically—a similar type of language and symbols, the EU makes things easy for critics. However, the EU's attempts at mimicking the nation are only one superficial aspect, and being embedded in a new context cannot be assumed to have the same results and significance. The EU is not a state, certainly not of the national type, so its interest in pursuing a cultural policy and what it means for a European identity could be different from the national case in ways that are not easily seen if we make of the latter a fixed, essential term of comparison.

One way to proceed, therefore, is to take a closer look at the local implementation of these self-defined identity-building measures, to have a more informed insight about the everyday and diffuse translations of 'unity in diversity' (a formula that has in the meantime been crystallized into the official motto of the EU) beyond Brussels's official documents. This approach follows from the realization that we can no longer assume that by looking at the center we will understand all the rest, as we have been doing for the national case. The fact that EU cultural action is implemented through local initiatives only makes more explicit what is always the case: especially in their symbolic impact on the social construction of reality, and more specifically as they contribute to shape individuals in their relationship with society (Shore and Wright 1997), policies should be studied from the point of view not only of their creators but also of their recipients, without assuming them to be passive carriers of fixed interpretations. In particular, the analysis of how an ambiguous rhetoric such as that of 'unity in diversity', informing Culture 2000 and more generally official EU discourse on European identity, turns into practice within locally implemented identity-building policies might reveal how Europe is being imagined today, both in and especially beyond Brussels.

An Example: Culture 2000 in a Local Context

I will now present some results of empirical research, conducted in 2003–2004 in the Italian region Emilia-Romagna, on the internationalization of cultural policies as seen from the local context.[6] A significant part of the study concerned the impact of the Culture 2000 program on the regional cultural sector. Emilia-Romagna is a relatively rich, northern Italian region—one of the hubs of the so-called third Italy, based on districts of small to medium-sized enterprises where social and economic development are integrated (Bagnasco 1977)—and is characterized by a high level of public services as well as cultural production and consumption. Emilia-Romagna evidenced the successful implementation of Culture 2000 within Italy, which, together with France (often a co-organizer), submits more applications and obtains more funds than most other countries.[7]

Quantitative analysis, however, would not bring us very far, not only because we are talking about small numbers, making statistics hardly significant, but mainly because, according to the approach espoused here, one requires a qualitative analysis in order to grasp the impact and even more the meaning that the introduction of a new subject of public policy, such as the EU, brings to the cultural field. Not only is each actor essential for the construction of a field (in the sociological, Bourdieusian sense), but the field is constructed by the structure of opportunities and constraints that result from the interaction of the different actors (Le Galés 2002). A new agent thus means a new relational configuration. To describe this, even the classical distinction between institutional (top-down) or grass-roots (bottom-up) action loses interpretive grasp, as does possibly even the distinction between local and European. As we have seen, the style of the policy is precisely to displace these two fundamental, analytical distinctions, finally also affecting the national level. As these analytical devices are not of use here, one possibility is to assess EU cultural action in its own terms, trying to see how it relates to the other forces in the field.

A good starting point is to look at the 'European added value', which we have identified as the EU's main evaluation criterion. Let us consider how it is officially defined, this time not by reading an official document but through the direct words of an EC official, whom I interviewed following a seminar for local cultural operators during the launch of Culture 2000 in Bologna, the regional capital:

> Projects ... are required to explain the European added value ... This means general cultural cooperation in the conception, performance and financing of the project. I mean that we ask the experts to look at the quality of the European involvement. In some ways this is quantitative too (a project which involves 11 countries will be quite 'European') but it is also qualitative too in that the level and type of co-operation must be assessed. This can include looking at the financial involvement of the partners but also at *how* they will work together. So, you're right to say that we are looking more for a high level of co-operation than a 'European' theme. Many of the projects we support look at regional/local culture, but are promoting them at European level.

This is a good illustration of what Europeanization as a process of abstraction might mean. As we can see, the control is not focused on the content but more on the form, or format, of projects. Of course, this has an impact on content as well: the analytical distinction is there precisely to highlight reciprocal correspondences and to draw attention to how this implies a different approach compared to the national one.

This emerges also in the declarations of local cultural operators whom I interviewed. Following is how the national support office for Culture 2000 in Italy (Antenna culturale) interprets Culture 2000:

> The program Culture 2000 asks precisely that these projects are oriented to Europe, because it has to last in Europe ... the outcome of the project has to be there for Europe. Projects have to be aimed at the largest possible range of citizens; cultural operators have to think of the lay citizens. Projects have to diffuse. The idea is that the citizen should feel as European as possible, without losing their national identity obviously, but by feeling European, citizens will be more interested in knowing what happens in Greece, in Slovenia, in Lithuania, or even where Lithuania is, because not everyone knows ... This is, so to speak, a chain reaction.

There is not, as one might think, a European vs. local dichotomy, in which one would be the means/cause and the other the end/effect. On the contrary, the emphasis given to one of the two terms is seen as positive as long as it is successfully combined with an emphasis on the other. Also, the initiative is not attributed exclusively to the EU. Indeed, a clue to identifying a successful project is the fact that it entails local subjects stimulating their own territory in a European key, as the same interviewee suggests:

It should be a drive that starts autonomously. The project, the co-operation of three or five countries, everyone putting a part of themselves in this container, when the container is full the project is ready and is poured onto the citizens. The citizens receiving this rain of extra knowledge feel part of Europe, without losing sight of where they come from, but exchanging, mentally making a sort of cultural exchange ... The project is successful when those going to a show or an exhibition become interested in what happens abroad, feeling in that moment part of one big network.

On the one hand, we can say that it is the EU objectives that are emphasized, through the 'European added value' and its alleged impact on identities. But on the other hand, this is not something imposed from above onto a local base deprived of subjectivity. Following is the opinion of an official of a regional development agency that supports local cultural operators in the application and management processes:

There is certainly an opening up of identities. I think that the prize at the end of a project within Culture 2000 is not the [monetary] contribution, but the realization that there are distant realities with whom it is possible to share initiatives, to start a dialogue. This I think is the added value of the project. And of course, as always, sometimes this happens, sometimes it doesn't ... Anyway certainly both during the application process and in the realization of projects, a mechanism starts that goes beyond the economic aspect that normally is the trigger of the project. So we have to evaluate not only the 50 percent (of Community contribution) but the impact on the city ... thus cultural identity. Effectively, one enhances one's own identity, because it gets legitimated, and then there is knowledge ... [S]ometimes even small municipalities that normally don't even work outside their region find themselves in Prague or Ireland, then impressive things happen ... it is difficult to quantify, measure this.

These are still official voices, although locally based. But what about local cultural operators themselves? What do they think of the EU's ambitious aims, using projects of cultural cooperation as narratives of a European identity? What is their representation of the almost ubiquitous Europeanist rhetoric that they themselves use in their projects? Let us listen to three people from among those who have led projects under Culture 2000. The first is from an academic involved in an archaeological project:

Q. Many projects speak of Europe, even of European identity. How would you explain this?
A. That is said to be what Brussels likes. But actually, the community of academics to which I belong has always been so supranational, international, and we all feel European, also because we deal with a period in which Europe was really united [the Celtic and Roman era].
Q. Would you say that these international projects have an impact on identities? If so, how?
A. For the project proposer, European projects enhance the sense of belonging to a European culture. For the public of the projects (students, other researchers,

the wider population), it is still about European identity and also national pride because finally an Italian project gets some consideration.

The next two voices come instead from the performing arts world:

Q. Many projects speak of Europe, even of European identity. How would you explain this?

A. It is about the place where we live, the unity in diversity.

Q. What do you think is or should be the aim of Culture 2000?

A. To support the birth and development of international projects, so that relationships of 'sympathy' can become common work. Let's say, a kind of enlightened patronage that, whilst aiming at its own exaltation (that is, the European added value, as much as in the Renaissance the prince aimed at his own exaltation, of his own magnificence), supports the development of the arts and culture. Everybody gains: the 'prince' Europe, the arts, and the population. And, at least, unlike the majority of the patrons in history, in this case we have a 'prince' democratically elected according to principles of justice and freedom ... All this should not sound cynical, but positively realistic.

Q. Many projects speak of Europe, even of European identity. How would you explain this?

A. With the fact, as I hinted at in the previous answer, that this is what the EU asks for in the call of Culture 2000. This explains the flourishing of exaltations of the European added value that actually is really there, but that being so emphasized (after all, it is obvious that if I make a project with partners from other countries, this project in itself shows its relevance for the European perspective!) unveils the mechanism of patronage.

This working more as an "enlightened patronage," or as an investiture, is well represented by the case of Bologna having obtained the title of European City of Culture (ECOC) for the year 2000. Although this is a topic developed elsewhere precisely for its relevance (Sassatelli 2005), a consideration of Culture 2000 in Emilia-Romagna cannot gloss over its regional capital being awarded a title that has become increasingly prestigious and competitive, and that is both one of the oldest EU cultural initiatives and a key action of the new framework program.[8] This action, representative in its evolution and style of those typical of EU cultural policy described above, is meant as a macro-event concentrating attention on one city with the idea of providing a stage for its own cultural assets, as well as projects from the rest of Europe. Cultural exchanges and cooperation (the basis of all EU cultural support) are encouraged, often under the banner of culture-led urban regeneration (Gold and Gold 2005; Heikkinen 2000; Richards and Wilson 2004). However, especially in its first 20 years as an intergovernmental action, the ECOC was above all characterized by its diversity and lightness, as far as the program itself was concerned. The city received the title and a very small fund (covering, on average, 1 percent of the total budget and connected with the realization of 'European projects'), and was otherwise totally independent in the conceptualization, organization, and even evaluation of the year's events.

This means that the ECOC is particularly indicative of the type of connection that is taking shape between the European and the local. With regard to Bologna 2000, this aspect is made evident by the emphasis that the organizers put on the direct involvement of the city's very lively cultural sector, from single artists to the many small cultural associations. This is revealing because Bologna is internationally renowned as a "laboratory of cultural enterprises" (Bloomfield 1993), having been so identified in the early 1990s in an influential collection of studies on urban cultural policies in Europe (Bianchini and Parkinson 1993). In choosing to use the year as ECOC to continue supporting a wide range of projects from its local associations, Bologna thus chose continuity with its tradition. However, it also had to develop an aspect—the 'European added value'—that was marginal to that tradition and yet was required to be brought to the fore by the ECOC nomination. This was not a matter of the content of projects; rather, confirming what we have already seen for Culture 2000 in general, it was about the stimulation of cultural collaboration across Europe. Asked what had been the role and relevance of the 'European dimension' for the choice of projects to include in the program, the director of the cultural program of Bologna 2000 said that it was the most characteristic feature of the whole program, because it was cross-cutting, which meant, however, that it was often implicit and needed 'reading': "[Even the EU] is not interested in knowing if there is a dance festival rather than a big exhibition. What is of interest is that the sum of these events contains those elements of European dimension: identity, differences, dialogue … [Because] when you have a project and you feel part of a bigger program, it is inevitable that you will deal, directly or indirectly, with some European themes." It is in these terms that Bologna 2000 was presented as a "reconsideration of the town in a European dimension" (a turn of phrase that often emerged in the words of my interviewees). The European investiture is thus mobilized to give new energy and financial backing—the ECOC functions as a stimulus for both private sponsors and public funding—to what was already present in the city's traditions.

Accounts of the ECOC program in general confirm this picture, attributing its success to the flexibility of rules and the resulting great diversity: "The permissive rules of the festival [European City of Culture] ha[ve] always allowed host cities and their governments to reshape it, almost at will, to fit their agendas" (Gold and Gold 2005: 243). The EU itself has welcomed this, as a practical demonstration of precisely its 'unity in diversity'.[9] This should not be taken at face value however. The local exploitation of the European investiture (in the neutral sense of putting it to a specific use that corresponds to local configurations) and the resulting wealth of approaches and contents that have animated the ECOC year after year are not totally arbitrary or unexpected. On the contrary, they fall within the constellation of opportunities and constraints that the EU is framing for local actors. Moreover, even this formulation is simplistic, as no single actor has total control or remains unchanged. EU cultural policy, with its 'unity in diversity' rhetoric and project-based practices, does imply an openness toward contents that can find a space inside it—a space for the expression of contents that were not already there in the minds of those who designed the policy itself. Or, to use Marina Fokidis's expression (see her chapter in this volume), this leaves open the possibility for cultural operators to "hijack" EU cultural policy for their own contents, as long as they fit the frame.

Concluding Remarks

The EU has been able to generate new ties between Brussels and local actors, both institutional (local governments) and societal (NGOs, networks, etc.).[10] As the EU's intervention in culture was developing throughout the 1980s, within individual states a common trend was spreading—despite an otherwise very diverse administration of culture—a trend toward the decentralization of cultural policies in which cultural competence was partially devolved to subnational (regional and local) bodies (Bianchini 1993).[11] This opened up the possibility of a synergy between the local dimension and European agencies, which the latter have actively promoted. The plurality of actors and of their relationships may explain why interpretations still vary on the real impact of current cultural action. More varied still are the interpretations of how good or desirable that impact is, and how it affects the relations of pre-existing actors (for two opposing views, see Banus 2002 and Pantel 1999). At the core of diverging evaluations, however, is the question of institutional identity building. Much as the state patronage of the arts implied a process of abstraction, compared to private patronage, regarding both objectives and methods, today, considering the EU, the program of a national culture homogeneously promoted is also far too specific and essentialist. Still more abstraction is needed in order to accommodate at the cultural level the 'unity in diversity' that the EU is trying to promote to hold together the different national, regional, and local bodies (and other kinds of diversity) of which it is composed and that are not simply going to melt into a new, European homogeneous whole (Robins 2006).

Looking at the declarations of some local cultural operators, it appears indeed that EU cultural programs are not just a source of funding (limited and insufficient), nor do they involve full patronage and their own projects to realize. We have used the term 'investiture' to imply that the initiative is not torn away from the local level but instead legitimated as its competence. This is a competence, to reiterate, that depends on accepting the field of opportunities and constraints within which it emerges. Thus, on the one hand, local initiatives have to renounce imposing their specificity as hegemonic, and, on the other, the European investiture is embodied by contents that emerge 'from below'. What the observations of Culture 2000 from our local context suggest is that the emphasis on the 'European added value' results in this specific 'fit' between European form and local, diverse contents—a fit characterized by the exclusion of exclusivity that may point to a new way of imagining cultural identities. Europe is in the making, and this may be just a transitional stage. So it is this fit, these contents, and the resulting configuration that we should continue to inspect in a future that promises to be characterized by more and more Europeanized—and fragmented—cultural policies.

Monica Sassatelli holds a PhD in Sociology from the University of Parma. She has been Jean Monnet Fellow at the European University Institute in Florence, and she currently teaches sociology at the University of Ferrara. Her recent publications include *The Logic of Europeanizing Cultural Policy* (2006), *Nothing Changes and Everything Changes: Change, Culture and Identity in Contemporary Italian Social Theory* (2006), and *Identità, Cultura, Europa: The "European Cities of Culture"* (2005).

Notes

1. Abstraction does not equate with lesser control but rather with its displacement inside the policy recipients themselves. Modern cultural policies can thus be seen as key factor of this internalized control and as part and parcel of the disciplinary modern state 'as educator'. See, in particular, Foucauldian, 'governmentality' approaches to cultural policy (Barnett 2001; Bennett 1992; Foucault 1991).
2. For a more detailed description of the development of EC/EU policy—and of the unveiling and significance of the myth—see, for instance, Shore (2000) and Sassatelli (2006).
3. Even after the TEU, only 0.033 percent of the EU budget is earmarked for culture, about a tenth of what even the least interventionist countries in the cultural sector invest individually (Banus 2002: 160). However, a much higher level of support goes to culture via the structural funds (see Helie 2004, and note 10 below).
4. To give an idea, in the period 2000–2004, Culture 2000 received an average annual request for about 700 projects and financed over 200 annual, multi-annual, and special events projects, for a total allocation of about 30 million euros per year. See also PLS Ramboll Management (2003) and Efah-Interarts (2003).
5. How successfully the nation-state actually did so, and at what cost, is something that might be investigated further, also thanks to the new perspectives presented by developments such as Europeanization.
6. This project, conducted at the Fondazione di Ricerca Istituto Carlo Cattaneo research center in Bologna, was partially funded by the regional administration of Emilia-Romagna. Concentrating on the internationalization of cultural policies, the project investigated in particular the implementation of two initiatives, Culture 2000 (EU) and the World Heritage List (UNESCO), in the region. Emilia-Romagna is in fact interesting on both fronts, having an active presence in Culture 2000 and three World Heritage sites (Modena, Ferrara, and Ravenna) out of a total, at the time, of 37 nominated sites in Italy. The research on the World Heritage List, which is not included in this chapter, was conducted by Jasper Chalcraft; the other, partially described here, was conducted by myself. For more details, see Chalcraft and Sassatelli (2004a, 2004b).
7. In the period 2000–2003 analyzed by the research, Italy alone obtained 17 percent of all Culture 2000 financed projects—an average of about 38 projects per year with an Italian project leader. This should also be considered in connection with the high number of applications coming from Italy; for instance, in 2002, over 23 percent of applications were from Italian project leaders. Within Italy, Emilia-Romagna in the same period ranked fourth, after Lazio, Lombardia, and Toscana. The research is based both on document analysis and on interviews with several project curators, as well as other key informants (EU officials, the Emilia-Romagna representative in Brussels, the Culture 2000 national contact point, etc.).
8. ECOC is an action that started autonomously on the initiative of the ministers of culture of the member states, and thus at intergovernmental level, in 1985. It was then subsumed under Culture 2000, becoming a direct action of the EC in 2005. Up until 1999,

one city had been nominated per year. In 2000, due to the special significance of the year and to the impossibility of reaching agreement otherwise, nine cities were jointly nominated (see Cogliandro 2001; Myerscough 1994; Palmer/Rae Associates 2004; Sassatelli 2005, 2006).

9. See the recent official evaluating report prepared by Palmer/Rae Associates (2004).
10. These ties have been created not only through the Culture 2000 program. The EU has also encouraged the use of the much more generous structural funds for cultural projects. According to an official document of 2001, structural funds give to culture about 400 million euros per year, that is, 12 times the total annual provision of Culture 2000 (33 million euros). However, the relevance of structural funds for the cultural sector has the effect of putting "culture at the service of local development" (Helie 2004: 67, 71). On the relationship between cultural policy and cohesion policy, see also Delgado-Moreira (2000).
11. Indeed, the TEU itself mentions the regional level next to the national one in the title on culture.

References

Anderson, Benedict. 1983. *Imagined Communities*. London: Verso.

Bagnasco, Arnaldo. 1977. *Le tre Italie: La problematica territoriale dello sviluppo economico italiano*. Bologna: Il Mulino.

Banus, Enrique. 2002. "Cultural Policy in the EU and the European Identity." Pp. 158–183 in *European Integration in the 21st Century: Unity in Diversity?* ed. M. Farrell, S. Fella, and M. Newman. London: Sage.

Barnett, Clive. 2001. "Culture, Policy, and Subsidiarity in the European Union: From Symbolic Identity to the Governmentalisation of Culture." *Political Geography* 20: 405–426.

Becker, Howard S. 1982. *Art Worlds*. Berkeley: University of California Press.

Bennett, Tony. 1992. "Putting Policy into Cultural Studies." Pp. 23–37 in *Cultural Studies*, ed. L. Grossberg, C. Nelson, and P. Treichler. London: Routledge.

Bianchini, Franco. 1993. "Remaking European Cities: The Role of Cultural Policies." Pp. 1–20 in Bianchini and Parkinson 1993.

Bianchini, Franco, and Michael Parkinson, eds. 1993. *Cultural Policy and Urban Regeneration: The West European Experience*. Manchester: Manchester University Press.

Bloomfield, Jude. 1993. "Bologna: A Laboratory for Cultural Enterprise." Pp. 73–89 in Bianchini and Parkinson 1993.

Calhoun, Craig, ed. 1994. *Social Theory and the Politics of Identity*. Oxford: Blackwell.

CEC (Commission of the European Communities). 1977. *Community Action on the Cultural Sector*. Reprinted in *Bulletin of the EC Supplement*, 6/77.

_____. 1996. *First Report on the Consideration of Cultural Aspects in European Community Action*. Com (96) 160. Brussels: European Commission.

Chalcraft, Jasper, and Monica Sassatelli. 2004a. *Identità locale e processi di internazionalizzazione degli interventi di politica culturale: Il posto dell'Emilia-Romagna*. Research report. Bologna: Fondazione di Ricerca Istituto Carlo Cattaneo.

_____. 2004b. "Identità locale e internazionalizzazione delle politiche culturali: Il caso dell'Emilia-Romagna." *Il Mulino* 2: 217–220.

Cogliandro, Giannalia. 2001. *European Cities of Culture for the Year 2000: A Wealth of Urban Cultures for Celebrating the Turn of the Century*. Final report. http://www.europa.ue.int.

Delanty, Gerard, and Chris Rumford. 2005. *Rethinking Europe: Social Theory and the Implications of Europeanization*. London: Routledge.

Delgado-Moreira, Juan M. 2000. "Cohesion and Citizenship in EU Cultural Policy." *Journal of Common Market Studies* 38, no. 3: 449–470.

Efah-Interarts. 2003. *Report on the State of Cultural Cooperation in Europe*. Report for the European Commission Directorate-Generale for Education and Culture. http://www .europa.eu.int.

Forrest, Alan. 1994. "A New Start for Cultural Action in the European Union: Genesis and Implications of Article 128 of the Treaty on European Union." *European Journal of Cultural Policy* 1, no. 1: 11–20.

Foucault, Michel. 1991. "Governmentality." Pp. 87–104 in *The Foucault Effect: Studies in Governmentality*, ed. G. Burchell, C. Gordon, and P. Miller. London: Harvester Wheatsheaf.

Gold, Margaret M., and John R. Gold. 2005. *Cities of Culture: Staging International Festivals and the Urban Agenda, 1851–2000*. Aldershot: Ashgate.

Heikkinen, Tim. 2000. "In From the Margins: The City of Culture 2000 and the Image Transformation of Helsinki." *International Journal of Cultural Policy* 6, no. 2: 201–218.

Helie, Thomas. 2004. "Cultiver l'Europe: Elements pour une approche localisée de 'l'europeanisation' des politiques culturelles." *Politique européenne* 12: 66–83.

Ifversen, Jan. 2002. "Europe and European Culture—a Conceptual Analysis." *European Societies* 4, no. 1: 1–26.

Le Galés, Patrick. 2002. *European Cities: Social Conflicts and Governance*. Oxford: Oxford University Press.

Lewis, Justin, and Toby Miller, eds. 2003. *Critical Cultural Policy Studies: A Reader*. Oxford: Blackwell.

Mackey, Eva. 1997. "The Cultural Politics of Populism: Celebrating Canadian National Identity." Pp. 136–164 in Shore and Wright 1997.

Majone, Giandomenico. 1996. *Regulating Europe*. London: Routledge.

Mazey, Sonia, and Jeremy Richardson. 1995. "Promiscuous Policy-Making: The European Policy Style?" Pp. 337–360 in *The State of the European Union: Building a European Polity*, ed. C. Rhodes and S. Mazey. Boulder: Lynne Rienner.

McGuigan, Jim. 2004. *Rethinking Cultural Policy*. Maidenhead, UK: Open University Press.

Meinhof, Ulrike H., and Anna Triandafyllidou, eds. 2006. *Transcultural Europe: Cultural Policy in a Changing Europe*. Basingstoke: Palgrave.

Miller, Toby, and George Yúdice. 2002. *Cultural Policy*. London: Sage.

Myerscough, John. 1994. *European Cities of Culture and Cultural Months*. Full report, unabridged Version. Glasgow: Network of European Cultural Cities.

Palmer/Rae Associates. 2004. *European Cities and Capitals of Culture*. Study prepared for the European Commission. http://www.europa.ue.int.

Pantel, Melissa. 1999. "Unity in Diversity: EU Cultural Policy and Legitimacy." Pp. 46–65 in *Legitimacy and the European Union*, ed. T. Banchoff and M. Smith. London: Routledge.

PLS Ramboll Management. 2003. *Interim Report on the Implementation of "Culture 2000" in 2000 and 2001*. http://www.europa.eu.int.

Richards, Greg, and Julie Wilson. 2004. "The Impact of Cultural Events on City Image: Rotterdam, Cultural Capital of Europe 2001." *Urban Studies* 41, no. 10: 1931–1951.

Robins, Kevin. 2006. "Towards a Transcultural Policy for European Cosmopolitanism." Pp. 254–284 in Meinhof and Triandafyllidou 2006.

Sassatelli, Monica. 2005. *Identità, cultura, Europa: Le "Città europee della cultura."* Milan: FrancoAngeli.

———. 2006. "The Logic of Europeanizing Cultural Policy." Pp. 24–42 in Meinhof and Triandafyllidou 2006.

Shore, Cris. 2000. *Building Europe: The Cultural Politics of European Integration*. London: Routledge.

Shore, Cris, and Susan Wright, eds. 1997. *Anthropology of Policy: Critical Perspectives on Governance and Power*. London: Routledge.

Chapter 9

POLITICAL ART, CULTURAL POLICY, AND ARTISTIC AGENCY

Jeremy Valentine

The topic of this chapter is something rather banal and ordinary. It concerns recent developments in the nature of the bureaucratic and administrative conditions of the production and distribution of culture, and the political and economic drivers of change in those conditions. By describing and problematizing those changes, the chapter will also discuss some of the implications of their impact on the relations between art and culture. In particular, responses at the level of production and distribution to government actions within the broad context of neo-liberal welfare regimes authorized by the state and the assumptions that underpin the legitimacy of government-funded art and culture will be analyzed. The consequences of these changes are summarized by George Yudice's (2003: 13) description of the arts and cultural sector as an "enormous

Notes for this chapter are located on page 141.

network of arts administrators who mediate between funding sources and artists and/or communities. Like their counterparts in the university and business
world, they must produce and distribute the producers of art and culture, who
in turn deliver communities or consumers."

Political and Aesthetic Causality

There is an obvious economic dimension to this scenario, in that its participants get paid; however, this chapter will argue that its emergence is politically
driven. Yudice's focus is on the Latin American context and in particular the
growth of 'NGO-fication' and the 'UNESCO-racy' in culture. These phenomena
suggest that state commitment to forms of liberal-democratic rule in that region
is a matter of appearance rather than reality, as they are continuous with established pathologies of mundane corruption and the clientelism normally associated with it. That may be true, but if so, it is not confined to Latin America
in that these scenarios are expressions of more widespread and underlying
processes present in the European and particularly the UK context associated
with the systemic instabilities that characterize neo-liberalism.

One consequence of the dominance of instability and the well-known
characteristics of disorganization, risk, and uncertainty is the emergence of
a specific relation between politics and culture that can be characterized as
'organizational gaming'. This phrase can be illustrated through an analogy
with situations in which rules exist but are subject to change without players
necessarily knowing what they are. In other words, the rules become the stakes
in the game itself, with success defined as the capacity to determine rules to
one's advantage while at the same time keeping the other players playing and
in the process altering what one's advantage or interest is. Although the sense
of politics that the analogy invokes is not equivalent to ideological notions such
as socialism or conservatism or values such as democracy or pluralism, such
concepts are not necessarily excluded from it.

To provide an initial theoretical context for the emergence of these developments, we can begin by considering questions about the relations between
social, aesthetic, political, and economic causality. If old positivist explanations of causality no longer hold water, despite, as we shall see, their official
persistence at the level of state and government action, and in particular policy
formation and implementation, then equally traditional assumptions about the
causality of art and culture have also evaporated and persist as a set of ambiguous and subjective normative beliefs that do not enjoy much force. Although
political causality is often theorized in terms of micro- and macro-levels of
prediction and calculation, at bottom these rest on structures of authority and
command that can no longer be taken for granted by political actors. This
has given rise to various explanations, ranging from 'legitimation crisis' to
the unpredictable distribution of 'exit, voice, or loyalty' preferences among
political subjects, none of which could be considered definitive. Similarly,
assumptions about the causality of art and culture, which allows one to make

statements along the lines of "looking at this painting produces this effect," are usually categorized in terms of aesthetics, whether as the arbitrariness of individual pleasure or as an objective hierarchy in which, classically, beauty is the sensible form of the good or as modernist predictions of the dislocating effects of art and culture on the taken-for-granted understandings of every-day life. Again, explanations are varied, but one could point to the success of the critique of aesthetics from within cultural production itself, as well as the decline of aesthetic attachments within classes associated with dominant social forces. However, when these developments in the political and aesthetic spheres converge, one can refer to what George Yudice has called a "crisis of the political causality of art."[1]

However, the consequence of such a crisis is not an abyss in which notions of politics and culture, no less of economy and society, have become com-pletely indeterminate on the model of the postmodern mishmash. Instead, claims about causality no longer reflect objective and independently verifiable observations, if they ever did. Rather, they have become politicized, embedded in political and aesthetic projects as solutions to the problems that such pro-grams exist to solve, and in so doing are the means with which these projects can become solidified and maintained. At the same time, such enterprises co-exist and compete with other rival projects, especially insofar as they take place in contexts characterized by finite resources and struggles over their allo-cation or, in another idiom, the appropriation of the surplus.

This chapter does not seek to adjudicate between competing aesthetic-politi-cal projects or attempt to provide grounds for doing so. Instead, the ethos of this chapter is Machiavellian, in the political science sense of identifying the relative strength and weight of competing forces. The chapter is also Gramscian, bear-ing in mind Gramsci's debt to Machiavelli. In that respect, the chapter hopes to show some of the indicative aspects of the dynamics through which relations of politics and culture are articulated. Yet it would be misleading to assume that such relations can be described as hegemonic in any straightforward way. Hegemonic articulation is normally understood on the Laclauist model of an equivalence between heterogeneous terms that are unified with respect to a transcendental point that is itself defined with respect to an 'other', which func-tions as an enemy to be opposed, or the populist 'them-against-us' model.[2]

That model is insufficient to capture the nature of articulation in the circum-stances that this chapter will lay out. Instead of the stability of antagonistic frontiers, this chapter describes articulation itself as a mobile and flexible prac-tice that seeks to establish contexts of meaning and relevance for actions and objects without becoming tied to attempts to maintain those contexts. Perhaps the fashionable notion of 'networking' most approximates such a regime of articulation. An additional consequence is that the value and causal assump-tions of alterity and heterogeneity, with respect to both politics and aesthetics, are also rendered moot, since the frontiers and relations of exteriority and inte-riority that they maintain are no longer fixed. The agency formerly attributed to frontiers, in the sense of the capacity to establish distinctions between an inside and an outside, has declined, and in certain cases one might conclude that these distinctions are no longer determinate. Equally, one might say that transgression has become routine, albeit without the frisson of excitement that used to be associated with it.

Audit and Causality

A good example that illustrates these phenomena is audit, which is perhaps best described as a system that seeks to make bureaucratic and administrative actions accountable and predictable under conditions of generalized contingency. Audit is a method or technology for counting actions and relations in order to make them objective; in other words, it represents actions as measurable and in doing so transforms them into something that can be quantified and evaluated. Audit is a machine for turning actions into things and for representing things as objects that obey laws like those that are believed to govern physical reality. Hence, the dimension of causality is preserved in conditions where no one knows what will happen next, or even which actions and events are linked to other actions and events. Social scientists may conclude that audit is a form of practical positivism. However, its existence is purely political because it depends on encouraging accounts of actions to conform to a range of possible descriptions so that these actions can be mapped as a quantity of desirable actions. These descriptions are then inserted into larger narratives that provide purpose and direction to actions that are commensurate with a wider field of actions governed by a larger framework. The actual content of audit is arbitrary and subject to change. If it happens to be discovered that in reality there is a discrepancy between an action and a description, then such knowledge is simply an occasion for more audit. Audit is a method for producing representations in terms of aims, objectives, and outcomes, and linking those representations with other representations. To be auditable becomes the telos of actions, and actions become teleological.

How has this situation come about? According to Power's (1997) description and analysis, audit derives from the failure of financial accounting practices and specifically from the series of spectacular financial scandals and frauds that emerged as part of the postmodernizing re-regulatory process of the 1980s and that continue to the present and beyond.[3] On that account, bearers of capital invented ways of outmaneuvering the disciplinary systems of financial representation in which they were caught by producing multiple representations of the same thing so that the objectivity of representation weakened. Ironically, accountancy firms volunteered to solve this problem of their own creation by developing technologies that would audit the systems and procedures in which actions and exchanges took place. This development emerged in parallel with the growth of management consultancy in which accountancy firms commodified specialist knowledge that was then sold to managers as a product that would provide better tools with which to exercise control over their organizations. At the same time, as decision-making authority is outsourced, it becomes harder to attribute causal chains to actions and the moral and economic responsibilities that depend on them. In broader terms, audit can be subsumed within the dialectic of trust and risk which characterizes societies structured by contingency and the elimination of guarantees. To trust is to risk. Therefore, there is no 'trust in trust'.

It would be a mistake to reduce audit to the requirements of capital accumulation, not least because of the costs it generates. Rather, it might be better explained as an attempt by administrative and organizational forces to maintain some control over the appropriation of surpluses in conditions of disorganization. To a certain extent, the economic dimension is captured by the notion of 'rent seeking' that is central to public choice theory. That is to say, audit is a means to accumulate unproductive and thus 'unearned' income. Indeed, audit may well be characterized in terms of Bourdieu's notion of cultural intermediaries.[4] In fact, the success of audit as a regime of verification stems from its pathological and perverse nature. Although audit seeks to establish compliance between systems, actions, and meanings, compliance is never enough, as it may simply be an effect of audit itself. As actors become subjected to audit, they learn its requirements and so adapt to meet them. They comply, but for the wrong reasons. Thus, Power (1997: 135) maintains that "[a]ssumptions of distrust sustaining audit processes may be self-fulfilling." In such circumstances, audit simply devises more things to audit. Not surprisingly, the symptom of audit is an adversarial environment of blame allocation and risk displacement and competition between and innovation within the performance of impression and reputation management. Hence, Power (ibid.: 67) asserts that "audit and inspection are also seen to constitute the conduct of politics by other means, a conduct they share with war." He provides an excellent historical analogy for the logic of audit with the detailed output targets of the former Soviet Union: "This was a situation characterised by pathologies of 'creative compliance' ... poor quality goods and the development of survival skills to show that, often impossible, targets were achieved. Games are played around an 'indicator' culture where auditable performance is an end in itself and real long term planning is impossible" (ibid.: 121).

The absence of trust in and knowledge of organizations and systems is sublimated by the displacement of trust onto the process of audit through which organizations and systems are represented as knowable, which, of course, is distinct from knowledge of what is represented. In fact, audit is sustained by this distinction between representation and that which is represented, as audit itself resists representation. It can be known only by its effects, the becoming auditable of the world, which audit verifies. Or, put simply, audit cannot be known except by more audit. The productivity of audit is secured on the grounds that there is always one more thing to audit, as a representation can never be completely objective until the world stops. Power argues that auditing works through a "dialectic of failure" that is expressed positively as "the expectations gap." More and more audit is required to fill the gap between representation and represented that is created by audit. Thus, Power (1997: 141) states: "The problem of the epistemological obscurity of audit means that it is difficult to disentangle instrumental effects from a certain staging of control; audit practice is a form of social control talk."

As such, audit is a form of power that gives rise to a peculiar form of politics that Power (1997: 95–98) describes as a "reverse effect" and that works in two complementary ways. The first is 'decoupling', which refers to the creation of agencies within an organization tasked with managing the auditing process and making the organization auditable. In order to benefit from resource allocation, these agencies advance their own agendas within the organization, promoting distrust and undermining confidence by representing the organization as lacking objectivity. As a consequence, organizational activities become consumed by the infinite task of representing in an auditable way the structures, systems, processes, and procedures that are supposed to make organizational activities possible. Thus, auditing is the cure for the disease that it creates. The circle is not entirely closed, however, as the organizational autonomy that audit aims to weaken, or 'professional capture', is replaced by the autonomization of the audit process itself. In a reversal, audit becomes the profession that 'captures' the organization. This gives rise to the second consequence of audit—'colonization', the creation of a new organizational actor that challenges the power of an organization by subjecting its activities to the technologies of audit. This works because audit is promoted as a benefit that will provide the objectivity that audit has weakened, repairing the damage to trust and confidence that audit has caused, and thus delivering a measurable improvement in the performance of the organization. Audit can simply point to the transformation of actions from non-auditable to auditable as verification of its own effectiveness and causal agency.

Audit and Cultural Governance

To the extent that the sphere of art, aesthetics, and culture enjoys significant relations with bureaucracy, this sphere will be subjected to a regime of audit insofar as it can be characterized in terms of a crisis of causality. In general, this occurs due to the necessary relations of financial dependency that the sphere enjoys with public bureaucracies and administrations. Audit is a response to the increased contingency characterizing public bureaucracy and administration, for which constant 'review' and 'reform' are reliable symptoms.

  In this section, I would like to discuss the logic of audit in the Scottish context in order to show how audit works as a linking process between government, in this case the Scottish Executive, and various non-departmental public bodies, here primarily the Scottish Arts Council (SAC) and other agencies of varying size, such as Scottish Enterprise, the main economic development agency for Scotland, and smaller training organizations, as well as artists and artist-run organizations.[5] Hence, the context includes various scales of scope and purpose. Indeed, representing the context as relatively unified is an effect of the extent to which its elements have become auditable, in this case through subjection to a policy framework in a report produced by the Scottish Executive (2001). This framework is known as Scotland's 'cultural strategy', suggesting that culture in Scotland is in some way Scottish and at the same time can be acted upon. The subtitle of the report, *Creating Our Future, Minding Our Past*, gives some indication of the compromise between conservative and modernizing forces in the formulation of the strategy. The policy is concerned above all to represent culture in terms of the cultural continuity of Scotland during a process of devolution. Although the content of this continuity is never explicitly described, the effects of culture are stated quite categorically and unambiguously. Culture does, and therefore will, contribute to Scotland's economy. Culture does, and therefore will, contribute to the formation of Scotland as an inclusive society. Culture does, and therefore will, reflect the excellence of Scotland's culture and represent Scotland to the world.

In this respect, the Scottish Executive has made a decision about the causality of culture, having determined what culture does and therefore what culture should do in order to be what it is. No one would like to say that culture does not do any of these things, but demonstrating that this is the case is harder to accomplish. However, there are certain tensions present. For example, for some political forces, cultural excellence is regarded as elitist and thus exclusive. For others, subjection to logics of government dilutes and compromises the autonomy of the aesthetic sphere. At the same time, external forces can also shape the play of art and politics, for instance, through a skeptical response to claims for the contribution of culture to economic activity, which is hard to demonstrate, especially if the justification is that the contribution is greater than the subsidy received, a criticism which has been directed at all government intervention in economic activity where economy is equated with market. Similar skepticism can be directed at the assertion that the provision of art and culture leads to social, welfare, health, and even behavioral benefits. The problem of public participation, a value that usually trumps other measures of legitimacy, remains consistently difficult to resolve. The effect of audit is to prevent these tensions from becoming antagonisms. Audit simply allows agents to demonstrate that they are engaged in activities commensurate with the policy framework, even if these are contradictory as a consequence of the requirement that contesting positions are included in the context. By inclusion, agencies are linked to other agencies engaged with other elements of the framework. Hence, the causality of art and culture is linked with the causality of administration and policy. Behavior is changed in order to maintain participation in the framework. Competition over resource allocation is regulated through participation in an auditable framework, a process that skims off a portion of the surplus itself.

Thus, as a condition of audit, cultural activities have to be represented in a way that is auditable and that fits with the narratives of the policy framework. Here we can consider the case of the SAC, the agency with primary responsibility for the allocation and distribution of funds to support art in Scotland. In 2002, the Centre for Cultural Policy at the University of Glasgow published a report by Hamilton and Scullion (2002), which had been commissioned by the Scottish Executive. The report analyzes the effectiveness of the SAC's links with other agencies including "local authorities, social inclusion networks, the enterprise and tourism networks, artists and the cultural community more widely." The key point to note is that the existence of links is by itself considered evidence of effectiveness, as it verifies the causal model that the policy seeks to implement. As links are part of the Scottish Executive's requirements, their existence shows that these requirements are being met and that therefore the Scottish Executive's requirements are effective. The report simply asks the agencies with which the SAC has established links to evaluate their experience of working with the SAC. On the whole, these experiences are reported as positive, although some agencies express the political view that funding could come to them directly, which raises issues of the balance of power between the SAC and other agencies. Interestingly, the bureaucratic requirements are experienced as burdensome, especially with regard to application procedures for funding. All of which happily leads to the conclusion that such links should be strengthened by virtue of the fact that they exist. Art and culture are represented as a network of activities, each of which aims at contributing to one aspect of the policy framework by participating in a network that exists as a consequence of adherence to the policy. In other words, audit demonstrates the existence of the network because participating in the network is a requirement of audit.

The audit regime in politics and culture in the UK has attracted various types of criticism from across the political spectrum (see, e.g., McGuigan 2004; Mizra 2006).[6] An interesting academic critique of the phenomenon focuses on its instrumental aspect, whereby culture is intended to attain changes or effects in non-culture, insofar as the distinction can be made, such as wealth creation and social inclusion (Belfiore 2004). Of course, the instrumentalist analysis of culture and politics is not new and informs the development of Bennett's (1995) Foucauldian approach. However, the justification for subsidy has increasingly become posed in terms of investment, rather than a simple 'civilizing mission'. The positivist methodologies associated with audit provide an expectation that a return on investment can be shown by measurement, with the self-serving consequences of measurement failure being remedied by more measurement. More often, as Belfiore points out, the findings of audit are simply ignored, irrespective of their contribution to the success or failure of a project, as this preserves the political flexibility of the project itself. So on the one hand, the apparent depoliticization that follows from the force of the objectivity and neutrality of measurement gives rise, on the other hand, to a politics that shapes a non-auditable and non-representable space of action. Audit is a way of formulating politics in non-political terms or, perhaps, of creating a new type of politics. The dynamic of such a politics is suggested by Belfiore's (2004: 195) observation:

> Even more than other areas of public policy the arts have found in the justifying practices of audit and performance measurement a precious form of official validation. This, it could be argued, might represent for the arts a means to filling the legitimacy void caused by the erosion of cultural authority that followed the diffusion of theories of cultural relativism within the post-modern theoretical discourse. What we are suggesting is that, to a certain extent, rituals of verification (e.g. the obsession for policy targets and outcomes evaluation) might be seen as a surrogate for the arts' lost authority and legitimacy.

If this is so, perhaps demonstrating outcomes is less important than contesting authority and legitimacy. The following sections will try to show that the dependency within which art and culture are inscribed is not simply an effect of their participation in games of sticks and carrots. It is inherent in the notion of aesthetics itself. To establish that claim, the chapter will proceed to a discussion of the causality of aesthetics and then of government to determine which features of each combine in a regime of audit culture.

Games of Art and Life

To address the first point, we can turn to a larger account of the modern relation between aesthetics and politics, which has been recently outlined by the French political thinker Jacques Rancière (2002).[7] For Rancière, this relation is organized in terms of various permutations of the opposition between autonomy and heteronomy. The scope of Rancière's discussion is broad, ranging from Kant to Jeff Koons, but the decisive point concerns Schiller's *Letters on the Aesthetic Education of Mankind*, first published in 1794. The significance of Schiller's text is that it proposes a radical division between aesthetic experience and the objective position of aesthetic experience within life on the condition that art enjoys a privileged relation to aesthetic experience, and that aesthetic experience is understood in terms of the freedom and autonomy of 'play' rather than a strictly determined causal sequence to which the body is subordinate as the locus of aesthetic experience. For Rancière (ibid.: 137), this formula provides the basis on which "the division of our forms of experience" is framed and acts as a code from which a subsequent series of formulations emerge: "The key formula of the aesthetic regime of art is that art is an autonomous form of life. This is a formula, however, that can be read in two different ways: autonomy can be stressed over life, or life over autonomy—and these lines of interpretation can be opposed, or they can intersect." So on this basis we can outline three basic positions that give rise to innumerable possibilities which navigate relations between culture and politics. Such possibilities constitute moves in the game, or what Rancière calls 'emplotments', through which (1) art can become life, and life can become autonomous; (2) life can become art; and (3) art can become heteronomous. From the various combinations of these elements arises a 'meta-politics' of aesthetics, such as the demand that actual politics be subjected to aesthetic criteria, reconfiguring art as a political issue or asserting art as true politics.

The problem for Rancière (2002: 146) is that these possibilities have become too successful and familiar, since "nothing, however prosaic, escapes the domain of art." Even the critical denunciation of the banality of aesthetics has become part of the plot. Similarly, with postmodernism, the entropy of modernist aesthetics, the autonomy of art can be affirmed only by representing itself as heteronomous, at which point the relation between art and politics becomes a matter of bouncing between these various possibilities, depending on who is doing the politics and who is doing the art. Consequently, Rancière (ibid.: 151) maintains: "This means that there is a certain undecidability in the politics of aesthetics ... Aesthetic art promises a political accomplishment that it cannot satisfy, and thrives on that ambiguity." Which is to say that the political dimension of art rests on a paradox. Art aspires to something that is not art—even if this is understood as life becoming art—and cannot be achieved. Yet this does not cancel out the aspiration; rather, it confirms it by reference to that which would prevent it, that is, everything to which art is opposed. Hence, the politics of art is more art because the political dimension of art hangs on the failure of art to achieve its political objectives. Hence, insofar as art fails its political dimension, it is preserved. Hence, the paradox. Success depends on failure. This summarizes the political causality of art within modernity. As art fails to achieve its political effects, the solution is more art. This paradox has now become incorporated into the practice of audit, and, in the process, the political dimension of art has shifted. The relation between art and politics has been relocated from an antagonistic relation between art and that to which it is opposed to the internal workings of the promise and failure of art itself or to the uncertainty of the causal relations of art or to the undecidability of the relation between aesthetics and politics.

At stake in this suggestion is the axiomatic and self-evident status of the opposition between autonomy and heteronomy discussed by Rancière. To illustrate this opposition, and to understand its collapse, we can consider a classic formulation in which cultural autonomy is opposed to the heteronomy of administration, such that, within administration, culture aspires to be heteronomous in order to preserve its autonomy. The formula derives from Adorno's (1991: 93) proposition that "[w]hoever speaks of culture speaks of administration as well, whether that is his intention or not." Adorno was resigned to the total domination of what Max Weber had analyzed as the 'iron cage' of bureaucratic rationality simply because administration is the condition of existence. There is no position available to occupy that is radically exterior to this state of affairs. Nevertheless, Adorno (ibid.: 109) locates the promise of aesthetics within this dominated space—characterized by the clash of two autonomous logics, each heteronomous to the other, and where administration has the upper hand—in terms of an opportunity to preserve the autonomy of culture and thus redeem its political promise. Everything hinges on the structural limits of administration, the practical impossibility of administering everything, or the victory of time over space in which the contingent "planning of the non-planned" opens a space for excessive demands that are a "sublime form of sabotage." Such demands are enunciated by experts in culture in an antagonistic relation to specialists in administration. Thus, Adorno (ibid.: 113) outlines the ethical responsibility of the cultural expert in the following way: "The minimal differences from the ever-constant which are open to him define for him—no matter how hopelessly—the difference concerning the totality; it is, however, in the difference itself—in divergence—that hope is concentrated."

Through the unpredictability of culture, critical jurisdiction and aesthetic experience coincide in the sublime moment of administration, the moment in which administration does not know what to do precisely because the objectivity of administration is ruined. Yet this means that the political promise of culture is exhausted by the very act through which its negativity with respect to administration is affirmed and verified. Its effect is its cause. This is, as might be expected, of some consolation. But even in these circumstances, such an act depends on an opposition in which administration can be known objectively as a series of vertical and horizontal relations that organize the social totality, and culture can be experienced only contingently as an exception that falsifies the objectivity of administration. Today, this opposition can no longer be sustained because, at the risk of only a bit of exaggeration and distortion, culture has become everything and administration has become nothing. To put it another way, the objectivity of those structures and organizational forms that would determine action and causal relations has dissolved. This situation is referred to across the humanities and social sciences as 'postmodernity' or 'postmodernism' or 'postmodernization'. It is characterized by the generalized contingency of structures in which organizations are no longer understood as things but as processes and practices of organizing. In turn, these processes are overdetermined by globalization and deregulated regimes of capital accumulation and by an expansion of the politics of liberty and freedom, which lessens any possibility of subjection to hierarchical forms of rule and authority. The expansion of contingency even destabilizes the causality of communication itself, with meaning remaining tied to contexts that are opaque within acts of communication—hence, the dominance of the 'phatic' and 'indexical' dimensions of communication.

These developments allow for an explanation of the force of audit in relations between culture and politics that is not a simple reduction to the domination of heteronomous administration or capital accumulation over aesthetics at the price of the autonomy of the latter. This can be shown by reference to transformations of cultural policy itself. In their analysis of this sphere, Miller and Yudice (2002) summarize its characteristics in terms of institutions that link culture as an aesthetic hierarchy, established through criteria of judgments, with culture as a way of life, established through anthropological description. The institutional sphere is itself characterized by goal-focused regulatory activity that is organized through bureaucracies where objectives are set by wider political processes, including forms of democratic representation and participation and state support for economic and social development. However, the relation between these elements is far from that of a self-regulating, cybernetic system of control—even if the agents within it believe that it should be—and corresponds more to shifting and differentiated responses to unpredictable and unrepresentable events.

Hierarchies of judgment change, not least because of their critique, and opposing criteria can co-exist. Hence, Miller and Yudice (2002) point out that the self-image of policy as a direct causal link between the formation of political will and action is misleading, if not ideological. The institutional locations of policy formation, which are not confined to state and government, are also characterized by internal conflicts such that political action is never as consistent and homogeneous as it would like to appear. Consequently, Miller and Yudice (ibid.: 2) hold that "[p]erformativity, rather than constativity, characterises policy, and it is frequently made 'on the run', in response to unpredictable pressures." In that context, any conception that the political objective of cultural policy is to produce citizen-subjects regulated by hierarchies of taste will at best be marginalized, not because such a project is incorrect or opposed, but because it constitutes a commitment to permanence and fixity that cannot be sustained. Instead, cultural policy becomes characterized as the expansion of the administrative, managerial, and technocratic sectors into the production, distribution, and consumption of culture. Even more perversely, cultural policy is sustained by a client base that lobbies for cultural protection on aesthetic, anthropological, or economic grounds. Hence, the self-sustaining strategy of cultural policy is to play these conflicting demands against each other without becoming restrained to a fixed position. It can do this insofar as it develops the capacity to exploit its own failure to produce structures of linear causality in a context where that has become impossible. As Miller and Yudice (ibid.: 25) summarize the process, the aim of cultural policy has become the creation of "bureaucracies that deal with the problems that the very institutions of policies create."

In a subsequent argument, Yudice (2003) proposes that these developments become more intelligible if it is understood that culture has become represented in political models of causality as a resource. This is because the notion of resource is neutral with respect to projects and goals and condenses most of the claims made for the causality of culture at a general and abstract level, thus enabling its deployment in a variety of contexts where it can be subjected to calculation, planning, and molding, according to diverse and contradictory criteria of legitimacy. Thus, culture is an economic good in its own right in its commodity form, a means to preserve or transform established economic practices, and a general attribute of social well-being. All of these aspects of culture can be concretized in particular ways without fatal conflicts of incommensurability and contradiction arising.

Yudice is especially concerned to reveal how phenomena such as identity politics and notions such as cultural rights fit into and sustain this logic, whereby cultural difference has become a resource that trumps content in any allocation contest in neo-liberal regimes. Not only is the communitarian turn in social thought and policy overdetermined by the systemic requirement to manage the dislocations of capital accumulation, but also cultural policy seeks to establish communitarian enclaves against the cultural dislocations associated with the logic of capital accumulation, such as modernism and its avant-gardes and the stimulus to moral transgression provided by the culture industries. Hence, the modern conflict between culture as emancipation and governing as regulation can be squared insofar as emancipation becomes the acquisition of the status value fixed as different through the regulatory practices of intervention and representation. For Yudice, these logics are understood in terms of 'flexible articulation' in which claims for the subversive power of performativity—the idea of making up rules against the fixed conventions of a dominant culture and its symbolic representations—become otiose as there is no all-encompassing oppressive stability to subvert. Thus, Yudice (2003: 59) maintains that advocates of such positions, such as Butler, are "caught up in the very fantasy" that they aim to elucidate. If anything, the failure of the repetition of normative behavior enhances the logic of capitalist dislocation, and reactions to that process sustain capital accumulation.

If that conclusion might appear to be too neatly dialectical, it would be a mistake to assume that it leads to a telos of reconciliation. Rather, cultural policy sustains a regime of rule that may be characterized as liberal-democratic, but which nevertheless constitutes a process of 'governmentalization', according to Yudice's (2003: 49) analysis of Foucault, in which "the identitarian ticket to negotiate for respect and resources" is caught. Conflict is not eliminated or pacified but encouraged and managed in an interminable process of demands for recognition, in which the rule is to evade fixation through the others' understanding as a means to advance advantage and maximize interest on the basis of one's own exceptional predicament. Thus, with some permissible exaggeration, Yudice (ibid.: 55) claims that all group members seek to take their place "within the ensemble of recognized groups or to mobilize to be recognized as such on the basis of 'their culture.'" The old notion of a national/popular hegemonic unity defined against a common enemy has become irrelevant (ibid.: 90).

Beyond Audit

One of the assumptions underlying this chapter is that the instabilities of neo-liberalism signify that nothing is permanent and that attachment to specific forms and procedures reduces the opportunity for movement and thus, potentially, for dominance or, to use more neutral language, for winning the game. While audit may be experienced as coercive, the dimension of consent is usually underemphasized in terms of the benefits that agents receive from compliance. If the consensual aspect preserves some room for maneuver, it is also enjoyed by those forces seen as dominant. After all, getting 'locked in' to particular practices is disabling to those forces that implement them. If that is the case, it would be prudent to assume that the regime of audit is internally animated with questions about how to 'move on'. By the same token, that possibility ought to be taken into consideration by any forces that wish to shift the balance of power.

With that in mind, we can conclude by considering some of the implications of an argument by Canclini (1999) insofar as they address some of the issue raised in this chapter. Canclini accepts that the contemporary context is characterized by constant reorganization through the intersection of multiple and simultaneous processes in which relations between local, deterritorialized, and transcultural forms of art and communication oscillate. This process cuts across the antagonism between autonomous aesthetic experience and rationalistic hierarchies of judgment. In light of these phenomena, Canclini (ibid.: 373) suggests the importance of posing new conceptual and empirical questions appropriate to the context: "We need to discover if the actual organisation of the aesthetic field (producers, museums, galleries, historians, critics and the public) contributes, and in what way, to the elaboration of shared imaginaries ... In posing the problem in this way, it is possible to include in the question something about how art thinks today, even its innovative gestures: what capacity to think about a world orphaned of paradigms do transgressive or deconstructive works possess that are submitted to the order of the museums and the market?" Here the question is a matter of research at the meso-level, and the object is the formation of shared imaginaries. But notice how the causality of art is reconfigured as the action of thinking itself, without the guarantee of a paradigm. Most importantly, the aesthetic field is not external to the organizational processes of the museum and the market, as these processes contribute to the construction of a shared imaginary.

In fact, I would like to add that organizational processes themselves lack a paradigm in the sense of a ground of activity. Or, to put the same thing differently, organizational processes take place within a groundless context. Similarly, contemporary capitalism seeks to avoid being grounded in anything, as this might restrict the flexibility of capitalism. One of the reasons for this is that organizations—across the public and private spheres and across civil and corporate society—have not understood postmodernization as a problem to be solved and have not worked on a solution. Instead, they have just got on with it, responding and adapting pragmatically to their changed circumstances. Hence, the problem for aesthetic thinking is perhaps to establish its own groundlessness, which is distinct from simple modern autonomy. In this respect, a politics of art may involve a sort of counter-audit, a discovering, representing, and making objective of that which cannot be audited, and thus of that which is without grounds.

Acknowledgments

A version of this chapter was presented at the workshop on "The Arts and the State: Changing Discourses of Power and Influence in the Post-National State" at the University of Bergen, 16–18 September 2005. I wish to thank Judith Kapferer for the invitation and the participants for the stimulating discussion. An earlier version was presented at "Contemporary Art: The New Paradigms" at the Caixa Forum, Barcelona, 13–14 March 2004. I wish to thank Helena Tatay for the invitation and the participants and audience for the stimulating discussion. I would also like to thank Neil Cummings and Marysia Lewandowska in particular.

Jeremy Valentine works at Queen Margaret University, Edinburgh, where he teaches and conducts research in the area of culture and politics. He is co-author, with Benjamin Arditi, of *Polemicization: The Contingency of the Commonplace* (1999) and co-editor of the monograph series *Taking on the Political*. His publications deal with the intersections between political thought and cultural analysis.

Notes

1. Yudice coined this phrase in a paper presented at a conference, "Contemporary Art: The New Paradigms," at the Caixa Forum, Barcelona, in June 2004.
2. Laclau elaborated this model in *Hegemony and Socialist Strategy* (Laclau and Mouffe 1985) and has recently reaffirmed this notion of hegemony (Laclau 2005).
3. Audit is not reducible to the literal and usually neutral practice of making things accountable. Rather, audit is a method in which the literal sense is a technique of subjection and subjectification. As a consequence of its dominance, other forms of accountability, such as democratic ones, are usually neutralized, marginalized, or eliminated. Strathern (2000) and Shore and Wright (1997) provide good ethnographic accounts of how the audit regime is enacted and placed in various contexts. A simple, personal example might serve to illustrate its insidious nature. As an academic largely engaged in teaching, I am required by the institution I work for to provide a list of 'learning outcomes' for everything I teach. These have to be intelligible to administrators who are indifferent to content. Instead, they require 'learning outcomes' that verify that my teaching has modified the behavior of those I teach, a process that is called, without irony, 'quality audit'. Modified behavior is thus the outcome of the quality of what I teach. For more on this predicament, see Strathern (1997).
4. Arguably, audit regimes have been submerged within the profession of public relations. See Coffee (2006) and Valentine (2004).
5. The Scottish Executive, which was created in 1998 as part of the devolution process in the UK, is the legislative arm of the Scottish Parliament and the bureaucracy that supports it. Although it has some limited taxation powers, these have never been used. Thus, Scotland is subject to a dual system of government—the Westminster Parliament and Whitehall and the Scottish Executive. Elected Scottish MPs sit in the Westminster Parliament, and many are members of the UK government. The Scottish Arts Council also exists within this dual political structure. Formed through devolution, it mirrors the UK Arts Council and receives funding from both the Scottish Executive and the Whitehall-based Department for Culture, Media and Sport.
6. The magazine *Variant* is also very useful. See http://www.variant.randomstate.org (accessed 29 September 2006).
7. Rancière was one of the original authors of Althusser's *Lire le Capital* (Reading Capital).

References

Adorno, Theodor W. 1991. "Culture and Administration." Pp. 93–113 in *The Culture Industry: Selected Essays on Mass Culture*. Ed. J. M. Bernstein. London: Routledge.

Belfiore, Elinore. 2004. "Auditing Culture: The Subsidised Cultural Sector in the New Public Management." *International Journal of Cultural Policy* 10, no. 2: 183–202.

Bennett, Tony. 1995. *The Birth of the Museum*. London: Routledge.

Canclini, Nestor Garcia. 1999. "Remaking Passports: Visual Thought in the Debate on Multiculturalism." Pp. 372–382 in *The Visual Culture Reader*, ed. Nicholas Mirzoeff. London: Routledge.

Coffee, John C. 2006. *Gatekeepers: The Professions and Corporate Governance*. Oxford: Oxford University Press.

Hamilton, Christine, and Adrienne Scullion. 2002. *The Effectiveness of the Scottish Arts Council's Links with Other Agencies*. Glasgow: Centre for Cultural Policy Research, University of Glasgow.

Laclau, Ernesto. 2005. *On Populist Reason*. London: Verso.

Laclau, Ernesto, and Chantal Mouffe. 1985. *Hegemony and Socialist Strategy*. London: Verso.

McGuigan, Jim. 2004. *Rethinking Cultural Policy*. Basingstoke: Open University Press.

Miller, Toby, and George Yudice. 2002. *Cultural Policy*. London: Sage.

Mizra, Munira, ed. 2006. *Culture Vultures: Is UK Arts Policy Damaging the Arts?* London: Policy Exchange.

Power, Mike. 1997. *The Audit Society: Rituals of Verification*. Oxford: Oxford University Press.

Rancière, Jacques. 2002. "The Aesthetic Revolution and Its Outcomes: Emplotments of Autonomy and Heteronomy." *New Left Review* 14 (March–April): 133–151.

Scottish Executive. 2001. *Scotland's Cultural Strategy: Creating Our Future, Minding Our Past*. http://www.scotland.gov.uk/nationalculturalstrategy/docs/cult-00.asp (accessed 29 September 2006).

Shore, Chris, and Susan Wright, eds. 1997. *Anthropology and Policy: Critical Perspectives on Governance and Power*. London: Routledge.

Strathern, Marilyn. 1997. ""Improving Ratings': Audit in the British University System." *European Review* 5, no. 3: 305–321.

_____, ed. 2000. *Audit Cultures: Anthropological Studies in Accountability, Ethics and the Academy*. London: Routledge.

Valentine, Jeremy. 2004. "Audit Society, Practical Deconstruction and Strategic Public Relations." *parallax* 10, no. 2: 19–36.

Yudice, George. 2003. *The Expediency of Culture: Uses of Culture in the Global Era*. Durham, NC: Duke University Press.

Chapter 10

THE FEELING FOR GRAY
Aesthetics, Politics, and Shifting German Regimes

Inger-Elin Øye

Arriving in February 1991, my first strong impressions of eastern Germany, the former German Democratic Republic (GDR), were the looks and smells of the place, the physical, sensuous traces of a worn-down industrial, socialist society. Starting in Rostock on the Baltic Coast, I took in the gray, monotonous forms and colorings of docks, wharves, and huge concrete building estates, accompanied by the smells of Trabant[1] and coal pollution. The rural landscape in northeast Germany, the endless, rolling morainal pastures cultivated by collective farming, was consonant with this picture. The northern city of Schwerin,

Notes for this chapter are located on page 164.

capital of the present state of Mecklenburg-Vorpommern, offered some relief from this monotony with its beautiful lake surroundings and architecture: a fairy-tale castle with courtly gardens, the seat of the dukes and grand-dukes of Mecklenburg; a range of representative buildings in Gothic, baroque, Tudor, neo-classical, and art nouveau styles; and narrow winding alleys with traditional cottages, as well as functionalist brick housing estates.

However, the architectural variety was also draped in a gray, austere uniformity of an impoverished kind. Many buildings were in need of much more than paint and freshening up of ornamentation after decades of neglect. I heard west Germans proclaim that socialism had done more damage to cities than World War II. The condition of the buildings was read as a sign of a state ideology that constrained individual economic initiative as well as creativity. There was no elaboration of beauty for beauty's sake or for the sake of commercial interests. This was no shopping mecca; little energy was invested in window decorations or advertisements to attract people's attention. The remaining traces of the GDR's planned economy and restricted supply contributed to an image of eastern Germany as visually undernourished and less eventful, suggesting that East time had lagged behind West time. This image was reinforced by uniformed Soviet soldiers strolling Schwerin's streets, reminders of wartime and post-war occupation, and by unfashionable interiors of public buildings, such as the disco at the previous House of Soviet Friendship on Leninplatz, with its artificial colors and green plastic palms.

Complementing the monotonous, still standing images of the city center were the giant, pre-fabricated concrete housing units in the suburbs. In spite of its kinship with American Fordism, this type of building estate, called *Plattenbau*, was regarded as the epitome of GDR modernity. The estates' size, ubiquity, and monotony made them potent emblems of socialism. Celebrated by GDR officials as part of progressive, anti-fascist policies, they were decried by GDR critics as *Gleichschaltung*, brutal mechanical erasures of individuality. In 1989, the largest *Plattenbau* in Schwerin, Grosse Dreesch, housed 60,000 of the town's 130,000 inhabitants. Dreesch was bordered by woodlands and lakes, but to me these surroundings were a faint background to the sterile dormitory town's display of faith in social engineering and rational mastery over nature. Rows upon rows of yellow-gray building blocks, devoid of decoration, individuality, and spontaneity, were carved in straight lines—strict geometrical forms that were repeated in long and broad avenues for traffic.

I was soon fascinated by east German readings of and feelings for this, to me, drab, gray environment. Like my own understandings, theirs were imprinted by ideology and deeply engrained Western values. However, their perceptions were richer and more elaborate, expressing complex, tense relations between 'insides' and 'outsides'. I listened to how gray forms were endowed with warm, human qualities, including an *Innerlichkeit*, a sincerity, depth, and soul, that I, the outsider, had not discerned. Such readings were highly articulate in 1991 and 1992 on car trips to the old *Länder*. Returning home, crossing the old border, my east German co-passengers compared the prevailing physical differences between east and west. Western Germany stood out with its more colorful, busy, and lively commercial centers, its well-kept old public buildings, and its affluent housing estates. My co-passengers found these western façades shiny, clean, well-kept, and *bunt* (meaning colorful in a literal and metaphorically sense of being mixed or varied), in comparison to the east, which was acknowledged to be more gray, even dusty and dirty. Despite its less attractive appearance, the eastern environment was described as being more honest, modest, natural, human, and *innerlich*. It was in the east that these people felt *zu Hause* (at home).

Throughout the 1990s, Schwerin was marked by intense construction activity. Old buildings were torn down or completely renovated, and new buildings were erected. Parts of the city center went through a massive restoration. Years of deterioration were wiped out, and the decorative ornamentations of previous epochs and various architectural styles were highlighted. Sections of Grosse Dreesch were upgraded and painted in brighter colors; balconies were built, and a new infrastructure of shops was provided. Distinct GDR looks were disappearing. Russian soldiers, the Iron Curtain protectors, no longer traversed the streets. Apart from west Germans, global flows of travelers, goods, and consumption, including Italian, Greek, Chinese, Thai, and Turkish gastronomy, had found their way in. At Leninplatz, renamed Marienplatz, the House of Soviet Friendship was torn down and replaced by Schlosspark Center, the largest, most exclusive shopping center and boulevard in the city. Schwerin had become part of the big wide world, more commercial, beautiful, and *bunt*, attracting tourists with increasing success. How did east Germans experience this changing environment?

Renovation as the Deceptive Façades of the Market

In 1991 and 1992, I lived in the same neighborhood as Karl,[2] in a worn-down part of the city center in the typical two- or three-room flats in brick houses lacking maintenance on the outside and modern sanitary facilities on the inside. The flats had no private bathrooms, showers, or toilets; the communal toilet was in a cold corridor. The homes were heated by coal stored in the basement. Heavy loads of coal bricks were carried daily up several flights of stairs. By 1997, many buildings in this neighborhood had been renovated, and a lot of people had been on the move, some seeking a better place to live, others moving because they could not pay the raised rent. Karl, who was about 60 years old, stayed on in his non-renovated flat. One day, after a walk in the city, I asked Karl: "Don't you find Schwerin more beautiful?" Karl replied that he is not able to enjoy this or that façade, although they actually are beautiful. He finds them more sterile: "The modest and *beseelte* (spiritual) façades in the GDR were more human. The new façades and houses give an optical illusion of an improvement, but behind them is an ice-cold calculation, a very strong drive to make money." Karl's reaction did not come as a surprise but rather expressed what I have learned over the years are deep-seated views.

My first meeting with Karl took place in 1991, as I sat on a bench in the city center reading *Neues Deutschland*, a socialist paper and previous organ of the GDR ruling party, the Sozialistische Einheitspartei Deutschlands (SED).

Karl, sitting beside me, commented that this was the only newspaper depicting what was "really going on." He pointed at shops in front of us owned by west Germans, drawing a connection with the fact that east German products were no longer available in stores, that east German industry and agriculture were being downsized, and that unemployment in eastern Germany was rampant: "What is going on is a straightforward *Anschluss* (annexation) by west Germans." He compared post-unification capitalism to fascism, which to him indeed was much the same thing. Karl was afraid that this new, big Germany, where capitalism reigned, would bring a new Hitler to power.

Karl rooted his outlooks in his personal experiences: a simple, harmonious peasant childhood in East Prussia, followed by war, flight, and years spent in Soviet work camps that damaged his health and soul, and his hopes for and experiences with socialism. After World War II, Karl, one of the 12 million Germans expelled from Eastern Europe, chose to settle in the Soviet zone. He believed it was the better Germany in its break with fascism. Being himself a war invalid, retired early from work, and a single father of four children, Karl considered social security and *Geborgenheit*, the protection from capitalistic forces in the socialist GDR, invaluable. Karl had had no worries about work, income, education, or housing for himself and his children. Like many others, Karl's concern after unification was with what he referred to as an 'existential anguish' connected to how to make a living in a society marked by unemployment, eroding social security, and a growing gap between poor and rich.

By 1997, Karl was personally affected by the changed property relations. His perception of capitalist façades was fed by his dealings with his west German house owners, descendants of the original owners who had left the GDR and activated their property rights after unification. The house owners first gave an extremely friendly impression, but Karl soon discovered that they were trying to lure him into changing his GDR rent contract. Karl and his house owners were, like many other proprietors and renters, in a prolonged legal conflict with different interests at stake. The house owners presented themselves as offering *Wohltaten* (good deeds) by renovating and upgrading the flat; however, it was apparent to Karl that their motive was not his well-being but profit. He sees his situation in relation to other east Germans, who were forced to move from homes they had lived in for decades because they could not afford to pay the raised rent.

Karl proclaims that he does not want to renovate his flat, not even to refurbish it with new paint or furniture. He has everything he needs: "Old people, like small children, don't like changes ... If I won in Lotto, I wouldn't change a thing." In his flat and neighborhood, where he has lived for nearly 40 years, he enjoys family and friends and a sense of well-being. His understanding of the modest, spiritual, and human GDR is expressed in his distinction between living standards and life quality. Karl says that he had a relatively low living standard in the GDR, but the quality of life was higher in terms of social security, community, and solidarity. He used to call his neighborhood "the most beautiful village" in Schwerin, measured by the *Gemeinschaft* among the mainly simple, honest people living there. If Karl wanted to talk, he only had to stand outside his house for 5 or 10 minutes; somebody would stop and engage in a conversation usually lasting more than 30 minutes, often continuing in his flat over a cup of coffee. This hardly happens any more. Karl has seen how the community promoted by state-run organizations such as Nationale Volksfront, Hausgemeinschaft, and Strassenorganisation, as well as informal contact among people in the neighborhood, has crumbled after unification. The new anxieties accompanying capitalism, mainly regarding how to make a living, have resulted in people withdrawing from social life.

Socialism and the Bracketing of Beauty

Apparently for Karl, beauty in the form of renovated façades is bracketed, or comes in second place, in relation to compelling material and social concerns tied to the 'battle of existence'. Karl's story also indicates how state policies are filtered through particular life circumstances, including experiences of social vulnerability. His background as an empty-handed war refugee, an invalid, and a single parent helps explain why GDR policies that promoted equal life chances, social security, and communal solidarity found resonance in him and still guide his views on aesthetics.

The way that Karl ranked the modest, human, and spiritual GDR façades in his neighborhood above the beautiful renovated buildings resembles how other east Germans have evaluated Dreesch. During my first encounter with the building blocks, I was accompanied by a man who commented on my unspoken thoughts: "It isn't beautiful to look at, but during the GDR, these flats were attractive. Doctors, artists and dustbin men lived side by side here." He explained that this attraction was due to the shortage of housing in the GDR: old buildings could not be maintained because of the lack of craftspeople and building materials, and because it did not pay to do so. Compared with the living quarters in the old city, the flats at Dreesch offered comfort, with their inside toilets, bathrooms, and central heating. Others told me that the beauty of houses and historical buildings was indeed appreciated as an effort of human labor during the GDR, but that rich ornamentation was regarded as extravagance—a luxury for the few at the cost of the many.

Even more than views on Karl's neighborhood, views on the Dreesch revealed how ideas about attractiveness were conditioned by social and economic circumstances. Those who could afford it, moved away from Dreesch. As elsewhere in the GDR, the *Plattenbau* was regarded as becoming socially degraded, with a high concentration of unemployed and state benefit receivers and incidents of street aggression and violence committed by youths. Increasing economic and social stratification, as well as social avoidance among different groups, went hand in hand with residential segmentation. The inhabitants were no longer a composite slice of the population—manual laborers, doctors, and artists living side by side.

The housing shortage during the GDR was overtaken in post-unification eastern Germany by the problem of 'shrinking' towns and regions, manifested in abandoned flats. By 2003, Schwerin's population had shrunk from 130,000 to under 100,000, a depopulation tied to persistent high unemployment after unification. Amid renovated buildings and commercial liveliness, empty flats and houses manifested economic, social, and political disillusionment, circumstances used to explain youth violence and right-wing radicalism. The "blooming landscapes" prophesied by Chancellor Kohl in the 1990 elections were rather barren. Mecklenburg was soon nicknamed Germany's *Armenland* (poor land) and was perceived as a periphery in a globalized economy. The region's ability to catch up with the west in terms of work and prosperity was increasingly doubted. Eastern Germany was perceived as being left behind.

Dreesch, more than other residential areas, exemplified the negative aspects of economic development after unification—superfluous labor and human beings, abandoned homes, and islands of increasing poverty in the midst of plenty. The 'existential anguish' experienced by Karl and other east Germans was also informed by a historical understanding of the Third Reich catastrophe. In post-war GDR, *Aufbau* (building up), in contrast to restoration, referred to the double task of overcoming fascism and constructing a new, socialist state. This implied a constitutional right to a place to live and to work. Building was both a pressing practical problem in a post-war situation characterized by *Wohnungsnot* (lack of housing) and an ideological task that involved breaking free from the economic and social conditions that had favored fascism. Following Soviet guidelines, GDR building policies diminished the role of architects as form makers by placing them under state control and substituted them with building engineers who abided by efficient, low-cost industrial production (cf. Hannemann 2004). Issues of form and beauty were subordinated and fused with social function and socialist goals.

The socialist, anti-fascist 'functionalist' meanings of buildings and building policies can be found in samples of *Bauzeitung*, the newspaper of the building cooperative in Schwerin in the 1950s and 1960s, and in a promotional book published in connection with the fortieth anniversary of the GDR (Büttner 1989). Schwerin and the Mecklenburg region, characterized by previous agrarian backwardness, figure as prime examples of socialism's advantages. Dreesch, awarded the GDR Architecture Prize in 1979 and presented as the largest, most beautiful *Plattenbau* in the area, is given a prominent place in this history. The natural surroundings of Dreesch's beauty are outlined, but also its social facilities and generally improved living conditions for ordinary people. When such improvements are quantified in sanitary facilities—in 1961, only 12 flats out of 100 in the inner city had a bath or shower and 22 of 100 a toilet, whereas in 1985, 73 flats out of 100 had a bath or shower and 71 of 100 a toilet (ibid.: 314)—the backdrop of historical class cleavages and the reasons for fascism are evoked.

The duchy of Mecklenburg's long-term history, more than that of most German lands, supports a broadly shared historical hypothesis that absolutism, feudalism, and class cleavages provided fertile ground for the acceptance of Nazism (see Karge, Münch, and Schmied 1993). The Nationalsozialistische Deutsche Arbeiterpartei (NSDAP, or Nazi Party) gained the majority of votes in the Schwerin Landtag (regional parliament) in 1932, one year before Hitler won the national elections. The alliance between Nazis and Mecklenburg's rural estate owners, the Junkers, who held on to an antiquated feudal system at great cost to peasants and commoners, was given great weight in the GDR, as was the Nazis' tendency to invent and thrive on rural traditions and folklore. In Marxist understandings of how agrarian backwardness led to support for the Third Reich, Dreesch emerged as a multi-layered symbol of progress. Overcoming fascism was fused with faith in urbanization, industrialization, and the forging of an empowered, enlightened working class.[3] The building of Dreesch in the 1970s combined these factors, linking urbanization, as Schwerin attained the attractive status of *Grossstadt*, passing the 'magic' number of 100,000 inhabitants (a near doubling of the population after the war), to the growth of industrial plants and a labor force.

People's readings of and feelings for the built environment must be seen in relation to an understanding of such ups and downs in a personal, regional/ national, economic, social, and political history—a history in which a Marxist interpretation of the evils of capitalism, including its relationship to fascism, found resonance and new significance after unification. However, the perception of aesthetics, such as the bracketing of beauty of renovated houses performed by Karl and others, draws on an imagery of façades, which deserves more attention. The imagery leads us to look more closely at how people perceive capitalism and other powerful social forces impinging on their lives and to examine how they deal with them.

The Pervasive Imagery of Façades

To Karl, the bright and shiny façades of buildings are but one manifestation of capitalism, matched by the new façades of people's appearance and sociality. He critically comments on how shop assistants after unification are not so natural any more. Their use of make-up and manner of dressing, artificial smiles, and friendliness, combined with strenuous 'small talk' and the persistent question, "Can we help?"—all are efforts geared toward selling products. Karl has a daily walk in town with regular stops, including visits to several second-hand dealers. With these people, he does not have what he calls the "superficial five-minute chat." Like those he used to have in his neighborhood, the conversations can last for hours. He enjoys them because the second-hand dealers "nehmen alles wahr"—that is, they perceive the truth of what is "really going on" (underneath the surface of things).

In a similar way, east Germans would talk about west German bureaucrats, mostly men, who came to work in Schwerin's Landtag after unification. Walking around in suits and ties, and sometimes driving an expensive car, such as a Mercedes, they embodied *neue Zwänge*, new compulsions toward conformity connected to the market—to show through dress and consumption 'who you are' and to call attention to status differences. I was repeatedly told how this behavior contrasted with the GDR practice whereby employers and employees both followed the same, more casual dress code. To the east Germans, the suit-dressed west German men also embodied a system of deception. Their smart looks, I was told, often did not match their abilities. People voiced complaints: Why were all these west Germans offered jobs when so many east Germans were unemployed? Why were not east Germans offered re-education, a second chance? First, they accepted these west Germans, believing that they were better qualified. However, over the years, the perception was that the westerners coming to the East were often second- or third-rate professionals, individuals who, in contrast to former GDR citizens, had been given a superb chance to make a career after unification. Another group of west Germans perceived as deceptive, who also made their entry after unification in suits and ties, were the salesmen knocking on people's doors, trying to sell their carpets, vacuum cleaners, and insurance policies. At first, they made a professional, trustworthy impression, but they soon gained notoriety, being seen as sly or even fraudulent.

Although this deceptive, pretentious self-presentation was particularly tied to certain groups, it was also viewed as an intrinsic aspect of west German society. East Germans regarded themselves as more modest and honest and less self-assertive in conduct and self-opinion. They were not trained to stick out, to sell products or themselves. The saying was that west Germans learned in school, in work interviews, or through interaction with the media to be more *Selbstbewusst*, that is, self-confident and assertive. This image of the east being more modest and sincere than the deceptive, more impressive, and attractive façades of the west was tied to a multitude of events in people's everyday lives, including the wrapping of commodities. The attractive paper on everything people bought in shops, sometimes even single sweets, contrasted strongly with the modest, often non-existent wrapping paper in the GDR. This art of wrapping was considered an aesthetic, luxurious pleasure but also a big waste. Furthermore, the term *Verpackung* (packaging) functioned as a metonym, depicting the energy that capitalism channeled into shaping attractive, seductive façades in general, not only in the wrapping of commodities, but also in the conduct of people and politicians, who followed the same practice of 'selling' themselves in a seductive, appealing manner.

Contrasting the shiny façades of the market and west German society, east Germans were ascribed not only a modest appearance but also worthy qualities not visible on the outside. I noticed how people like Christina and Joachim, who worked in the culture sector, dressed modestly and discreetly, usually in earth colors such as gray and brown, as if they wore camouflage to blend in with their surroundings. I once asked Christina about her use of clothing, including colors, and was told it was a natural reflex. She found it comfortable not to stick out; it offered her a kind of protection so that she could spend her energy on other things. Not being quite conscious about it, I myself adopted a non-conspicuous, even austere dress code, something Karl noticed one day when we met by coincidence in town. He commented on my clothing as a good strategy for a researcher. I could more easily move about without people paying attention to me and take in all kinds of observations.

The Shadow Life behind Façades

Over the years I came to see how east Germans' notions of façades went along with modes of accommodation and resistance to regimes in the past and present. The imagery of façades played on relations, often tensions, between 'outsides' and 'insides', and was linked to notions of form versus content, and to pressures toward conformity against submerged forms of dissent. This impression was sustained by visiting and living with east Germans and by a fascination for the aesthetics of homes. In contrast to common views about the GDR as a socialist society forging equality and community at the cost of conformity, I came to see how homes harbored creative, individual, and critical expressions, revealing dimensions of life in the GDR not visible on the surface of buildings or when taking GDR official policies at face value.

In the autumn of 2002, Christina and Joachim, both born in the 1940s, were having one of their regular discussions about the pros and cons of the GDR and the Federal Republic of Germany (FRG) as political systems. Christina, highly critical of the GDR's authoritarian traits, used the *Plattenbau* as an example of a stereotyped, conformist GDR culture that eroded individualism. Joachim protested: "In those concrete buildings you might have an entrance 100 people used, with little signs of individuality. However, when you entered these flats, they were all different." Christina and Joachim continued disputing a while before they reached their usual, underlying agreement: "After unification, individual freedom is also harnessed. The market brought with it *neue Zwänge* (new compulsions) tied to consumption."

The individualism evoked by Joachim was something I had noticed and sensed but had not heard so clearly articulated in words before. Crossing the thresholds of people's homes, either in *Plattenbauten* like Dreesch or in the old city, I sensed a creativity hiding, or maybe just as much protected, behind the cloak of the monotonous, gray façades. I was taken by the energy and care spent carving out living spaces, and by the aesthetic preferences evinced in practical, functional solutions combined with organic features.

The young couple I lived with in 1991 and 1992, both of them *Handwerker* (crafts workers), were born in the late 1960s and lived in the same neighborhood as Karl. Their three-room flat resembled many young people's homes, with its minimalist touch. The walls were white and mostly naked. There was no 'sitting room' or couch, but a multi-purpose wooden dining table with old wooden chairs, an antique wardrobe, and a wooden bookshelf. Green plants, a bird in a wooden cage, and earth-colored pottery gave an organic feeling, as did the open use of rooms, one with a handmade bed. Sleeping, eating, working, and other activities were not sharply separated into different spaces. Books, sports gear, camera equipment, and a carpenter's bench were evidence of a life filled with numerous hobbies and activities. Handmade shoes, clothes, and jewels, which had been cherished in the GDR with its limited supplies, contributed to a personal, creative atmosphere. The organic-like interior extended to a backyard, a natural, lush place with an unmowed lawn, trees, weeds, and flowers, where breakfast was eaten on warm mornings.

My insight into the interior of houses changed my opinion about the shabby exteriors of the worn-down buildings. The gray façades no longer denoted a sterile conformity. I came to see how gray walls, with their earth-like colors and their state of deterioration, resembled organic life processes: the development of individual differences, coming of age, and decay. I developed a better feeling for gray. The notions of modest, natural, human, and *innerlich* east German façades gained meaning, not only in relation to socialist policies that supported equal life chances and social security, but also with regard to the use and meaning of homes as living spaces in which people creatively arranged their lives in accommodation and resistance to GDR economic and political structures.

I was told and saw how east Germans, due to the sluggish economy and shortage of crafts people and goods during the GDR, had been urged to improvise practical solutions. Many houses and pieces of furniture were partly made by people themselves or with the help of friends. My hosts, the crafts workers, were still visited regularly by friends and acquaintances, who asked them to repair or make things. Shortages in the GDR had fostered a second economy built around personal networks for exchange, in which crafts people were important nodes. I was told that money used to have little value in relation to *Beziehungen*, the informal networks for the exchange of goods and services. Taking part in a work party of a sports group that was helping a couple move into a new house, I was informed, with regret, that such forms of reciprocity are in decline. The GDR shortages had forged a *Notgemeinschaft*, a community based on scarcity, in which people were locked into relations of interdependency as they coped with the practicalities of their daily lives. After unification, people increasingly purchased services and materials on the market, with its impersonal relationships. Likewise, the political pressure toward conformity during the GDR was acknowledged as having generated specific networks and forms of solidarity. The pervasive surveillance of the secret police, the Stasi, in public spaces made the home a vital arena for critical discussions about the state in small, trusted circles of family members and friends. The home was furthermore associated with the GDR as *Leserland* (reading country). I was told how people immersed themselves in cherished books that had been forbidden by the GDR state and secretly passed on by friends. Officially permitted literature by GDR or Soviet authors, such as the books of the most celebrated GDR author, Christa Wolf, also had an important critical function by giving voice to a subjectivity and to critical aspects of everyday life, challenging official representations and glorifications of the GDR.

Without intending to, the GDR state's attempts at social engineering and control forged a rhizome-like counter-society of activities and networks, including non-prescribed interpretations, that spread their roots in and between the more sheltered spaces of homes, taking the form of a shadow life, not only in conflict with but at times symbiotically feeding on, reproducing, intertwining with, and modifying official GDR structures. This counter-society displayed an intricate balance of resistance and accommodation. The GDR state's effort to control also nourished 'inward-bound', withdrawn articulations of individual-ity—'night shadow' flowers, not daylight flowers—that flourished behind gray, seemingly conformist façades, sometimes permeating official policies.

The shadow life of intricate, double-layered meanings of GDR literature also characterized the theater. A play script, which had passed through the organs of censorship and had been deemed politically correct, could still convey a powerful critique. Meaning could be manipulated by the inter-textuality of words and staging, costume, and tone of voice. Again and again, I heard people say that the Schwerin theater, rated as the third best in the GDR, was not only politically engaged but *anspruchsvoll* (demanding, of high quality), referring not only to the director and performers, but also to the effort demanded of the audience, in their reception, digestion, and discussion of the plays. Early in 1989, the much admired theater director Christoph Schroth staged *Wilhelm Tell* by Schiller, which had been banned by the Nazis, to celebrate the 200th anniversary of the French Revolution and 40 years of GDR rule. Symbols and texts were twisted into a critique of the existing GDR socialism, and this played an important role in mobilizing people during the revolutionary autumn of 1989 (cf. also McGowan 2001). Again, the imagery of façade was in play. The seemingly conformist GDR theater encouraged a critical political engagement involving a decoding and search for hidden messages, tied to what people called "durch die Blumen reden" (to speak through flowers, or to read between the lines). After 1989, the *anspuchsvoll* GDR theater was placed in opposition to the 'entertainment' theater—a theater that had been granted economic and political independence and was no longer charged with educating the people. Under the reign of market forces, the theater to a greater extent had to gener-ate income, and did so by staging what people perceived as 'light' operettas in order to satisfy the tastes of broader west German audiences, who were bussed into town to attend the productions.

After unification, the shadow lives—the withdrawn forms of individualism, creativity, political commentary, and critique—seemed to live on in relation to capitalism. Not renovating, not shining up homes or 'catching up with the Joneses', not investing in the new façades of the revised economic and social order went with a sophisticated aesthetic resistance, which was symbolic and embodied in practices not always articulated in words. Although Joachim and Christina had strongly conflicting political opinions on the GDR and FRG, they shared critical views about the market and consumption, its waste and environmental problems, with implications for their life-style. Neither Joachim nor Christina had renovated, decorated, or invested in new furniture after uni-fication. They spent their little money and more abundant energy on cultural activities and socializing apart from work.

Their homes, like many others, are marked by a functional, practical use. The lack of refurbishment adds to their outspoken organic, creative qualities. Joachim's two-room flat on the Dreesch consists of a bedroom, small kitchen, bathroom, corridor, and living room. The living room, as in many alterna-tive homes, does not have a 'sitting-room arrangement' with a couch as the fulcrum; rather, there is a multi-purpose dinner table, used for eating meals, socializing, working, and creating, that is usually crowded with items needed for his last activity. The shelves in the living room are filled with books, records, and equipment tied to his previous work at the Schwerin theater. Joachim does not feel comfortable in *kleinbürgerliche* (bourgeois arrangements). His creative disorder is signaled by his non-attention to a bourgeois façade of exaggerated order and by his paying attention to cultural and social activities that matter more. Christina has a similar functional and practical arrangement. She also has held on to her old GDR interior. The aged appearance of her apartment, with its well-used furniture and white goods, gives her flat a homey, natural look. Signs of creativity and anti-materialism go hand in hand. Christina has no couch. The middle point in her living room is a multi-purpose single table (the kind usually reserved for gardens) that is made of plastic and painted blue. Numerous paintings, photos, and books decorate her walls. From the ceiling hangs a self-made lamp with various waste-plastic items painted in cheerful colors and glued on as decorations. On her bookshelf are arranged some of her art pieces—small cardboard boxes onto which are glued motifs cut out of colorful advertisements. One cardboard box is completely covered with cutouts of eyes in different varieties and sizes; one is covered with mouths, another with hands, and one with meat.

Karl's perception of the renovated buildings after unification, which he links to a capitalist system generating profit and inequality, has its counterpoint in his resistance to changing anything in his sparsely furnished flat. The painted walls and ceiling bear the marks of age and cigarette smoke. To Karl, the deceptive façades of the market are contrary to his appreciation and cultivation of what he refers to as "natural." His feeling for the natural permeates his aesthetic judgment and practice and is applied to a better, truer mode of existence, to his sense of true self, his individuality and idea of democracy. This thinking is most strongly expressed with regard to the garden plot that he calls his "exile," which is basically as he describes it: "500 square meters of wilderness," "a garden with old fruit trees, flowers, weeds, and grass growing naturally together." It lies at the end of a long row of other allotment gardens and purposely stands out with untidy life processes. Karl is conscientious about not mowing the lawn, not pulling out weeds, not organizing the natural processes of difference, growth, and decay.

Karl's self-understanding as an individual is expressed through these aesthetics of home and garden, in resistance to market forces and a bourgeois order and conformity, and is guided by his understanding of the Nazi past. Karl proclaims no identification with anything German, rejecting its orderliness and conformity, even its high culture. Karl identifies himself as Eastern European— if German at all, then east German, as they, in contrast to west Germans, "have a soul." The wilderness of his garden plot, where plants and weeds grow side by side undisturbed, is what he refers to as his idea of democracy. Karl's garden 'exile' is more than symbolism: it was and remains his 'escape', where he, a strict atheist, receives sustenance for body and soul and healing for his wartime wounds. This is the place where he feels well-being and real life quality—it is the place he says he cannot do without.

Aesthetics, State Construction, and Reconstruction

How have all these powers and dominions, all those glittering prizes been won? Were they not gained at the price of spiritual death—enslavement to an inhuman, soulless, machine-like political, social, cultural system, all those arrogant French officials with whose aid the renegade Francophile King Frederick in Berlin is trying to crush all that is spontaneous and original in Prussian lands ... But there was one region which even the proud French had no access to, that of the human spirit, the true inner life—the free autonomous human spirit, which they, the Germans, had preserved inviolate, the spirit that seeks its own path to fulfilment and will not sell itself for material benefits. (Berlin 1996: 240)

England and Germany are related in the same way as form and content, appearance and reality ... [I]n England people are distinguished by outward packing. You need not be a gentleman, you must only have the means to appear one, and you are one, and you need not be right, you must only find yourself within the forms of rightness, and you are right ... The German lives in order to live, the Englishman in order to represent. (Theodor Fontane, cited in Elias [1939] 1994: 28)

East German interpretations and actions in a range of contexts—the built environment, the 'styling' or 'non-styling' of homes and gardens, dress and conduct, literature and theater—are guided by a visual imagery of façades and relations between 'insides' and 'outsides', echoing an age-old antithesis between *Kultur* and *Zivilisation*. Modest, sincere, natural, and spiritual conduct, associated with *Kultur* and 'inwardness', is opposed to and regarded as superior to the 'exteriority' of *Zivilisation*, with its shiny, flat, and seductive appearances (cf. Elias [1939] 1994). I suggest that east German aesthetic discourse, including subversive non-verbal, everyday acts of resistance to economic and political forces, has been formed and informed by a long, historical interpenetration of aesthetics and politics. This view does not presuppose a reified concept of German culture and character evolving smoothly through time. Indeed, assumptions about cultural continuities, including notions of a German *Sonderweg* (a special path of development) are increasingly questioned against a state history marked by fragmentation and fissures. A focus on imagery turns attention to how ideas and orientations at one and the same time have persistent and plastic qualities, and how they gain new relevance and are reproduced within particular social structures—in this case, early German state building and later efforts at state de- and reconstruction

Norbert Elias ([1939] 1994) gives insight into how the imagery of *Kultur* versus *Zivilisation* transformed from denoting a specific social stratum, the *Bildungsbürgertum* (middle-class intelligentsia) in opposition to other German groups, especially the Francophile aristocracy, into national emblems, particularly after the Napoleonic wars, symbolizing Germans in opposition to French. The upwardly mobile, increasingly educated but, in contrast to their French and British counterparts, politically disenfranchised bourgeoisie were the proponents of an extraordinary cultural and intellectual blossoming tied to a refinement of the German language, which had been discarded by the political elite. In this predicament, they demarcated themselves as proponents of *Kultur*, *Geist* (spirituality or creative genius), and *Bildung* (education or self-cultivation), associated with 'inwardness' in opposition to the aristocracy's 'outwardness', their refined, superficial, deceptive, and French-inspired courtly manners and speech. As highlighted by, for example, Dominic Boyer (2005: 46–98) and Eric Wolf (1999: 209–211), the contextual, intertwined semantic referentiality of *Kultur*, *Geist*, and *Bildung*, like the categorization of the *Bildungsbürgertum*, escapes a short (English) translation.

The intellectual bourgeoisie spearheaded the nineteenth-century formulation of the German *Kulturnation*, preceding the 'belated' German nation-state, but the antithesis of *Kultur* and *Zivilisation* lived a longer life. The imagery has proved throughout history to be powerful and enduring, yet also flexible, expressing resentment against French dominance and society, including the French Revolution, and a wide spectrum of modernizing processes—liberal democracy, industrialism, capitalism, scientific knowledge, the objectification of nature, and Western logocentrism. It channeled sentiments toward model countries of modernity and Germany's political rivals in the fight for supremacy: first France, later Great Britain, and then the United States. During the Weimar Republic, with its political and aesthetic radicalization and polarization, the imagery found expression in the German *Kulturkritik* of Americanism, in debates about conservative traditionalism and radical modernism.[4]

It is well-known that aesthetics was not an epiphenomenon but rather played a crucial role in Third Reich ideology and politics. Decisive action was based on fatal aesthetic criteria, such as those prescribed by Joseph Goebbels, the minister for public enlightenment and propaganda. One of the most influential Nazi political figures, Goebbels, who had been educated in philosophy, art history, and literature, was assigned by Hitler to become his heir. Apart from planning gigantic visual spectacles for the purpose of disseminating Nazi ideology, Goebbels put in motion the book burning at Bebelplatz, the Munich exhibition of degenerate art, including modernist art with alleged decadent Jewish/Bolshevist influences, as well as the *Kristallnacht* pogrom. The antithesis of *Kultur* and *Zivilisation* underpinned the distinction between 'beautiful' and 'ugly', 'healthy' and 'degenerate', while 'nature' and 'life' were associated with *Volk* on the side of that to be preserved against decadent forces and people. Aesthetic categories guided notions of purity and pollution that were employed in ethnic cleansing and the political persecution of Jews, Bolshevists, and other groups. During the Cold War, the imagery was transferred to German partition. The Soviet-controlled GDR employed the conceptual antagonism of *Kultur* and *Zivilisation* in its portrait of the FRG as a German colony, an Anglo-American civilization of consumerism, capitalism, and materialism. The GDR was portrayed as the 'better' Germany, with its heritage of humanism, spirit, and culture, and with morals and truth on its side (Gillen 1999: 87).

The imagery of *Kultur*, rather than supporting a nationalist narrative of a primordial culture, a German *Geist* evolving through history and eventually finding its true expression, may be understood as having been shaped by the absence of natural boundaries, be they cultural, political, or geographical. Aesthetics were at the center of internal and international strife and warfare, and were thereby charged with political meaning. As states and elites attempted to control artistic content, aesthetics were reproduced as potent expressions of compliance, withdrawal, and resistance. Among them were controversial acts of 'inner emigration', including the role of poets during the Third Reich; by dwelling on the experience of nature as a source of poetic inspiration and a refuge from the pain of the world, they were seen as supporting Third Reich policies (Leeder 1998: 200). The ruptured twentieth century, with its repeatedly perceived task of state construction and deconstruction, of breaking with the traditions of past regimes, sharpened the political potency of aesthetics. The abyss after the Third Reich, the crushing defeat, and the recognition, passed on by the Allied victors, of total moral failure charged aesthetics with an urgent political and educational task. This involved revising the content and forms of art and aesthetics.

Cultural and aesthetic guidelines in post-war Germany were defined by the victors within competing ideological frameworks. Occupied by the United States, Great Britain, and France, and equipped with a liberal democratic constitution, West Germany sought to break with the Nazi past by giving aesthetics an autonomous role. Inspired by Theodor Adorno—who, with the 'inner emigration' of poets in mind, coined the famous words, "To write poetry after Auschwitz is an act of barbarism," denoting the unbridgeable breach of civilization that Auschwitz represented and the impossibility of continuing any cultural tradition in Germany—poets, musicians, artists, architects, and designers sought to undertake an 'artistic' Marshall Plan. To break with the traditionalist approach promoted by Nazism, they embraced abstract modernism and drew on pre-1933 German modernist currents, such as the Bauhaus school, that had been condemned by Hitler (cf. Betts 2004; Heinze 1999: 73).

In the Soviet-occupied eastern zone, the failure of the German people to rise up against Hitler and the moral superiority of communism and the Soviet resistance were used as arguments to install an 'educational' Communist dictatorship over the populace (see Herf 1997: 30).[5] Classical German *Bildung* had not prevented the Nazis' descent into barbarism. The urgency to forge a politically engaged aesthetics was expressed by Bertolt Brecht in his famous complaint about the times, when "a conversation/About trees is almost a crime,/Because it includes a silence about so many misdeeds"[6]—a commentary on the 'inner emigration' and failure of Third Reich poets and intellectuals (Leeder 1998: 200). GDR cultural policies mainly followed the Moscow doctrine: progressive art was identified with realism, reflecting social reality, although there were exceptions, such as Brecht's theory of *Verfremdung* (distanciation). The GDR largely reproduced Third Reich forms decried in the West by duplicating the military spectacles of state parades, by embracing social realism and condemning abstract art, and by blending the true, the good, and the beautiful in representations of workers and their conditions. The pervasive control and censorship of aesthetics and the theatrical façades of public culture also had unintended consequences, forging submerged modes of resistance. According to art historian Eckhart Gillen (1999: 86), the monopolization of the GDR political sphere by the SED ruling party transplanted political discourse to aesthetics, which became a compensation for poor and bad politics, overloaded with issues about politics and morality, and a substitute sphere for critical discourse.

What I propose is that the imagery of façades inherent in the antagonism of *Kultur* versus *Zivilisation* also provided a lingua franca, a verbal and non-verbal 'vocabulary' feeding on a visual imagery of the distinction between 'inside' versus 'outside', form versus content, which transformed officially prescribed and censored GDR art. Aesthetic works and expressions were loaded with multi-layered meanings, stretching the state censorship's efforts to imprint univocal messages in the forms of social realism. According to Gillen (1999: 86), artists shared a quiet consensus to refrain from using confrontational titles for their works and also to avoid unequivocal interpretations. Through complicated allegories and metaphorical codes, literature, theater, and painting became a source of political discourse. State control of cultural expression enforced a resistance in terms of aesthetic 'readings' and of searching for hidden, deeper meanings and truths under the surface appearances of texts, actions, and buildings. This is the kind of interpretation that people in Schwerin refer to as reading between the lines. It is an art of interpreting and acting with parallels to what Paul Ricoeur has called a "hermeneutics of suspicion," associated with Marx, Nietzsche, and Freud, in their critique of modernity and shared suspicion toward surface meanings of cultural phenomena, "because their genesis is 'overdetermined' by motivational factors not immediately accessible to the producers of that meaning" (cited in Bowie 1998: 140). The imagery of façades depicts not only the dual character of social life in authoritarian states, but also how non-conspicuous 'shadow life' forms of individuality, creativity, and freedom thrive in these circumstances.

Protestant Aesthetics

In order to grasp the potent and subversive political import of aesthetics in everyday articulations, we must address aesthetics as culturally variable notions of self and personhood. Isaiah Berlin (1996) and Louis Dumont (1986) help us do this by tracing the German concept of *Kultur* back to the Reformation and its spiritual, inward-bound individualism. In the German lands, the spiritual individualism of the Reformation did not translate into the political individualism of liberal democracy, as it did in the constitutions of France, Britain, and the United States. The withdrawn, non-worldly religious spirituality of the Reformation transformed into the *Geist* of *Kultur*, a cultural spirituality with an intricate relation to state power, informing a radical individualism and resistance to worldly powers, as well as subjection to absolutist and authoritarian rule.

Berlin points to an interesting continuity in Protestant and Romantic thought: the Lutheran concept of *Beruf* (vocation) is exalted in Romantic philosophy with its new, revolutionary aesthetic ideals. Romanticism, a countermovement to the Enlightenment that had a particularly strong following in the German lands, defines the essence of humans not as the capacity to reason or understand, but as the faculty to create and express after the model of the artist: "Art is not imitation, nor representation, but expression. I am most truly myself when I create—that, and not the capacity for reasoning is the divine spark within me" (Berlin 1996: 179). It was this aesthetic model of humanness translated into social and political terms that was destined to play such a fatal role during the Third Reich. Doctrines of nationalism and fascism rest on models of morality and freedom derived from artistic creation. The support for a strong leader and dictator, along with accompanying non-egalitarian, hierarchical notions of humans, was underpinned by a celebration of the creative genius (ibid.: 188): "Men are not equally gifted; either men are endowed with creative powers or not. If they are 'asleep' or passive, they must serve the ends of the creators and achieve their fulfillment by being molded by them; and though violated, tortured or destroyed in the process, they are lifted to a higher level than that to which they could have risen by their own efforts." Berlin also points to the broad and at the same time fundamental understanding of creativity (ibid.): "What Napoleon did with people is the counterpart of what Beethoven did with music and Shakespeare did with words. All are vast creations of the human spirit." Berlin is in line with Walter Benjamin's characterization of fascism as the 'aesthetization of politics'. Both sidestep the issue of identifying a fascist style and address the explosion of aesthetics.

Berlin also gives an opening for acknowledging continuity from Protestant ethics of *Berufung* (inner calling) to a Romantic aesthetics of resistance. Protestantism's stress on the voice within—on withdrawal from the external world in order to cultivate the spiritual, simple life—informs a radical individuality. Berlin not only traces continuity from Protestantism to Romanticism, but also includes Kant's immense stress on inner-directedness and independence, and how it is intensified by his Romantic successors in their resistance to anyone and anything that diminishes or threatens their 'inner kingdom'. Protestant values of inner life and freedom are framed in a celebration of the heroic martyr, the lonely thinker or artist struggling against alien values. The ideal is to be true to one's inner vision and follow one's conviction, never to sell out or compromise for the sake of success, power, or peace—not even for survival. The consequence of the belief that men are the authors of values is that what matters is one's own inner state, motive, integrity, sincerity, fidelity in principle, purity of heart (ibid.: 185). Romanticism's Protestant heritage, with its emphasis on inner life, gives priority to the motivation behind acts rather than their results, to self-sacrifice over worldly rewards.

In Martin Ahrends's (1991) sorrowful yet highly ambivalent obituary to life in the GDR, we can recognize Protestant and Romantic themes. Ahrends applies the metaphor of Sleeping Beauty surrounded by a thorn hedge to depict the GDR as a Janus-faced system. The suppression of GDR life and its barbedwire encapsulation from the outside world also forged a sense of freedom, one associated with depth. Evoking visual differences between the drab east and sparkling west, Ahrends connects contrasting aesthetic façades to different ways of life, to 'inside' and 'outside' orientations and notions of freedom, which also characterize the labyrinthine forms of eastern prose. Ahrends, an author and former GDR citizen who moved to West Germany in 1984, due to his work prohibition in the GDR, gives a personally informed account of subtle forms of resistance in the GDR tied to a fuzzy counter-public sphere, in which people, juggling with state dictums and restrictions in their everyday lives, saw all kinds of acts, such as hand-crafting toys and composing music, potentially as acts of resistance that evoked meanings different from the official interpretation. His notion of resistance against state structures is intimately tied to a broad notion of creativity, which fits into Berlin's outline of aesthetics in the Romantic tradition.

Ahrends also foresees an afterlife for east German life forms and orientations. Ideas of inward-bound freedom, poetic imagination, the creativity of everyday life, and ascetic virtues, which the capitalist west threatens to deem passé, are ascribed a politically potent role after unification. Drawing ironically on the slogan of GDR leader Erich Honecker, "to take over, without catching up," Ahrends envisions east Germans as a post-industrial, post-capitalist avantgarde, celebrating the rich, creative forms of individual and social life behind the gray façades of materially and politically restrained conditions. Ahrends depicts what I call a Protestant aesthetics, which resonates with the 'readings' and actions of east Germans in Schwerin.

Concluding Remarks: Aesthetics and Politics after 1989

In contrast to Ahrends, other observers of German culture suggest that the societal context of art after unification, released from GDR state tutelage and its role as a substitute public sphere, combined with pressures from the market and profit making, will undermine its political significance (McGowan 2001). I suggest that aesthetics, from the viewpoint not only of high culture but also of people's everyday activities, will remain important in the understanding of politics and, moreover, that subversive praxis may translate into political mobilization. However, appreciating the intersection of aesthetics and politics also calls into question our comprehension of these categories of perception and action. If we want to understand them, we need to take into account peoples' viewpoints and how they are formed by and reflect on the historical contexts people act within.

For this reason, I have not started with definitions of politics or aesthetics per se, but have instead sought to unravel understandings of the meaning and relevance that aesthetics has for east Germans. These meanings are not captured a priori by tying aesthetics to predefined domains of experience. Aesthetic perceptions and acts are not restricted to the high arts but can include quotidian objects and events. Nor is aesthetic experience mainly an issue of beauty, clearly separated from issues of truth and ethics, according to a principal understanding of modernity and an interpretation of Kant. On the contrary, aesthetic judgment and praxis, guided by the imagery of façades, blends notions of 'beauty', 'the good', and 'truth'. The relation and tension between 'outside' and 'inside', form and content, *Schein* (what deceptively appears to be) and *Sein* (that which is) express values and ideals tied to an *Innerlichkeit* and *Geist*, sincerity and profundity, which touch on notions of deeper truths.

I have adhered to a 'thick description', progressively situating contemporary east German acts and interpretations in broader societal and historical contexts. This method, commonly associated with the anthropologist Clifford Geertz, is also an iconological method promoted by the art historian Erwin Panofsky, building on Ernst Cassirer's neo-Kantian theory about symbolic forms. Panofsky ([1939] 1972) sees the art historian's task, like that of other researchers, as arriving at the intrinsic meaning and evaluations of art and aesthetics. This takes synthetic intuition guided by knowledge of the larger society.[7] I started by outlining the views of one east German, Karl, on the built environment, linking the bracketing of beauty in his perceptions of the deceptive capitalist façades of renovated buildings to his concerns, anxieties, and changing life situation. The conjunction between individual east German views, like Karl's, and GDR anti-fascist, socialist policies is, I believe, fruitfully explored with an eye for life course development and personally accumulated experiences during shifting regimes, rather than viewing the conjunction as an expression of socialist indoctrination, an interpretation underpinning some of the simplified and politically biased notions of *Ostalgia*, a catchword referring to a generalized east German nostalgia for the GDR past.

Understanding the pervasive character of the imagery of façades also requires a historical perspective—one that goes beyond the legacy of the Cold War. I have traced aesthetic judgment and action back to Protestant notions of a spiritual, inward-bound, ascetic individualism informed by a hierarchical relation between the spiritual and worldly, where the spiritual ranks highest. Such notions were simultaneously reproduced and transformed in the imagery of façades and relations between 'inside' and 'outside', content and form. Influenced by Romantic aesthetic models of existence, the imagery surfaces in the antithesis of *Kultur, Geist*, and *Bildung* versus *Zivilisation*.

I suggest that the cultural reproduction of the imagery of façades is tied to the ruptured, non-linear German state trajectory. Efforts at state construction and deconstruction contained crude attempts to monopolize and suppress aesthetic expressions, most severely during the Third Reich. This turbulent and divisive history recharged aesthetics and the imagery of façades with political potency, also from the viewpoints of citizens balancing pressures toward conformity with efforts at maintaining a sense of individualism and integrity. Moreover, cutting across different mediums of expression, both verbal and non-verbal, in regimes where the possibility for open dissent was very limited, it provided a (submerged yet) salient political lingua franca. The imagery informed 'readings' and actions based on identifying hidden deeper meanings, truths, and morals beneath surface appearances—what we might call a 'hermeneutics of suspicion'.

The visual imagery of façade, and its play with relations between 'inside' and 'outside', builds on metaphors, which are 'good to think with' and moreover 'good to act with' because of their bases in spatial, sensuous, bodily experiences. Yet being in a sense concrete, they are also plastic and fluid. They are adaptable to changing circumstances and can figure in very different ideologies. In this regard, the intersection of aesthetics and politics in German history supports cognitive theories of culture, wherein the most fundamental, long-lived values with relevance across many domains are tied to experiential-based metaphors that are highly flexible and have little specific content (Lakoff and Johnson 1980; Shore 1996). Cognitive theory may also help us grasp how metaphors translate between different domains of experience, including sensory mediums of language, vision, and sound, and how the imagery of façade functions as a political lingua franca, building on non-verbal acts.

This view on aesthetics as metaphors should be complemented with Alfred Gell's appeal to engage with art objects themselves, with their specificity and efficacy, by appreciating dimensions that are not necessarily in opposition to a semiotic or cognitive approach, nor are they exhausted by these approaches. According to Gell (1992), material art objects motivate inferences, responses, and interpretations. They are not merely objects in the sense of being end products of action, but are the distributed extension of agents. Gell seems to draw on Romantic notions of humans as creative and expressive beings, reconciling subject and object, man and nature and the material world. His view on art does not draw a sharp distinction between different kinds of practices or objects, such as art and technology. Rather, he sees the material world as aspects of 'being' and 'acting', which captures east German readings of their environment and their everyday aesthetic acts. When east Germans like Karl, Christina, and Joachim resist mechanisms of power in the former GDR state or in the present-day market by 'styling' or 'non-styling' their homes, gardens, or clothing, they see the material world not just as mere objects, but as extensions of their own and others' intentional acts.

How might such perspectives on aesthetics, as those above, inform understandings of politics? Apart from helping us identify the political in submerged, everyday actions, I believe they can sharpen our conceptualization of the public sphere in socialist, authoritarian societies—and in general. Research on eastern Germany naturally brings into question Western-biased conceptions of the political. Since 1989, discussions about 'civil society' and the 'public sphere' and their status as distinguishing marks of Western democracy, as well as their absence in Eastern bloc states, have occupied a central place. Chris Hann (1996: 3–7) points at how standard receptions of 'civil society' imply dominant Western conceptions of the person as the "autonomous agentic individual" (Seligman 1992: 5; quoted in Hann 1996: 5) or the liberal individual, building on preconceptions of modernity. The inward-bound notions of individuality that I have portrayed display how 'individualism', taken to be a hallmark of Western modernity, is not of one piece. Addressing the variable character of self and personhood may offer one valuable factor in discussions about the public sphere and politics. Discussions about East Germany have moreover circled around whether and how theater and literature, apart from the church, qualify as a critical public sphere in accordance with the works of Jürgen Habermas, whereby spaces for open, rational debate are seen as the very core of the concept of the public. The idea of the public sphere is closely linked to voice and language as the vehicle for communication. It is acknowledged that in the realms of theater and literature, east Germans have practiced a sensitive habit of decoding language, demonstrating what Silberman (1997: 30) calls a "multilingual talent" for distinguishing between authentic and strategic speech, an ability that he sees as a potential critical contribution to aspects of unified Germany.

My proposal is to extend an understanding of this habit of decoding to a notion of a lingua franca, including non-verbal aesthetic expressions, such as those I have described above. Such a wide view on the intersection of the political and the aesthetic figures in Betts's (2004) account of industrial design objects in post-war Germany. In West Germany's attempt at 'cultural denazification' and a transition to a modern liberal democracy, the promotion of Werkbund Bauhaus and its industrial design played a crucial role by offering modern forms that drew on aesthetic traditions banned during the Third Reich, and by forging an alliance with US modernism. The Bauhaus style was also conceived as a language, 'a morality of forms' and 'honesty of materials', which invested everyday objects with German idealism and Romanticism, with transcendental ethical qualities and spiritual essence. It drew on pre-war German traditions, including the *Kulturkritik* of Americanism and its conflation of design and cosmetic styling. Moreover, Bauhaus design, with its code of forms, represented one of the rare instances of East and West German consensus and cooperation during the Cold War.

I suggest not only a notion of aesthetics as political and critically informed actions. I also propose that the inherent aesthetic character of politics be reconsidered. Is not Habermas's outstanding and influential work on the public sphere and democracy (work that is not usually associated with Romanticism)—a theory whose goal, in a parallel way to post-war Bauhaus style, was to promote a German post-war transition to a modern democracy—also guided by 'a Protestant aesthetics', an underlying 'honesty of forms'? The ideal of a public sphere tied to language as a medium of *Verständigung* (mutual understanding) is based on the exchange and appreciation of convincing arguments, on the virtues of sincerity, commitment, and critical thinking, and not on the deceptive ornamentations of form in manipulative speech. This echoes an old distinction between rhetorical principles of conviction versus persuasion, informed by more recent American pragmatism and inter-subjective communicative rationality. It also builds on a German *Kulturkritik*, refined in the Frankfurt School's criticism of capitalism and modern mass culture.

Acknowledgments

The author gratefully acknowledges the support for the research for this essay provided by the Faculty of Social Sciences and Centre for European Studies at the University of Bergen, the Institute for Social Anthropology at the University of Tromsø, and the Nansen Foundation. An earlier version of this chapter was presented at the conference "Arts and the State" at the University of Bergen led by Judith Kapferer. For reading and commenting on drafts, I would like to thank Shawn Kendrick, editor at Berghahn Books, Marie-Theres Federhofer, Narve Fulsås, Bruce Kapferer, Judith Kapferer, Michael Schmidt, Øyvind Stokke, and Trond Thuen. Last, but not least, I extend my special gratitude to 'Christina', 'Joachim', 'Karl', and other people in Schwerin.

Inger-Elin Øye is Lecturer in Social Anthropology and Social Sciences at the University of Tromsø. She has carried out 26 months of fieldwork in Schwerin in eastern Germany between 1991 and 2006. Her PhD thesis, with the working title "Precarious Democracy: East German Political Culture and Its Challenge to Occidentalism," discusses personhood and modernity theory in cross-cultural comparison, and furthermore explores life courses and life histories, party politics, memory, the critical public sphere, and aesthetics.

Notes

1. Trabant, a GDR-produced car, was a materialized symbol of socialism. It was practical and cheap to manufacture and maintain, with a two-cylinder engine, a plastic body (in order to save on expensive steel imports), a basic design, rattling engine noises, and smoky exhaust gases that resulted in pollution above the permitted standards in the Federal Republic of Germany.
2. All the names of east Germans have been altered.
3. Herf (1997: 74) points out how fascism and anti-fascism in the judicial setting were tied to social categories in post-war eastern Germany, while the Western zones operated with categories of individual responsibility. In the Soviet zone, the aristocracy, officer corps, and bourgeoisie were assumed to be followers of National Socialism, while the working class was, a priori, assumed to be anti-fascist.
4. Americanism, or America as a mythologized modernity in terms of ideology as well as everyday life, was a primary target of the German *Kulturkritik*. As Peukert (1993: 178–179) points out, Americanism was just as much a debate about German society itself, a passionate enthusiasm for rationality and efficiency, on the one side, and hostility to modern civilization, a rationalized form of life emptied of tradition, on the other side.
5. In the east, the Soviet Union emerged as the main victim of fascism (with 20 million dead) and positioned itself as morally superior, with its Communist resistance fighters and the Red Army's decisive battle force ending the war in the European theater.
6. "'Was sind das für Zeiten, wo/Ein Gespräch über Bäume fast ein Verbrechen ist/Weil es ein Schweigen über so viele Untaten einschliesst!' from Brecht's poem 'An die Nachgeborenen' (To Posterity)" (Leeder 1998: 211). The poem was written in exile in 1938.
7. "The art historian will have to check what he thinks is the intrinsic meaning of the work or group of works, to which he devotes his attention, against what he thinks is the intrinsic meaning of as many other documents of civilisation historically related to the political, poetical religious, philosophical and social tendencies of the personality, period or country under investigation" (Panofsky [1939] 1972: 16).

References

Ahrends, Martin. 1991. "The Great Waiting, or the Freedom of the East: An Obituary for Life in Sleeping Beauty's Castle." *New German Critique*, no. 52: 41–49. (Special issue on German reunification.)

Berlin, Isaiah. 1996. *The Sense of Reality: Studies in Ideas and Their History*. Ed. Henry Hardy. London: Random House.

Betts, Paul. 2004. *The Authority of Everyday Objects: A Cultural History of West German Industrial Design*. Berkeley: University of California Press.

Bowie, Andrew. 1998. "Critiques of Culture." Pp. 132–152 in Kolinsky and van der Will 1998.

Boyer, Dominic. 2005. *Spirit and System: Media, Intellectuals, and the Dialectic in Modern German Culture*. Chicago: University of Chicago Press.

Büttner, Ulrich. 1989. "Schwerin." Pp. 303–323 in *Die DDR im Spiegel ihrer Bezirke*, ed. Werner Ostwald. Berlin: Dietz Verlag.

Dumont, Louis. 1986. *Essays on Individualism: Modern Ideology in Anthropological Perspective*. Chicago: Chicago University Press.

Elias, Norbert. [1939] 1994. *The Civilizing Process: The History of Manners and State Formation and Civilization*. Trans. Edmund Jephcott. Oxford: Blackwell.

Gell, Alfred. 1998. *Art and Agency: An Anthropological Theory*. Oxford: Clarendon Press.

Gillen, Eckhart. 1999. "Ostkunst-Westkunst: Anmerkungen zum deutschen Bilderstreit." *Zeichen und Mythen in Ost und West: Rostocker Philosophische Manuskripte, Rostocker Universität*. New series, no. 6: 85–88.

Hann, Chris. 1996. "Introduction: Political Society and Civil Anthropology." Pp. 1–26 in *Civil Society: Challenging Western Models*, ed. Chris Hann and Elizabeth Dunn. London: Routledge.

Hannemann, Christine. 2004. "Architecture as Ideology: Industrialization of Housing in the GDR." *Stadt- und Regionalsoziologie*. Working paper no. 2A, Humboldt Universität zu Berlin, Philosophische Fakultät 111, Institut für Sozialwissenschaften. http://www2 .hu-berlin.de/stadtsoz/mitin/ch/slab_of_gdr_eng.pdf.

Heinze, Helmut. 1999. "Ostkunst-Westkunst: Anmerkungen zum deutschen Bilderstreit." *Zeichen und Mythen in Ost und West: Rostocker Philosophische Manuskripte, Rostocker Universität*, new series, no. 6: 73–79.

Herf, Jeffrey. 1997. *Divided Memory: The Nazi Past in the Two Germanys*. Cambridge, MA: Harvard University Press.

Karge, Wolf, Ernst Münch, and Hartmut Schmied. 1993. *Die Geschichte Mecklenburgs*. Rostock: Hinstorff Verlag.

Kolinsky, Eva, and Wilfried van der Will, eds. 1998. *The Cambridge Companion to Modern German Culture*. Cambridge: Cambridge University Press.

Lakoff, George, and Mark Johnson. 1980. *Metaphors We Live By*. Chicago: University of Chicago Press.

Leeder, Karen. 1998. "Modern German Poetry." Pp. 193–212 in Kolinsky and van der Will 1998.

McGowan, Moray. 2001. "Staging the 'Wende': Some 1989 East German Productions and the Flux of History." *European Studies* 17: 73–90.

Panofsky, Erwin. [1939] 1972. *Studies in Iconology: Humanistic Themes in the Art of the Renaissance*. New York: Harper & Row.

Peukert, Detlev J. K. 1993. *The Weimar Republic: The Crisis of Classical Modernity*. Trans. Richard Deveson. New York: Hill and Wang.

Seligman, Adam. 1992. *The Idea of Civil Society*. New York: Free Press.

Shore, Brad. 1996. *Culture in Mind: Cognition and the Problem of Meaning*. Oxford: Oxford University Press.

Silberman, Marc. 1997. "Problematizing the 'Socialist Public Sphere': Concepts and Consequences." Pp. 1–37 in *What Remains? East German Culture and the Postwar Public*, ed. Marc Silberman. Washington, DC: American Institute for Contemporary German Studies.

Wolf, Eric R. 1999. *Envisioning Power: Ideologies of Dominance and Crisis*. Berkeley: University of California Press.

INDEX